THEO GIVE
US A BALL

A LIFE IN FOOTBALL

THEO GIVE US A BALL

A LIFE IN FOOTBALL

THEO FOLEY AND PAUL FOLEY

Foreword by George Graham

APEX PUBLISHING LTD

First published as an eBook in 2018, updated in 2018 for paperback by

Apex Publishing Ltd

12A St. John's Road, Clacton on Sea, Essex, CO15 4BP, United Kingdom

www.apexpublishing.co.uk

British Library Cataloguing-in-Publication Data
A catalogue record for this book
is available from the British Library

ISBN 978-1-911476-19-1

Typeset in 11pt Baskerville

Production Manager: Chris Cowlin
Cover Design: Hannah Blamires

Publishers Note:
The views and opinions expressed in this publication are those of the
author and are not necessarily those of Apex Publishing Ltd

Copyright:
Every attempt has been made to contact the relevant copyright holders,
Apex Publishing Ltd would be grateful if the appropriate people contact us on:
01255 428500 or mail@apexpublishing.co.uk

For Joe and John

CONTENTS

Acknowledgements, Cover Details and Testimonials   vii

Testimonials   ix

Foreword by Paul Foley   xii

Foreword by George Graham   xv

Chapter 1 - From Inchicore to Anfield - the Pinnacle   1

Chapter 2 - Once a Dub, always a Dub   6

Chapter 3 - Turfed to Devon   19

Chapter 4 - On the up with the Cobblers   37

Chapter 5 - One Night in Paris   61

Chapter 6 - Whistle and Stopwatch   89

Chapter 7 - Bobby Moore's Leather Coat   103

Chapter 8 - Into the Lion's Den   125

Chapter 9 - The QPR Academy   142

Chapter 10 - Strolling back to The Den   160

Chapter 11 - Marble Halls and Heated Floors   180

Chapter 12 - The Prodigal Son Returns   211

Chapter 13 - From a Gunner to a Cockerel   223

Chapter 14 - Still Working   232

About the authors   235

ACKNOWLEDGEMENTS

With special thanks to:
Sheila Foley, Teresa Foley, Adrian Foley, Sean Foley, Terry and Maurice O'Loughlin, Ralph and Anita Waldron

Northampton Town FC
Graham Carr, Mick Everitt, Pat Kiernan, John and Nan Kurila, Pete Norton, Frank Grande, Mark Beesley

Charlton Athletic FC
Dietmar Bruck, Mike Flanagan, Derek Hales, Keith Peacock, Colin Powell

Millwall FC
Gordon Jago, Billy Neil, Terry Brisley, Nicky Johns, Trevor Lee, Jon Moore, John Seasman, Phil Summerill, Les Briley, Dave Cusack, Andy Massey, Alan Walker

QPR FC
Wayne Fereday, Peter Hucker, Gavin Maguire, Gary Micklewhite, Warren Neill, Ian Stewart

Arsenal FC
George Graham, Pat Rice, Tony Adams, Paul Davis, Lee Dixon, Perry Groves, David Hillier, John Lukic, Kevin Richardson, Alan Smith, Mickey Thomas

Tottenham Hotspur FC
Clive Allen, Les Ferdinand, Jamie Redknapp

Liverpool FC
Mark Lawrenson, Ronnie Whelan

Republic of Ireland
Jimmy Giles, Johnny Giles, Stephen Finn, Dec Finnegan, Stephen

Harte, Sean Little, Martin Prendergast, Irene Stevenson, Gerry Reardon, Paul Rowan, Paul Whelan

General
Amanda @GoonerGirl1969, Paul Baker, Rob Brennan, Iain Cook, Chris Cowlin at Apex Publishing Ltd, Dean Frost, Getty Images, David Goldblatt, Chris Guy, Stuart Izzard, Andy Kelly, Amy Lawrence, Alasdair Norrie at Colorsport, Mike @GoonerFanzine, Myles Palmer, Ray Richardson, Ben Sharpe, Susan Shipp, Gordon Tomkins, Steve 'Bernie Taupin' Tongue, Colin White, Layth Yousif

Cover Front Sleeve
Theo Foley leading out Northampton Town 2nd October 1965 away to Leicester City
Leicester City 1 *(Goodfellow 28)* Northampton Town 1 *(Foley 47 Pen)*
Reproduced with kind permission of Pete Norton (NTFC Photographer)

Cover Artwork Back Sleeve
'Who Luvs Ya Baby' by Ray Richardson
Medium – Conté Drawing and Oil Glazes on Board 2015/16
254 x 254mm Keith Peacock and Theo Foley away to Luton Town 1 Charlton Athletic 2, 6th November 1971

Inside Sleeve Photo
Theo Foley heading the ball away away Eire v Belgium, Dalymount Park 24th March 1965, Eire 0 Belgium 2 (Jurion, McAvoy o.g)
Reproduced with kind permission of The Irish Times

TESTIMONIALS

'To be playing out of position and marking one of the best players in the world, and playing well is a huge achievement, he wasn't overawed by it, he'd a good temperament.'
Johnny Giles on the World Cup qualifier against Spain about marking Suarez in Paris in 1965 – Manchester United, Leeds, West Bromwich Albion, Shamrock Rovers and Republic of Ireland

'I've always thought highly of Theo, he gave me my opportunity which I thank him for.'
Mike Flanagan – Charlton Athletic, Crystal Palace, QPR, Cambridge United and England B

'I'll always be appreciative for the start in the game given to me by Theo – when you've been in the game as long as Theo has, it's in his blood.'
Derek Hales – Luton Town, Charlton Athletic, Derby County, West Ham United and Gillingham

'When he got the sack, he shook everyone's hand but the ones he felt had let him down he ignored, he shook my hand, so I was alright – results weren't great but you could see we were getting there and with his team, we went up the next season.'
Colin Powell – Charlton Athletic, New England Tea Men and Gillingham

'Theo was Robin to Gordon Jago's Batman, a very positive influence on the dressing room, we all had a fantastic bond.'
Terry Brisley – Leyton Orient, Millwall, Charlton and Portsmouth

'Thanks to Theo I was given my chance after a few other clubs had looked at me without signing me, he took a chance. Theo was one of the first coaches to work with goalkeepers, every day he'd take me away for an hour or so to work on things. We spent hours and hours

on the training ground.'
Nicky Johns - Millwall, Charlton Athletic and QPR

'This mad Irishman came into my life, a total football nutcase.'
Dave Cusack - Sheffield Wednesday, Southend United, Millwall, Doncaster Rovers and Rotherham United

'He was a huge help to me being a boy from the sticks and we've remained friends ever since. The bloke is a legend.'
Alan Walker - Lincoln City, Millwall, Gillingham, Plymouth Argyle, Mansfield Town and Barnet

'Later that day, George called me to say Theo would apologise if I returned to Millwall.'
Ian Stewart - QPR, Millwall, Newcastle United, Portsmouth, Brentford, Aldershot, Colchester United and Northern Ireland

'There are not enough Theo Foleys in football any more, he is a diamond, give him a ball.'
Tony Adams, Arsenal and England

'He's the best 'cone' coach I've ever seen!'
Steve Bould - Stoke, Arsenal, Sunderland and England

'The legend that is Theo. We all loved him. He was a big part of that team's success and, let's not forget, he knew the game.'
Lee Dixon - Burnley, Chester City, Bury, Stoke, Arsenal and England

'Theo was a very important element of our (Arsenal) success. He had a wonderful way with him and was always laughing and smiling. It was a big loss when he moved to Northampton.'
Kevin Richardson - Everton, Watford, Arsenal, Real Sociedad, Aston Villa, Coventry, Southampton, Barnsley, Blackpool and England

'We all missed Theo when he left. One of the biggest characters I ever met in the game.'
Alan Smith - Leicester, Arsenal and England

'I wanted a move away, Theo kept me going and I can't speak highly enough of him. We all loved him; it was a sad day when he left. We missed him a lot as we couldn't talk to George in the same way. I've never heard any of the lads say a bad word about Theo.'
Michael Thomas – Arsenal, Liverpool, Middlesbrough, Benfica, Wimbledon and England

'Everyone was sad when he left the club as we'd lost a great coach, character and friend.'
Pat Rice – Arsenal, Watford and Northern Ireland

'It was a real pleasure to work with Theo but he should have been a newsreader, as he knew more about what was going on than Trevor McDonald and Alastair Burnett put together.'
Les Ferdinand MBE – QPR, Newcastle, Tottenham Hotspur, West Ham, Leicester City, Bolton Wanderers, Reading and England

FOREWORD BY PAUL FOLEY

For years I kept asking Dad to write a book about his life in football. He would always reply, 'Now, who would want to read that?' While I admire his modesty and humble approach to everything he has achieved, I always disagreed, as I felt it was a life definitely worth writing about. For various reasons, it has been a rewarding and difficult task for us both in equal measure but we got there and I, for one, am glad we got it all down. What was particularly pleasing was the undoubted warmth and love people still have for him which says more than any of his achievements in the game. Talking to former players he coached or played with and hearing the kind words means more than any medal or trophy to Dad. As he always says, 'It's nice to be important but it's more important to be nice,' or 'self-praise is no recommendation.' The number of times I have heard both of those sayings over the years, they are mantras by which he has lived his life and, hopefully, these beliefs come through in this book.

He has enjoyed a unique professional career in football that spans over 60 years taking in all four Football Leagues, playing in World Cup games for Eire whilst achieving the Holy Grail of the old First Division title as assistant manager of Arsenal. From the streets of Dublin to the hallowed Turf Moor at Burnley he started out on a journey as he has said many times 'with just his boots in a bag'. These real football people are now few and far between and in these heady days of Premier League money and fast cars, we should remind ourselves of the real reasons why we love the beautiful game. As you will see from these pages and his character, and the things he had to do, he was, and still is, a pure football man with no ideas above his station. He has loved the game his entire life and appreciates all it has given him. Whilst I have always loved the game and enjoyed playing, my appreciation is minimal compared to his. He would watch a kickabout in the back garden with the same enthusiasm as a World Cup game.

His journey as a player took him by ferry to Burnley and then on to the south west Coast at Exeter City where he met and married my mum. From there he joined Dave Bowen's progressive Northampton Town. The Cobblers' remarkable journey from the Fourth to the old First Division brought the FAI scouts to watch their inspirational full back captain. Full Eire caps soon followed with some rave reviews in the Irish press for his 1966 World Cup qualifier displays. In the months leading up to the World Cup in that golden year for English football, he tossed the coin at Upton Park with the great Bobby Moore in the First Division and over the course of the season played against the entire England World Cup winning squad. Not to mention playing against the likes of Dennis Law, George Best, Dave Mackay, Billy Bremner, Johnny Giles, Johnny Haynes and Ron Yeats – giants in the game of football. For the full sweep, he lined up for Eire in Dublin against Franz Beckenbauer and the West German World Cup finalists. After transferring from Northampton, he headed to South East London and Charlton Athletic as a player with a nagging, troublesome injury.

This injury meant just a handful of appearances at The Valley and marked the start of a longer, and arguably, more successful career on the coaching/management side. This 'second career' spanned nearly 40 years taking in spells at Charlton, Millwall twice, QPR, Arsenal, Northampton Town, Southend, Fulham, Leeds and, finally, Tottenham Hotspur.

For me, summer school holidays meant I could go training with him every day for six weeks, kick a ball all day and just soak up the magical world of pro football. What a thing for a young football-mad boy. This all seemed very normal to me but I now realise how lucky I was to be immersed in this wonderful sport and life. The odd treat of a McDonalds at Shepherds Bush or an ice cream from the parlour at the Elephant & Castle on the way home made it even more idyllic for a 10-year-old.

During secondary school days, I would stagger down the stairs in the morning to see the smiling face of the late David Rocastle sitting in the front room waiting for Dad to head to London Colney together. Hearing Dad on the radio or seeing him on TV seemed normal back then. To us he was just our dad, but to others he was Theo Foley. Hearing the famous North Bank at Highbury sing in unison, 'Theo, give us a ball, Theo, give us a ball,' is a strange thing to witness but also one to make an 18-year-old boy unusually proud of his dad. That's the key message really here, from all of his family – how proud we all are of him.

This is his life in football.

Paul Foley

FOREWORD BY GEORGE GRAHAM

When Theo asked me if I would write a foreword for his autobiography I didn't hesitate as I consider him to be one of my best friends in the game. It got me thinking about how we first crossed paths and when I sat down recently with his son, Paul, we looked at the records and they showed that we had played against each other only twice, either end of 1965, in January and December.

Theo was the right back and captain of Northampton Town at the time who were on their amazing rise to the First Division and I was a young lad trying to make my name at Chelsea. We beat them in January 1965 in the third round of the FA Cup 4-1 at a packed Stamford Bridge with Theo scoring their only goal from the penalty spot but he also scored an own goal, something I shall have to remind him of forever more now. Northampton were a strong Second Division side back then and, in the following 65-66 season, we played them again at the Bridge in their one and only season in the top flight. We won again, this time 1-0. Two games and two wins so, as he proved to be many years later when we worked together, Theo always was a lucky omen for me.

Little did we know that those fleeting encounters on the pitch in the mid-60s would end up with the highly successful management pairing we had at both Millwall and then Arsenal in the 80s, not to mention the early success we had at QPR with the youth players. We still meet up every Christmas with a few of the ex-coaches and scouts for a meal and we are still the same with each other, we will always have that strong bond. We had some great times together as a management pairing with plenty of laughs along the way. Theo is a lovely, warm character who is well thought of in the game and by those who have worked with him. People always talk fondly about him when I meet up with ex-players or staff. He was the king of the banter in the dressing room, always in the thick of it, that's where he belonged.

Our first involvement working alongside each other came at QPR when Theo was the reserve team manager and I was looking after the youth team. Theo was the more senior guy back then and I fed players into his side to prepare them for the first team. Well, we hit it off straight away and I remember him making an impression when you first met him – I thought what a friendly, likeable guy and a larger than life character.

We helped so many players along in that outstanding youth system at QPR and got a huge thrill out of seeing these young lads making the grade and carving out careers. We won our respective leagues and people started to ask why we were so successful, what was our secret. Then along came Millwall with an offer for me to manage them. When I told Theo he just laughed and said they would eat me alive at The Den but he soon stopped laughing when I said he was coming as my number two.

Looking back on those times, when I was learning the ropes as a manager, Theo's input was invaluable. He put me straight on the 'Millwall way', what the fans expect of their team and he astutely told me that, once they were onside, they were the most loyal fans around. Theo knew the club inside out having worked there before, he knew the area having lived there and he knew the people around the club. I am still so proud of what we achieved together at The Den and we both still have a lot of warmth for the club.

The team were really struggling at the bottom of the old Third Division when we took over but we steadied the ship and then got promoted to the Second Division. We won the first of many senior trophies together along the way and made some key bargain signings scouring the lower leagues. I even recall the time we managed to get squaddies from Woolwich Barracks to paint the Old Den in blue and yellow paint for nothing in the close season. In those early days we begged, stole and borrowed to improve the facilities off the pitch and try to entice players down to the club.

The people around the place were great and would just do anything to help the club out. This was a great nuts and bolts introduction to how a club worked and we used what we had learned at Millwall and improved it when we went to Arsenal. When I got the call from Arsenal there was only going to be one man who I would be taking with me, the genial Dubliner, so we set about doing the same at Highbury. Arsenal were a bigger club but the same rules still applied. In a similar way to Millwall when we took over, Arsenal were struggling and needed an injection of something new and different.

Well, it wasn't rocket science but, after a few weeks at training, they knew what we were about. We sat them down in the first week and told them straight that we would expect full commitment and 'wet shirts' in games and at training. If we didn't see enough of this at the end of the six weeks we would get people in who would fit the bill. With a combination of the experienced lads reacting in the right way, some excellent young players coming through at that time and some important signings, it worked better than we ever could have hoped.

We were top of the league in our first season and flying; Theo and I thought we had cracked it. We missed out that first season on the league title but we beat the mighty Liverpool in the Littlewoods Cup at Wembley in '87, Arsenal's first trophy for eight years. The following season we reached Wembley again and had our one and only defeat in a final but made up for it the next season winning the league title with the last kick of the season at Anfield. Who can forget that amazing climax to an emotional season when the tide finally turned, Liverpool knocked from their perch as Alex would say and Arsenal a force once more?

I know how much Theo loved those Arsenal days and when he left to manage his beloved Northampton in 1991 it was a sad day for me. I wanted him to stay and look after the reserves but he didn't want to step down and I would think, looking back now, he probably wishes he'd stayed, he could have been there for years. But Theo being Theo he wanted to take up the challenge and his fierce pride got in the way of settling for something comfortable. I know he considers his time at Arsenal to be the pinnacle of his career and in his house in SE London there is a great photo of him holding the League Championship up to the fans with a huge smile on his face.

Even when he left the club he would always ring to congratulate me on any success we had, there was never any bitterness which says everything about him as a man. We worked together again at Leeds when he scouted for the club when I was the manager and then again at Spurs as he was already there coaching when I got the manager's job. We won our last trophy together at Spurs in the Worthington Cup Final at Wembley in 1999, both of us back in the dugout again. It was another day in the sun for the two Celt boys who just so happened to form a great team together.

George Graham

Playing Career – Aston Villa, Chelsea, Arsenal, Manchester United, Portsmouth, Crystal Palace, California Surf and Scotland

Manager – Millwall, Arsenal, Leeds, Tottenham Hotspur

CHAPTER 1
From Inchicore to Anfield –
The Pinnacle

'We wouldn't have won the league if he'd listened to you.'
1989

The tragic and avoidable disaster at Hillsborough dominates and affects the football and UK landscape forever, the Berlin Wall comes down as West meets East, Ceausescu and wife are deposed and executed in Romania and there are student demonstrations in Tiananmen Square, China, in iconic images in front of advancing tanks, De Klerk begins dismantling Apartheid – the world landscape is changing – known as the year that changed the world.

Thatcher goes in hard a la Miners dispute with New Age revellers, this time at Stonehenge.

The brilliant 'My Left Foot' is released starring the excellent Daniel Day-Lewis, a local lad from SE London, and Harrison Ford dons his brown Fedora for the first time,good music is harder for me to find, apart from the old favourites like Rod Stewart, Billy Joel and Roy Orbison stretching out their careers.

As John Lukic gathered the ball in front of the Kop I remember screaming over and over, 'Just fucking kick it, Lukey!' Bouldy (Steve Bould), who was sat next to me having come off for the second half, reminded me of this recently when we spoke, as he always bloody does, 'We wouldn't have won the league if he'd listened to you.' He was right but, thankfully, in the cauldron of Anfield, Lukey couldn't hear me and I doubt he would have listened anyway – as the game approaches the closing stages, footballers tend to go onto autopilot.

Some things are just meant to be and, after 37 games and

90 plus minutes, we were reaching the last optic in the last chance saloon – this was the whole season condensed into a power play – as that familiar panic and dread set in little did we know this would turn out to be a unique and never to be repeated finale. This was 'Mickey time', the day a legend was born. Michael Thomas was destined to pop up in the dying seconds and, after the days I'd spent working with these lads and bringing Michael on as a player, I felt a part of his destiny.

The game had gone exactly as George had said it would just without that crucial second goal. Genuinely, he had called it spot on. We were starting with three centre backs or a sweeper, if you like, with David O'Leary, Tony Adams and Steve Bould which was a curveball that no one expected. This enabled us to keep the game tight and really play on the fears of Liverpool as they were under pressure and George knew it. We'd paid our respects to the tragedy of Hillsborough by handing out bouquets before the game and a cheque for £25,000 for the fund, lovely gestures and all very 'Arsenal' – now it was time for business.

George had said if we scored in the first half, or early in the second, they would play with a fear of losing. As was usually the case with George when it came to football, he was right. If you watch any pre-match interview with him you can see it, he has this inner calm and his belief shines through.

Smudger (Alan Smith) had glanced a free kick home on 52 minutes which he swears to this day he got a touch on from Nigel Winterburn's excellent indirect left foot free kick. I've no reason to doubt him, there's no more honest boy than Alan in football. As they always did, the Liverpool players surrounded the ref claiming there had been no touch, another sure sign that they were panicking, heads had gone. Arsenal had not won at Anfield in 15 years, never mind come up and won by two goals.

George used to hate that you'd go there and play well, deserve to win and get beat then they'd take you into the boot room and tell you how well you'd played and so on. It rankled with him and George wanted to knock them off their perch long before Sir Alex ever did. Mickey had a great chance with a few minutes to go in the box that he'd snatched at. We'd had Steve McMahon giving his 'one minute, come on', finger pointing instructions as Richo (Kevin Richardson) got treatment for cramp. Then John Barnes, who knows why, dribbled into the box with two minutes left and Kevin did what he did so well and dispossessed him, and George's masterplan was clinging by a thread. Richo rolled it back to Lukey, as you could back then, John gathered the ball, prompting me to bark out my basic panicked instructions which were thankfully ignored.

Lukey spun it straight to Lee Dixon, out on the right, who took one touch and looked up as McMahon ran out to close him down. Dicko clipped a ball to Smudger who was 20 yards inside their half, as they sat deeper and deeper at the back. Fear does strange things. Why did John Barnes dribble into our box instead of running down the clock, why was McMahon dragged out of position, why were Alan Hansen and Gary Ablett so deep? They were five yards off Smudger when he controlled the ball on his thigh. Fear. That couple of yards allowed Alan to get on a half turn and look up, seeing Mickey making a great burst clear, the type he was discouraged to do by George, ironically – 'sit in Mickey, break things up, play it wide.' Smudger lofted a great ball, as we'd come to expect, into Michael's path, he got that lucky ricochet off the last man Steve Nicol – fate and destiny. He was on the edge of their box through on goal, little Ray Houghton catching him with each stride, another player caught out high up the pitch supporting John Barnes.

Mickey set himself and took another deft touch, another small touch in the box, as the Arsenal fans behind that goal lurched forward, our whole bench stood up in anticipation and the world watching on TV took a sharp breath. Mickey, the most laid-back man on the planet, the South East London Brazilian, with the world at his feet, steadied himself, taking one more touch, waiting for Bruce Grobbelaar to blink first. With Nicol and Houghton both sliding in from behind, Michael looked up and flicked the ball in true Mickey Thomas style with the outside of his right foot over

Grobbelaar and into the bottom right corner. Pandemonium. Chaos. Jubilation. Jumping up, I banged my head on the dugout, something else Bouldy always reminds me of. Gather your emotions, see the game out, get back on the bench, still seconds to play.

If you watch the aftermath of the goal and Mickey's famous forward roll and interrupted flip off the ground celebration, have a look at Nigel Winterburn who was the highest player up the field, God knows what he was doing up there. Well, he ignores Mickey and arcs past the goal at full pelt towards our fans as Hayesy (Martin Hayes) and Smudger smother the scorer. Good old Nutty Nidge, funny lad.

Now, what often gets lost when looking back at that game, is what happened after the goal. We still had to see out the last few seconds and control our emotions, get our heads back on and kill the game off. They attacked down the right with McMahon straight from the kick off and Tony Adams sprinted out to win the ball with the best sliding tackle you'll ever see, given the situation. There are good centre backs and then there are great ones, Tony was the latter and one of the best leaders of a team I've ever seen. From the throw Ronnie Whelan lofted the ball into a packed box, it dropped loose and was picked up by whom? That man Mickey again, he just took a touch in our box this time, and casually rolled it back to Lukey, again with the outside of his right boot, like he was playing with his mates as a 15-year-old back at Kennington Astro turf. You've got to love Mickey, he was such a talented player.

From the goal kick the ball broke to Steve Nicol who just jogged it into touch, probably the only one who'd heard the whistle. It was over, 38 games in an emotional season had finished in a way that has never been seen before or since. We were beside ourselves on the sidelines; the hugs, the emotion, the joy. Then you had to shake hands with the Liverpool bench, beaming from ear to ear. I shook hands with Kenny Dalglish, Ronnie Moran and Roy Evans, all three of them so gracious in defeat and real football men I've always got on well with and respected. I didn't have George's Liverpool chip if you like, I've always loved Liverpool as a club, one of the best around. But this night belonged to Arsenal and to us. After a brief return to win it the following year, Liverpool never really got back onto their perch again, forever wounded by the Gunners.

It doesn't get better than that. Me, plain old Theo from the Inchicore Road to winning the First Division title at Anfield. It had been some journey.

CHAPTER 2
Once a Dub, Always a Dub

1930s – Glenn Miller, Billie Holliday, Bing Crosby and Count Basie on the wireless and 'King Kong', 'Gone With the Wind' and 'The Marx Brothers' on at the cinema.
The Second World War came along at the end of the decade and times were tough with money and jobs scarce. As long as we had a ball and a place to play though, we were happy on the streets of Dublin.

At the back of the family house at 149 Inchicore Road in Dublin you could see the ground of St. Pats' Football Club. In fact, you still can as I went back to the house recently. The yard in our back garden was a typical backyard to a row of terrace houses; small with walls all round so you couldn't see much. If you looked out from the back bedroom window though, you could see the pitch and the simple stands of the local football club that my dad loved so much. To me as a kid growing up this was like Wembley and, growing up with a football stadium as a backdrop, it's no wonder I wanted to be a professional footballer more than anything else in the world. It seeped into my blood at a young age and has stayed there ever since.

Why should my story be any different to the many stories already told by ex-pros in many books? Well, although I had my fair share of success as a player, coach and manager, my career may not be as successful as some but it is definitely as long as any in the game that's for sure. Having left my beloved Dublin at the age of 16 and signing pro forms at 17 for Exeter City, I have been involved in football in some capacity ever since. That is a span of over 60 years so, it is fair to say, I have seen a fair few things and now is as good a time as any to share my stories, as the game changed so much during that period.

Dublin was a very different city then but it was a great place and still is. I was born just before the Second World War to Theo and Agnes Foley, the second of four children and the second son. I grew up with the war going on and, although we knew what was happening, it wasn't as much of a worry as, say, in England but the prospects of jobs and money were both slim. I was born on 2 April 1937 although my youngest son Paul has always said I was born on April Fool's day but mum changed it to the 2nd to spare my blushes.

Dad was more of a rugby man than soccer, as we called it, he played the oval ball game but his brothers Jimmy and Gerard both played soccer and Jimmy turned pro playing in the League of Ireland. Dad also loved soccer (Gaelic was known as football) and he always loved St. Pats more than any other team. You could keep your Manchester Uniteds and Arsenals, Dad loved St. Pats who only played a long punt from our home on Inchicore Road. He never taught me how to play or anything like that, as it wasn't his thing, but he always encouraged me in his own way to play the game.

It helped having my older brother Jimmy around to get me into the games in the street round our way or up at Keogh Square with the older boys. Now, where I lived was tough enough, and you needed to look out for yourself, but Keogh Square was for the real tough boys. No doubt this stood me in good stead in later years when I had to stand up for myself on the pitch as some of the lads on the square wouldn't think twice about giving you a whack. Luckily, I had 'big Jimmy' to look out for me, he was four years older than me and I idolised him. Jimmy was big and strong and could box well, and as a young 10-year-old those were reasons enough to look up to my big brother.

He always stood up for me and, better still, he invited me to play football with the 'bigger boys' and that was the trial run for when I got to play against the real big boys of the English Football League. From an early age I never feared anyone I came up against even if they were bigger or stronger than me. I would back myself on the square at Keogh and I would do the same in the English Football

League many years later. That's not being arrogant; it's what you need to succeed as a pro footballer.

Looking out onto St. Pats planted a seed in me that started a lifelong obsession. From as young as I can remember I have lived and breathed the game. Whenever I was able to, I was kicking a ball and when I wasn't, I was thinking about kicking a ball. I still do now, if there is a game on I am watching it live or on TV, if there is a programme on about football I am glued to it and I constantly watch Sky Sports in the house much to the delight of my long-suffering wife, Sheila. I love the game and everything about it, by far the best sport in the world, and it has been great to me, just a normal boy from Dublin City who was lucky enough to win international caps and win trophies as a player and a coach.

At home, there was Jimmy, myself and my two younger sisters, Terry and Anita. Now, I would have followed Jimmy into a furnace if he told me to. Four years younger than me was my sister, Terry, who was and, still is, a gas character and we have always got on great, ribbing each other and codding each other on. We still do. I was the one in the middle looking up to Jimmy and being protective of my younger sister, Terry, before Anita came along eight years after Terry in, what I can only assume was, Dad coming 'back on the scene'. When I left home to go and play football Anita was only four so I missed a lot of her growing up to follow my dream but we have always been a close family and I went home every year to make sure I stayed close to my friends and family.

Our family of six was tiny by comparison to others in the area with families of 12, like the Garlands and the Lynches, being quite normal. As I said, the war was on when I was born and this was Catholic Ireland, when the size of some families were huge by comparison to today. It's what you did, there was no worrying about how you would fend for them or keep them safe, they'd be alright because they had to be. Different times indeed, life was much simpler then with none of the worries that young people have now. It made for a great place to grow up though, as there was always someone to kick a ball about with, as so and so was out with his four brothers and what do you call him with his five brothers from down the road. Great times, and people just got on with it, no one had any spare money to speak of but it didn't mean you were any less happy. I look at young lads now and they are tapping away on phones and iPads and missing out on real life by imitating it on a phone. I even call my grandson Connor 'Didge' as he is always didging away on his phone.

I would say from a young age I could at least lay claim to being the best footballer in my family which may explain the absence of any insecurity about my ability. My younger sister, Terry, thought I was great and my older brother was a goalkeeper so he was never going to be a threat. Maybe my belief and determination had been cast at a young age as I have always had that inner mental strength and confidence in my ability. How else would I make it in England and then carve out a career coaching and managing? Thankfully I've never been one to doubt myself which anyone who knows me will testify. In my view, if you have a chink in your armour and self-doubt creeps in, you have had it in football. I've seen it so many times with lads with all the ability but they're weak mentally, you've no chance in the cauldron of a football club. Luckily, I was the best at football in my family and soon got a reputation around the streets as a decent soccer player.

Our house was typical for the area, a mid-terrace and I know it's a cliché but the door really was always open. We had three bedrooms upstairs and two rooms downstairs with an outside toilet. We never had a bathroom as such for years and the turf fire was always on, kept going by Mammy. Nobody closed their front door in Inchicore, but you wouldn't dream of whipping anything as everyone knew what went on. There was one policeman who would larrap you with the stick if you 'gave out' to him and if you ever were caught nicking or told off at school then your dad would go mad. You'd get a whack from the Christian Brothers at school for stepping out of line and when you got home you'd get another telling off from your mum or dad who would know straight away if you'd been up to no good. That's just how it was back then, you got away with nothing and you learnt very soon the difference between right and wrong. Remember that this was before phones were in general use, never mind mobiles, but you can guarantee everyone knew if you had been up to no good the day you did it, everyone knew your business. We would go to the local shop, Bonhams, and try to push the cakes on to the floor and run off with them but they always caught us and gave us a whack so it was a waste of time and effort.

Mum was called Agnes, nee Cassidy, she was a wonderful woman and the matriarch of the house. She made dresses and adjusted clothes for anyone who asked and never took a penny. She was the homemaker and dad the provider as that was how it was. Back then you would get things on tick and then go and 'pay the man'. I can remember her arguing with the shopkeeper at the end of the week when she had to settle the bill saying, 'I never had that' or 'go 'way, that wasn't me' as she didn't agree with his list. Mum was from Merrion in the south of Dublin and her mum was called Hannah Cassidy from Kilkenny. Nanny Cassidy was a remarkable character who lived well into her 90s yet she'd smoke a fag and light another while one was still in her mouth. She could literally sew anything, having had no real training, and obviously passed this on to her daughter, Agnes, along with Mammy's love of Sweet Afton fags. Nanny Cassidy moved from Kilkenny when she married a baker and ended up in Merrion, Dublin.

Dad was called Theodore too but his first name was actually Cornelius although no one ever called him that, he was just Theo. I was christened Theodore Cornelius, which always raised a chuckle in England, but I was honoured to be named after my dad. Dad worked a lathe, turning wood into any shape imaginable, he was a skilled man and very bright too. He was one of the few people I know who could multiply and divide fractions in his head. He always wanted to be a draughtsman but he never got around to training himself so stuck to his trade. He'd come home with bits of wood offcuts stuffed down his trousers to stick on the fire, something I obviously got from him in later years with toilet rolls stuffed down my trousers. Every day he would cycle back from work in his lunch hour to stand and pray in front of St. Mary at the grotto at Oblates Church in Inchicore which had an exact replica of the Lourdes Grotto. Dad never missed a day of work and never missed going to Oblates. Religion was the bedrock of life back then around Dublin, it was huge. Cursing and swearing were not allowed, having a pint and a few bets was okay though. It was a common sight to see the women waiting outside the pubs, or the bookies, for their husbands to come out hoping that they hadn't spent all of their wages. Dad liked a little bet on the horses, that's for sure, easy come easy go, but it was all harmless enough and we always had food on the table, thank God.

Mammy was a strong character, if she told you off then you knew about it alright and Dad was a big man too so, if we ever got in trouble, it was double trouble. Dad was a good rower and he also threw weights, similar to a discus. One day, Jimmy and I got in trouble for pinching apples and Dad stood us in the hall. We'd only taken a few apples that had fallen off the stall so didn't think there was a problem. He asked us if we stole them and we both said no, not knowing that Mrs Kinnard had already told him that we had so he said he'd give us one more chance to tell the truth. I looked at Jimmy and he looked at me and we both said no. Well, he went to hit Jimmy, who used his boxing skills and dodged the blow, and Dad's hand caught me full on the side of my head and knocked me flying down the hall. He must have knocked me about four feet. Jimmy owed me that day for taking his dig.

If you broke a window then you had to all chip in to replace it and if you lied about it you were in bigger trouble. That's how they were, people at that time were very proud even though they never had that much. You didn't steal from your own and you definitely didn't tell lies, the Catholic Church was the bedrock to all of these traditional values. Those values never leave you and you try and pass them on to your family and, I would say, in my job too. When I look at some of the players today in the game I think they need some of these core values, not all players, as some are great role models, but definitely some of them need bringing back to reality.

We had a simple enough house with no bathroom originally, which was to come many years later when Dad converted a bedroom to a bathroom which was the high life alright. We were lucky though, as we actually owned a house when loads of my mates I used to play with didn't. One lad in my school, Patsy Lynch, never wore shoes at all. When I tell this to my kids, they think I am joking. Some families didn't have much at all but they never moaned about their lot, you just got on with it. Patsy was one of 12 kids, a great lad who was a mate of mine, shoes or not, a real gas character. If you went round to his house there were kids everywhere but his mum would always find me some jam and bread from somewhere, a lovely lady no taller than 5 feet. The Kennerks down the road had 14 kids and the Garlands had 12, it was nothing unusual then. We didn't have the benefits systems you have in place now in the UK, if you had a job you were one of the lucky ones. We would be considered 'posh' as we had our own house, which was rented, and at the end of the week you 'paid the man' again.

To sum up Dad's love of St. Pats, when he got made redundant from his job he got a £200 payout and he gave £100 to be a director of the club but he never told Mammy. It came out many years later when he wasn't well and they were working out where his money had gone and Mum was livid. We never had a bath in the house yet he put money into a silly old football club, or so she thought. That was Dad though, easy come easy go, much like the horses he'd back now and then. I don't recall ever hearing him swear, just a lovely genial man but you didn't want to cross him or Mammy, for that matter. It's no wonder I had a fierce temper on the pitch at times with the blood of those two coursing through my veins. Eventually, Dad had what they called a 'geyser' put in so the water came out hot and you could have a nice hot bath but before that we always had cold water. To this day, I still shout down to my wife Sheila to see if she wants my bath water, she never does which is hardly surprising after I've been in it but, I guess, I have my dad to thank for that water saving habit.

Mum always kept us well fed and my favourite thing would be to come in from school and she'd have a load of potatoes on the go so we'd grab them and run out to play football with them still hot in our hands. I would stand on the wing eating my spud if the ball wasn't near me and run with it in my hand if I had the ball or it was near. What more could you want, football and a lovely hot spud. We would play wherever we could or until we told to clear off, usually after a window had been broken and we'd been chased down the street.

Early school years were at the Model Primary school in Inchicore and then I went on to St. Michael's school in Keogh Square which was run by strict Christian Brothers who were another lot to watch out for. They ruled with an element of fear and if you stepped out of line you'd get a whack for your troubles. If you deserved it though, or even if you didn't, you didn't moan about it or you got another one. At St. Michaels we played hurling (an Irish game, a bit like hockey) and Gaelic but no soccer which was considered to be an English game then. If people knew you were playing soccer you would get a bit of stick as some of the feelings ran deep with the troubles and events in the past at Croke Park and so on. I didn't care much for the stick though as I just wanted to play the game I loved; it was what I was best at. I wasn't bad at Gaelic but I was always small so got a good bashing on the field but I was better at it than hurling which is a wild game. I tried a bit of boxing at the CIE club in Inchicore, like my big brother, Jimmy, but I got mashed a couple of times and didn't fancy getting 'bet up' for a bit of fun.

I got cut above the eye at boxing one day and the trainer just mopped it up with a towel which was covered in the blood gushing out of my face. I said, 'Look at all that blood,' as it wouldn't stop.

He just said, 'Piss off and get some cotton wool.' He couldn't give a bollocks.

To pass the time and keep off the streets we would all go to a club at St. Josephs to play snooker where Mr Lacey turned his whole house into a place for kids to play games. They had a football team too but I never wanted to play for them, as they weren't any good, so I headed to Richmond Rovers, at the age of 12, to play my first real games. I remember at Richmond there was only one lad that had a towel and we all used to share it and just hang it up to dry. Can you imagine telling young lads to do this now with their gelled hairstyles and fancy clothes? It's a wonder we never caught anything off each other but I guess that proves the old theory about building up resistance to infections. If we wanted to head further afield we would go into town, to Grafton Street, which was a real taste of the high life with its grand shops and lovely buildings. Another treat was to jump on a tram and head to the lovely sandy beaches at Merion or Portmanock. My two best mates who I knocked about with, and have stayed friends all my life, were Sean Little and Jim Wilson and we had some great times in the old town. I named my second youngest after Sean and Jim was my best man. I go back home as much as I can and the centre of Dublin still has the same charm no matter how much it has grown outwards over the years.

From Richmond Rovers I moved on to Bulfin Rovers, at the age of 13, but the following year moved on to the main junior soccer club in Dublin, Home Farm, having been spotted by the main man, Don Seery. If you get a chance, look up the history of Home Farm, a place with a remarkable record of producing full internationals that has been supplying the English Football League with talent for years. On the walls of Home Farm are the pictures of the full internationals or, at least, there always used to be. Famous names like Brady, Whelan and Giles with more recent internationals like Kinsella, Kavanagh and Cunningham.

It is a club based in Whitehall, Dublin, that grew from being a junior club to a full League of Ireland club but it still has its junior section, as far as I am aware, playing in the famous blue and white hoops. Players like Kevin O'Flanagan who played rugby and Soccer for Eire, Joey Carolan who went on to Manchester United and Joe Haverty who went on to play for the mighty Arsenal. At that time you also had Ray Brady,

Liam's older brother, and someone I went on to play with at international level and Ronnie Whelan Snr, who fathered another Ronnie who played for a while at Liverpool. I ended up working alongside Ronnie Jnr as assistant manager, many years later, in a short-lived spell at Southend United.

These and many more who cut their teeth at the Farm went on to become legends of Irish football which is remarkable for what was a little junior club in Dublin. As a comparison I would say it is like the Wallsend Boys Club in Tyneside or Senrab FC in London. Behind all of these clubs are a few unsung heroes who keep the club going, do all the chores that no one else wants to do and usually for no reward. At Home Farm those people were Don Seery and Bob Maddie who did the lot, organising training and games and making sure we knew where and what time we had to be places. They were marvellous men, looking back, as they had the same love of the game that I have and just wanted us kids to play soccer. Don's familiar phrase at games was 'you're better than this' which was hardly in the league of Jose or Pep for tactical analysis but he was a real football man and what he did at the club was remarkable with no funds to speak of.

When Dad realised that I was really into soccer, he bought me a pair of boots from the market on Moore Street which he probably would have saved up three bob over a few weeks to buy. They were high over the ankle and had a big cap at the front, not like the lightweight, fluorescent things you see now. It was impossible to run freely in these boots with leather 'taps' on the top and big studs nailed in to keep you on your feet. We should get the young players to play a game in these boots now and see how they get on. They were not great for developing skill that's for sure and heavy as you like. I never wore shin pads either, in fact I rarely wore shin pads as a pro until quite late as I found them to be a nuisance. Thinking back to some of the tackles I used to fly into, I really should have worn some but you learn to protect yourself.

After I had a pair of real football boots, they never came off. I wore them everywhere and it meant I could ditch the old shoes and wellies I used to play football in the street in. It was a common sight in those days to see boys playing football in wellies, it never seemed strange back then you played in whatever you could to cover your feet up. We played in the street, whenever there was a ball around, and on the grass at Keogh if it was really organised. Only one lad had a ball, Owen Murphy, so no matter what Owen was always invited to play even though he wasn't much good at the game.

So with my new boots and the skills honed on the streets or Keogh Square, I headed off to Home Farm via Richmond and then Bulfin Rovers. Well, if St. Pats looked like Wembley to me this was the next best thing. They had two pitches and changing rooms and it looked like a real football club. I loved it there; this was where I wanted to be. It was a fair trek across Dublin from home in Inchicore but I would have walked there barefoot on broken glass if I had to. It was a real football place, steeped in history, with a procession of players who had gone on to make it in the game.

They had produced Kevin O'Flanagan who played rugby and soccer at the top level, the great Joey Carolan and so on. As I said, I played with Ray Brady, Liam's older brother, and Ronnie Whelan's dad, also called Ronnie, as well as a lad called Tony Boyle who played League of Ireland for Shamrock Rovers. We played against the local sides like Stella Maris, Joneville, Beggsborough and Ringsend and you would get to know the best young players coming through like Johnny Giles who played for Stella. Johnny was younger than us but he stood out even then and he has to go down as one of the best I played with when we both turned out for Eire many years later.

Don Seery, the aforementioned driving force behind the club, was a truly great man whilst the priests were also a big presence behind the scenes. There is a plaque at the entrance to the club with Don's name on and rightly so. He did everything up there and was helped by Bob Maddie, who was the trainer, and he'd bring us down for a bottle of milk after putting us through our paces. There was no coaching to speak of back then, you'd play in practice games and hope to get picked for the real games when they came up. I was picked to play right back even though I always fancied myself as a midfielder, probably because I was difficult to beat and had good pace so they stuck me there and there I stayed. I obviously did okay in the games for the famous old club as a fella called Bill Hennessy spotted me and he had connections to a lot of the big pro clubs in England. Bill used to scout all the lads in Dublin who looked the part and he told me that I should go to England as he said I had what it took to make the grade. Without Bill's encouragement I would never have made the trip across the water to try my hand and for that I am eternally grateful. Bill had faith in me and that was good enough, I was sold on the dream.

Bill set me up with Burnley FC who were a huge club in the First Division then and regarded as one of the most forward-thinking clubs around. They were one of the forerunners of the youth system set-ups with a network of scouts, like Bill, getting the best players in. They even had their own training ground, the Gawthorpe Centre, which back then was unheard of. I went home and told Mammy and Daddy about the chance to go over and Dad was great even though he didn't want me to go, Mammy didn't say much. Dad said you don't even know where Burnley is but you may as well go as you'll only get £2 a week at St. Pats. Mammy had seen my brother, Jimmy, head off to Australia at the age of 20 and now her other son was off to England so she was not best pleased but what could she say, they both had to support me in my dream of making the grade.

I had not long been working at the local railway depot, driving the tractor in the yard, and I probably would have stayed there for years had I not gone and my life would have been very different. In Inchicore you had the railway depot which was the main employer or Kilmainham Gaol up the road which was the scene of the execution of the Easter Rising rebels in 1916. Those two places and St. Pats Football Club were the general options on offer, in Inchicore, so you took the railway for a job, you'd hope to stay out of the gaol and if you were lucky you might turn out for St Pats at Richmond Park. Lou Kelly of The Dubliners came from Inchicore so he managed to find another way out through music. Me, I was getting a golden ticket to the football League. It was never about the money, it was to be a professional footballer, to do the thing I loved and to get paid. I told my dad I would always go home but I never did and it broke my heart that I wasn't there when he had a massive stroke years later. He got made redundant and not long after had a stroke, he was never the same afterwards, dying much too young. Never heard Daddy swear, a lovely warm man who was as strong as an ox.

Having seen the big sides come over like Manchester United, Chelsea and Arsenal to play the League of Ireland teams, I was going to get the chance to go over there and, hopefully, one day play on the same pitch as these players I idolised. Players like Jimmy O'Neil, Tommy Eglinton and Peter Farrell who all played for Everton and came from my hometown of Dublin and the great Johnny Carey who played over 300 games for Man Utd. Here was I, trying to follow in their famous footsteps, and, even with all my self-belief, I didn't think I actually ever would.

Over the years, when I returned back to Dublin, I would bump into the man who persuaded me to go, Bill Hennessy, usually at the beautiful church in Inchicore, the Oblates. I always thanked him for telling me to go, for planting that seed in me that I really could play soccer for a living. Bill never moved from Inchicore and I guess it was fate that he lived on our road and spotted me. Bill wrote to Burnley and set up the trial period for me, I packed a small case with a change of clothes, an overcoat and my boots and I was off to Dublin Port with Mammy crying at the docks as the boat pulled out. It was 1954 and I said goodbye to my beloved Dublin but I never really left in my heart.

CHAPTER 3
Turfed to Devon
1954 – 1961

1950s Bill Haley – Rock Around The Clock, Buddy Holly, Elvis Presley, Bobby Darin – Mack The Knife over the airways and James Dean lighting up the screen in 'Rebel Without A Cause' while Marlon Brando was mean and moody in 'On The Waterfront'.

Britain was rebuilding post-war with the 1951 Festival and the Queen's Coronation in 1953. Edmund Hilary scaled Everest in 1954 and rationing ended in 1954 – anything was possible as optimism crept in and the space race to the moon dominated the news. TVs (black and white) became more and more common.

I was driving a black Ford Popular, my first car, with a crank start which always drew a comment or two if the lads saw me starting her up. I thought I was the bee's knees as I could get around, but popular was right all right, everyone bloody had one! No heater, semaphore indicators that popped out when you wanted to turn, only six volts power and issued with a starting handle. Imagine a young pro these days handed that to start up in the car park?

With the image of Mammy crying her eyes out Dublin Port, in the summer of 1954, burned into my memory I headed off to God knows what, full of excitement and trepidation of what lay ahead. I had packed an old brown suitcase with metal caps on the corners and leather straps round it, the likes of which you find in a loft these days maybe stuffed with programmes. What do you pack for an indeterminable trip to a place you have no idea about? Well I had packed six shirts, a spare of pair of trousers, underwear and my beloved football boots. I had on my best trousers, shirt and Crombie style overcoat so I was travelling light but, for all I knew, I could be heading back in few weeks. I genuinely had no idea; this was a punt with the mighty Burnley FC.

Before I'd left Mammy at the Port, I'd made a promise in the form of a pledge which is an undertaking under the eyes of the church, signified by a small lapel badge worn at all times. My pledge was not to consume alcohol as Mammy was worried I'd go off the rails in this foreign land and succumb to the devil of the dreaded drink, the scourge of so many back home. This tickled the kids when I told them recently, they just can't comprehend why I would do such a thing, religious or not. What you have to realise is that 1950s' Ireland was steeped in religion and it was the bedrock of society there, it really meant something. Alongside this sat the dark neighbours of drink and gambling which happily coexisted as long as you went to church and said the odd Hail Mary. It was a worry for Mum at a delicate time with my brother Jimmy off in Australia out of sight and she didn't want me to fall foul of the deadly drink. Now, Agnes smoked like a chimney but the drink was a worry. It seemed the right thing to do and I was happy to do it if it eased her troubles, but it wasn't lip service. A pledge was a pledge, I kept to it for years and, looking back, it helped me to stay focused on my career in the early days, definitely. I've seen many a real talent ruined by a liking for a beer or two. I wore that badge for years with pride and never really got the taste, which helped I have to say.

I caught the ferry to Holyhead for what was to be the first of many journeys across the choppy Irish Sea, heading to a country I'd never been to, trying to pass the interview of a lifetime with one of the big boys in the English Football League. Excited, and a little worried about it all but not half as much as Mammy. Dad seemed more relaxed but I'm sure he was apprehensive too, I doubt he actually thought I'd make it so probably said, 'Ah, Agnes, sure let him go and he'll probably be back in few weeks, but let the lad go.' I'm not sure even with my self-belief I actually thought I'd make it at Burnley so I wouldn't blame him for thinking that. On that four hour crossing to Holyhead, and the subsequent five hour train journey to Burnley, I had plenty of time to think about it. I spent the whole time taking the journey in as it was all a new experience for me, I wasn't a big reader then so it was look out of the window, maybe spend a few bob in the shop and soak it all in.

Burnley had paid the £4 ferry fare and train return while dad had given me some spending and spare should I need it to buy a few bags of chips when I wasn't eating at the digs. For that I'll always be grateful as money wasn't what you'd call 'spare', but he found it from somewhere. What was going to happen beyond the first couple of weeks was anyone's guess but I was promised at least a three week trial and that the club would put me up in digs so I'd be looked after.

After a couple of hours looking out from the ferry lounge the views of the Irish Sea got a bit boring so I had a walk around the deck. I nearly got swept away in the wind and I held on tightly to my old flimsy suitcase. Then I saw the Anglesey coast on the horizon and, with it, my first foreign land. When the ferry docked I was off the walkway and headed to the station for the train to Crewe and then another change at Preston. It was at Preston station that I asked a guard where I caught the Burnley train to which he replied in the first Lancashire accent I'd heard, 'No bugger goes to Burnley, lad.' He then pointed and said, 'That platform over there, Paddy.' Welcome to England, I thought.

On the last leg at Burnley I got on a bus to the hotel I had been booked into, it had been a long day but the excitement of it all kept me going. Tomorrow I'd be starting my trial period for The Clarets. The hotel was called the Yorkshire Grey and seemed nice enough, but what did I know? I was up and ready early then onto the bus heading to the Gawthorpe Centre. What a place, Burnley was one of the first clubs to have their own training ground thanks to their innovative chairman, Bob Lord. When Mr Lord walked into a room everyone stood up, he had that aura about him. We sat down to get changed in a spotless dressing room and the cotton drill training kit was all laid out for the triallists with that detergent smell of washed kit that would be a constant companion to me over the next 50 years. We headed out to join the warm up, as much as it was then, and I could sense the senior lads and other trialists thinking 'who's this scrawny Irish lad, what's he bloody doing here?' Now that's not me having a chip, it's just how the football world was, and still is. We are all after the same shirts, so people close ranks. They had the crop of northern lads there from Newcastle and Sunderland, big, strong and talented. No matter, I was here to give it my best, so I did and I thought I did well enough in the trial games.

I was training on the same pitch as the great Jimmy Mcllroy, the Northern Ireland international. I said, 'Hello Mr. Mcllroy,' on the first day and he asked where I was from and so on. There was always a bit of unity between the Irish lads as we were all in a foreign place missing home. Don't forget that this was 1950s' England and the Irish, whether it was from the North or South, just weren't generally welcome along with the Windrush generation from the West Indies. Unfortunately, there was fear and prejudice to the immigrants from those two regions at the time. Thankfully, this has now practically gone but it has reared its head again with different nationalities these days, sadly. Those signs in lodgings saying: 'No Irish, No blacks, No dogs' were no myth, believe it or not. What a thing to say, not only don't bother trying to pay for lodgings because of your nationality but you are grouped together with a four-legged animal. In many ways, we've come a long way in a short space of time but, sadly, there are always things to improve and some ignorant people still need to be educated. I didn't dwell much on it as I was here to make a life for myself and I wasn't about to let a few idiots stop that from happening. On the pitch you'd get called all sorts but opponents soon realised I wouldn't bite on any verbals and they might just get a bit extra in the next challenge. They soon stopped calling you derogatory names after that. I can safely say no one ever talked me out of a game by talking bollocks, they either got a smile or my best cold-eyed stare, followed by a whack when they least expected it. When you've played against some of the toughest boys in Dublin in Keogh Square kickabouts, there's not much that fazes you.

Over at the Garforth, I was rubbing shoulders with the likes of Jimmy Adamson, Jock Winton, Alex Elder, Brian Pilkington, and Brian Miller, all household names from the First Division I'd listened to on the wireless or read about in the papers. Burnley had finished mid-table the season before, they were a steady top division side at the time, obviously they are now back in the top flight after a few years in the wilderness. To think they nearly dropped out of the league altogether in 1987 but for a last day 2-1 win over Leyton Orient. Around the same time, I was at Wembley for the Littlewoods Cup Final with Arsenal watching us pick up our first trophy with a 2-1 win over Liverpool. I had no idea back then there would be a complete reversal in our fortunes.

I ended up doing a full month's trial playing in all the A games which were under 18s really, playing against the likes of Preston North End, Liverpool and Blackpool. These were the sides I'd dreamt about playing against and here I was, an ordinary boy from Dublin, wearing the famous claret kit of Burnley against these grand old clubs. Even just seeing the famous kits and badges brought it all home, I'd idolised the English League back home and now I was playing against these actual teams. I was loving it and couldn't wait to tell Mammy and Daddy all about it in my weekly updates.

In the digs, they'd put me in with three gas characters from Northern Ireland; Billy Marshall, Sammy McGrory and Sid Weatherall. Now, I was a Southern Catholic boy and they were three Protestant boys from the North, quite different, despite coming from the same island, but there was none of that nonsense about our differences. We were just four lads trying to make the grade, what did it matter what we did or didn't believe in? Sure enough, there was plenty of ribbing and mickey-taking but it was never nasty, just young fellas having the craic a long way from home. They could never get over me heading off to church every Sunday and their favourite when it rained was 'say a prayer for us, Theo' and 'surely to God you're not going to church in this rain?' I don't think they were too serious about their religion.

I came across Billy a few times later on in our careers as he went on to play for Oldham and Hartlepool, he always said the same thing, 'You're not still going to church in the rain?' With footballers the jokes invariably involve repetition.

The lady running the digs was a nice old lady who asked me the first day, 'Do you like greens, love?' to which I replied no. Well, she didn't pay a blind bit of notice, just kept piling on the greens every bloody day, which I just ate to keep the peace and now I love them, so she must have converted me.

After a month of training, working with the ground staff and playing in games, they took me into the office and told me they wouldn't be taking me on, saying I was too small. I was crestfallen, but they said they'd hook me up elsewhere so I dusted myself off and got my head around a new challenge. It was Billy Morris the youth team manager who broke the news to me, something I would have to do many times over the years, never an easy task crushing a young man's football dreams. Billy was a lovely fella who was a top player in his day, a Welsh international who was forced to retire early. I held no bad feelings towards him or the club, he was just doing his job and, with hindsight, he was right. He said I wasn't quite good enough and needed to go away and get stronger. Now those are harsh words to hear for the first time but there's no sugarcoating these decisions. He gave me some encouragement though, and said I'd make it somewhere but the group here included some of the best around.

He was proved right as Burnley went on to have unprecedented success with Billy's babes winning the First Division in 1960 with nearly all of the side coming through the ranks similar to the experience we had at Arsenal in 1989. The Clarets were even pioneers in international tournaments heading to the States in 1961 to play in the International Soccer League and also playing in the European Cup the following season playing against Reims and Hamburger SV. Burnley were the progressive team of the 1950s and early 1960s, thanks to the remarkable Bob Lord at the helm and Frank Hill managing the team. Little Billy Morris, the Welsh flyer, was a key part in the production line of top young players so I guess I should take something from the fact I got so close to one of the best youth set-ups in the country.

However, it never worked out at Turf Moor but they still managed to get me a trial many miles away on the Devon coast with Exeter City as there was a link between the two boards. The vice chairman at Exeter was a fella called George Gilhan and he knew the scout at Burnley, Tommy Coulter, probably through George's hotel in Torquay, The Belgrave, which was one of the biggest in the town. Tommy kindly recommended me so I was off, boots dubbed and packed in the old brown suitcase again. I had no idea where Exeter was really so had to ask a couple of the Burnley lads. Turns out it was a fair way down on the south west coast and they were in the bottom tier, playing in the Third Division South against the likes of Millwall, QPR, and my future club, Northampton Town, as well as current Premiership sides Crystal Palace, Bournemouth, Southampton and Watford.

They may well have been at the wrong end of the table in the bottom league but it made no odds to me as long as I made it as a professional. I was in no position to be choosy; clubs weren't queuing up for my signature that's for sure. I loved the idea of training every day as a pro footballer, improving my game and getting paid for it. That's what I wanted more than anything in the world. I wanted to follow my Irish idols like Frank O'Farrell and Noel Cantwell, both playing for West Ham in the Second Division, and Charlie Hurley playing for Millwall in the Third Division South. These were names I knew from the football scene at home who had made it in the English Football League, the finest around. What a thing that would be and it would make my parents proud. They were simple enough targets and, at that time, the dizzy heights of the First Division weren't in my thoughts, I just wanted to say I was a pro footballer.

I headed down on the train changing at Paddington and then on to the Great Western Railway which would become a prominent fixture over the coming years. The journey took forever so when I got to my digs near the ground I went straight to bed, banjaxed from the long day. I reported to the ground in the morning and they handed me some training gear and told me I'd be working with the ground staff which is one way of getting some return on your investment, I guess. I had to report to the ground and help the groundsman, Sonny Clarke, who was a great old stick. I don't think he was very impressed with my ground staff skills though, as he'd tell me regularly, 'You'd better bloody make it as a footballer, as you'll never be a groundsman.' I'd cut the grass, replace the divots, fork the pitch, paint the stand, you name it. It was never any bother as the longer it went on the more likely I'd be getting that golden opportunity to turn pro. I wrote home to Mammy and she'd reply with a note and a system that she followed for nearly 50 years, enclosing the main Irish papers for me to read up on, in case I lost my Irishness, I guess.

What I noticed about Exeter was that you'd always get compared to the local lads who have come through and cost the club nothing, even though I'd only cost them peanuts. Before I'd even signed they were complaining about the cost, it wasn't my fault I wasn't a local lad. Exeter City was a small club then, it still is, and it was trying to compete with bigger clubs in the same league with larger grounds and more money. It will always bring back fond memories for me, they signed me as pro and I met my lovely wife, Sheila, in one of my favourite cities. If that wasn't enough, I got spotted by the legendary Dave Bowen while playing there. When I arrived though, none of this seemed on the cards and I could see it all ending soon and hear me Da saying to Mammy, 'See Agnes, I told you he'd be back, will you ever listen to your ole' fella?' They stuck me in the reserves, I played all over the place in tiny non-league grounds smaller than St. Pats back home in Inchicore, places like Yeovil, Canterbury and Dover where my lads, Adrian and Paul, would also play many years later. They must have fancied me though, as I bypassed the youth team and they put me with the older lads so they seemed to have plans for me.

I enjoyed the work with old Sonny, who looked after me, and I did odd summer jobs to make up the money. I got on well with all of the youth team boys especially a Northern

Ireland lad, Roy Whiteside, who was from the Shankhill Road in Belfast and had seen some sights. Roy was a great lad, we got on really well, and these connections really helped me settle and concentrate on football whilst gaining life experience. Then it happened, on 28 March 1955 at the age of 17, Exeter City Football Club offered me a pro contract of £7 and £5 a week, which meant you got £7 during the season and £5 out of season. They could have offered me half a crown and I'd still have signed just to say I'd made it; I was a professional footballer. The first thing I did was ring Mrs Coogan across the road in Inchicore Road, as she was the only one with a phone, so she went and fetched Mammy and Dad and I told them my big news.

They were made up and so proud which made me even happier. Dad was pleased that I'd be earning much more than I'd earn at home even though I had to pay my digs money out of that now. It was a few zeros less than the likes of Gareth Bale these days but, as I said, they could have offered me anything, it was never about the money. That summer of 1955 I went home, for the first time, back to Dublin, as I did every year thereafter, for summer only, to return heavier which I did every year as Mammy fed me up. I'd end up running the last two weeks before I went back to make sure I was fit enough to go straight into training. There was the odd bit of hostility when you went back to Dublin and the odd comment. 'Who'd you think you are giving it the big I am,' which I never did but some people, especially when connected with England, were bitter. Then you'd hear, 'Why have they signed him, he's not even that good, no good in the air,' and so on. If you married an English girl, as I ended up doing, it was even worse – it had no effect on me, though.

I had to be patient and bide my time until my debut as the right back in front of me was a canny old pro called Brian Doyle who would have made it on the pitch on one leg if he had to. Brian had bronchial problems having signed from Stoke City on the advice of their medical staff, believe it or not, as they said the sea air should help. Now, I used to pick Brian's brains about positional play and learning the position so, for all his reluctance to give up his shirt, he was very

27

generous with his time and advice. I was always asking questions, keen to learn about body position, when to close down and when to jockey a winger and so on. In those days coaches were trainers just looking to reach a certain level of fitness rather than teach you specific parts of the game, never mind specific positions. Billy Morris was the trainer and if you needed to ask him something he would always try to help but there was no real coaching to speak of. Nowadays, you might have three goalkeeping coaches which is the other end of the scale.

I carried on as before, helping Sonny with the pitch, for about eight months more, although he'd probably say I wasn't much help. You'd see lads come and go, eventually moving from ground staff to full time playing staff. That waiting game watching others get their big chance was a killer as you kept trying your best in the A team games just hoping to get the nod. At the age of 18 I finally got my chance, making my professional debut a couple of years after heading over on the ferry. It was against Norwich City at home on a Wednesday night, 14 September 1955. I can still remember the manager, Frank Broom, bringing me into the office on the Tuesday to tell me I was in the side the next day and to get an early night. Those moments mean so much to a footballer, you've done all the hard miles, played all those games and run through pain with sweat just to get the chance and here it was. I was beside myself and as always, I rang Mrs Coogan again to tell Dad who was made up for me.

I played well enough in a 1-1 draw, stayed in for four games and then Frank took me out of the side, telling me I wasn't quite ready, that I was still a bit raw. Well, talk about crashing down to earth, I didn't like it, or agree with it, but I wasn't about to start shouting the odds especially with the fella who had signed me and given me my big chance. We'd drawn after Norwich with Coventry at Highfield Road, then lost midweek to Gillingham at Priestfield and at home to Brentford which was a poor result. The back to back defeats made it easy to drop the young lad, I suppose, and bring the old pro back in. I was sure I wasn't to blame, I couldn't even put a goal down to me in those four games. I was only 18 years of age so I had time on my side but I didn't expect to wait nearly two years for my next chance at home to Southampton in a 2-2 draw. I spent two seasons playing reserve football against some robust teams, which stood me in good stead, but six months or less would have done me fine.

Brian and his chest problem were back in the side. But that's football and it was an early lesson for me, you haven't arrived so don't get comfortable, son. I'm sure I did the same as Frank when I ended up sitting on the other side of the table later on. I said to myself the day he told me, 'Right, next time I get in he's getting no excuse to do that again,' and that stayed with me my whole career. Never ever give reasons to take your shirt away may sound obvious but people missing games with slight knocks, not putting in 100% in games, I never understood it for the life of me. It is your job, the thing you love. Sure enough, it didn't happen again so the kick up the jacksy worked. I knew I'd be back in as Brian was always struggling.

Exeter's ground, St James Park, was nothing like its namesake in the North East with a capacity of around 8,000 in those days even with everyone standing. The ground was named after the nearby railway station. Remarkably, they managed to get a record attendance of nearly 21,000 for a sixth round FA Cup game in 1931 against Sunderland. The fans must have been packed to the rafters as the ground was so small in every way, with three open sides, back then but it was a lovely little club and a great place to learn my trade. They were founder members of the old Third Division in 1920 and have occupied the lower leagues for most of their time, currently competing in Football League 2 or the old Fourth as I call it. The club have suffered financially in recent years much like my other old club, Northampton, but hopefully both can enjoy some stability and push forward like the trail blazed by the likes of Bournemouth recently.

Exeter's most famous player was born and bred in the city, the legendary Cliff Bastin who went on to play for Arsenal and become their record goalscorer until Ian Wright surpassed it. In all of my time at the club we played in the old Division 4 which was the bottom tier of the Football League. You would have to go to all manner of far flung places in rain, wind and snow and it was a real education into the brass tacks of professional football. Places like Hartlepool United and Carlisle United seemed like the other side of the world from Exeter. Teams like Gateshead, Barrow, Workington, Southport and Doncaster were all in the Football League then but are now plying their trade in the non-league pyramid and you had sides like Watford, Crystal Palace, Southampton and Watford who are all obviously in the top tier now. We also had sides like Northampton Town who I would eventually join and enjoy great success with and I had my first experience of the cauldron that was The Den at Millwall. As I would regularly tell my sons when they were growing up I played at all but two of the Football League clubs during my time playing which is not a bad record to have.

My eldest and youngest boys, Adrian and Paul, would come back with their claims of winning this and that at non-league level but I always won that battle, saying I'd never heard of those cups or those leagues. The middle son, Sean, would come back with some statistic about the Greenwich and Lewisham League on a Sunday, well, I didn't even bother rising to that one. All three of them got used to the well-worn question, 'How many international caps have you got, son?' They used to come back and say I must have collected enough coupons off the Corn Flakes packets to qualify to play and 'it was easy then' and so on. Although they'd never admit it, I would like to think that they are proud of their old Dad but they always gave as good as they got.

In my first game at the old Den the ball ran out of play and, in those days, the barriers weren't there like they are now. I was playing right back so went to get the ball for a throw in. Arnold Mitchell was an experienced straight-talking Yorkshire lad who was a key player and captain of our team at right half and someone who really took me under his wing. Arnold went on to become the record appearance holder for the Grecians playing in every position, including in goal. Well, as I ran off to get the ball on the main stand, with the enthusiasm of a young lad not quite aware of the surroundings, Arnold shouted over to me, 'Leave thee ball there, lad.' Arnold was well used to the Millwall 'atmosphere' and knew I would end up getting plenty of stick from the Dockers, either verbal or something worse. I learned very early on that Millwall fans were fiercely loyal of their own and were great when you were on their side but if you were playing for, or connected with, the opposition, then you were going to get some stick, that's for sure, even if you were a young lad who was a bit green round the gills. If you don't fancy it then they will spot it and they were the same with their own players, they would work you out straight away, no problem.

It obviously struck a chord with me that day as I became a lifelong friend of Arnold whose wife, Julie, was my wife Sheila's best friend and played a big part in us getting together. We would regularly go out together as couples to dances or for a meal and remained friends from the moment we met although, sadly, Arnold passed away in October 2014. Aside from being just a lovely man, he was a great help to me in my early days as a pro and a very good player in that Grecians' side, captaining them to promotion in 1963-64 after I had left the club.

Arnold also got me interested in the other sporting love of my life, golf. Arnold was a keen player and kept asking me to come and play at his beloved local club at Dawlish Warren, so when someone turned up at St James Park selling some golf clubs, I bought them in a flash, keen to get out with my mate Arnold and give it a go. It was only when I got them home I realised they were left-handed but I wasn't going to let that stop me so I taught myself to play left-handed, which I play to this day although nowhere near as good as I used to. Just goes to show what can be achieved if you put your mind to it but it also taught me to be wary of a good bargain. I got down to a 7 handicap during my best days with a golf ball so think how low I would have got if I'd bought a right-handed set? Also, with a handicap in the early 20s now, I've a great excuse for having a crap round – 'I'm playing with the wrong hand.'

In those days, when football was definitely less professional, you would generally get some high scoring games as sides had to travel for, what seemed like, ages to far flung places with none of the preparation you get now. We would spend a long time cramped in little coaches or, if we were lucky, on a train, have large pre-match meals and then expect to go out and run around for 90 minutes and get a result. There was none of the science behind the game and warm-ups were usually army type drills to get the body ready for some activity but no gentle stretching and gradual warming up of the muscles before building it up. Players would play with injuries, worried about their wages, and would try to get through games without getting found out. You would have no chance these days with microchips monitoring how far you run in a game and a number of physios and coaches watching your every move. It's no surprise that we lost a stack of games away in those days and managed to keep the season going by our home form. Exeter was not the easiest place to get to for the same reasons as we had getting to Carlisle on a wet Tuesday evening.

In my last full season at the club (1959–1960) we played 49 games with 26 at home and 23 away. At home we won 15 with a great run of six wins on the trot at home from October to December. That's a very healthy win percentage at home, whilst away we only won five out of 23 which is dramatically different. We relied on the fact that most sides had to travel down to the West Country to play us and we would hit them at home so it's no surprise we beat the likes of Oldham, Workington, Doncaster, Rochdale and Hartlepools. These were sides that had to travel the length and width of England to play us. We tanked Cloughie's beloved Hartlepools 5-0 in a rout at St James Park but, when we travelled away, we got a few good hidings in return, getting done 3-0 at Rochdale and Notts County and got spanked 5-2 away to Watford that year. Somehow, we managed to win 4-0 away to Carlisle which is practically in Scotland. In those days you wouldn't stop over in a hotel and get a good rest before you played, if you had a long journey you just met earlier and got on with it. The travelling was deadly, especially the midweek games, and all through my playing and coaching career it has been the least enjoyable part of life as a footballer. If you could just play the game it would the perfect job. For someone like me who loves the game it has been the best job in the world but you can keep the travelling for hours on dusty old coaches to far flung towns.

While on a night out at a dance hall, in 1958, I met my gorgeous wife-to-be, Sheila Smith, who was a couple of years older so, of course, I said I was the same age. I tried to impress her by saying I played for City but it didn't cut the mustard with her even though her dad was a big Grecians' fan. I even mentioned I was staying in digs with Vic Godber, who was the brother of Sheila's sister's other half, but not much swayed this cool customer, proving to be my most difficult opponent to date. We met for a date, one day, at a bus stop in Whipton where she lived and I brought a signed copy of me in Exeter colours for her which she still reminds me of to this day. I don't quite know what I was thinking there. She warmed to me over time though, and we started courting properly which meant I met their lovely family; father, Sam, and mother, Violet. Sheila had a large family with four brothers and two sisters, sadly one brother, Colin, died young of tuberculosis.

The family made me feel very welcome with meals at weekends and so on while I'd repay the favour with tickets for games for Sam and Sheila's brothers, Gordon and Alan. Samuel Smith was infamous in Exeter as he was a feared inspector on the Great Western Railway bringing people from London or the smoke as Exonians called it. Sam took no nonsense and was a highly intelligent man always working on something or other, be it his beautiful MG sports car, making wine from his two greenhouses full of grapes or in his fully stacked workshop, everything was painted GWR green around the house and garden. I got on great with him but I definitely wouldn't cross him, while Violet was the sweetest, kindest lady you could wish to meet and she did a mean Sunday roast which was like home from home for me.

Sam gave me a rollicking when we decided to get married as I was due to ask for Sheila's hand, all proper and above board, but the local paper leaked the story as 'local girl set to marry City player'. Well, he only had to tell me once barking, 'If I'm paying money towards this wedding, I don't expect to read about it in the bloody paper.' Good old Sam, one of life's characters. I doubt they were best pleased about their daughter running off with an Irish Catholic footballer but they never let on, always being supportive and I guess they could all see we were very much in love.

In 1960 we got married on Easter Monday at the beautiful Sacred Heart Catholic Church just a stone's throw from the impressive City Cathedral. It goes without saying we got married in the morning so I could play in the afternoon for the first team. I go back to my earlier promise of giving no reason to be dropped, even getting married. This may seem very single-minded but Sheila has always understood this and been fully supportive which sums her up. She has always been that way, giving up so much for me, even converting from C of E to Catholicism so we could marry on equal terms.

Most of the City team were there at the church in Exeter and my best mates from Dublin, Jim Wilson and Sean Little, came over on the ferry. Jim was best man and I still speak to him and Sean regularly, just three Dubs having the craic now the same as we did growing up, great lads the pair of them. We played Crystal Palace in the afternoon and managed to draw with the Eagles so my wedding day wasn't spoiled by a defeat and the lads had a whip round raising the princely sum of £25 as a wedding present including money from the Palace lads, fair play. This was a tidy sum in those days and would reflect more than a good week's wages so not to be sniffed at.

We set off after the game in the goalkeeper's borrowed car to Bournemouth for a three-day honeymoon and then headed to the Lake District to play two games away at Darlington and Workington. Again, I wouldn't let anything get in the way of the football which is why some of the things I read about now just don't make sense. It's still the same game, just played by people with different incentives, I guess. During all of this time, I'd had the same manager and Frank Broome had been a real influence on me during the early days of learning my position and becoming a pro. He had been a top player who'd played for Villa, Derby, Notts County and England. I realise now how lucky I'd been to have him as my first manager.

No sooner had we got married though, Frank left to manage Southend and they made one of the playing staff, Glen Wilson, the manager. Now, I never really got on with Glen as a player, a good one at that, and when they made him player-manager I knew it was bad news for me. We didn't get on from the get go and, to be honest, I thought he was an arsehole so I knew I'd have to move on eventually. It all started when I tore a thigh muscle in a game and he wanted me to play in the next game despite me telling him I was injured. Now, I've never feigned an injury in my life and, as explained, I never gave the opportunity to be dropped so why would I fake an injury. It summed up how much he knew his players. It is probably the biggest insult to an honest pro to accuse him of faking it and I lost all respect for Glen immediately. I played under duress but couldn't run or strike the ball, it was a waste of time and I made it worse as I knew I would.

To brighten the mood off the pitch, we had our first child on 12 February 1961 when beautiful, bonnie Teresa Marie came into our world. Being 23 years of age, with a mortgage and young family, I had more responsibility now and I began to worry about the future at Exeter especially with Frank Broome gone. It came as no surprise when Glen put me on the transfer list, disappointing though it was, and we had a few cross words, not for the first time.

In my final season at Exeter though, the FAI had seen my progress and I got the red letter day notice to call me up for international duty for Eire. I was the proudest man in Devon, it certainly lifted my transfer listed gloom and made me feel justified in my anger towards Glen Wilson. I rang Daddy straight away and he was as pleased as me, both excited at the prospect of wearing the famous green shirt and the shamrock badge. I had gone from kicking around with the other boys on Keogh Square in our shoes or wellies in the street, with the only borrowed ball in Inchicore, to eventually playing for the national side at Dalymount Park. I got called up twice but never got a shirt so no appearance caps but no matter, I was on their radar and I was improving so I felt sure the caps would come. Little did I know at the time though, that the kickabouts on the streets and on Keogh Square were not wildly different to the professionalism in place at the FAI back then. More of that later.

A few clubs were interested in me namely Chelsea, West Brom and Birmingham who were all bigger clubs. Then the great Dave Bowen came calling and, in no time, I was off to Northampton Town and, what turned out to be, a remarkable journey to the top. I signed for the Cobblers on 19 May 1961 for a small fee. Dave stepped in at a time when I really needed him and boy did he improve my situation. Little did I know at the time, but I was joining the club at the start of something fantastic with the maestro Bowen pulling the strings. The club has never seen anything like it before or since. It was the 60s, the country was changing and exploding musically and culturally, and the Cobblers were on the rise too with me driving them on with the armband. Time to up sticks, say goodbye to our family, friends and the city we loved to head to a new life and challenge. With the boots – better ones this time – dubbed again I was off to prove myself once more. Exeter had been great to me in a football sense and, personally, I still love the place, a great city with lovely people.

As part of my long service to the club I received a loyalty gift of £700 which was a lovely gesture as we were going to need it. Who knew what Northampton would be like but I was excited and life was great.

CHAPTER 4
On the up with the Cobblers
1962 – 1965

1960s The Beatles and Rolling Stones change music on two fronts, rock/pop and rock/blues – I loved Frank Sinatra and Andy Williams as Johnny Kurila my great mate at Northampton brought all these great new records back from the States. Elvis became The King and we jived away on the dancefloor. I dived into the fantastic spaghetti westerns of Sergio Leone like 'Fistful of Dollars' and 'The Good, The Bad and The Ugly'.

The whole country was going through a liberating rebirth, Ann Packer and Mary Rand excelled at the Olympics and London became a cultural centre for others to follow. Suddenly, it was the place to be, at the forefront of music, fashion and sport. The USA and Russia were racing to get to the moon first and literally anything had become possible. JFK lit up the world to new ideas of civil rights until that fateful day he was assassinated in Dallas in 1963.

Cassius Clay shook up the world before he became Muhamad Ali, he was The Greatest

I drove a Hillman Minx for the majority of my time at Northampton which was a fairly standard car back then, nothing fancy like the players have now but it did the job.

We loaded up the Ford Popular with our new baby strapped in and headed off to a new challenge in a new town and it was back to proving myself at another club, only this time I'd actually been signed first. Dave Bowen had seen something in the games against Exeter in the league and told me when we met that he thought I could be a leader on the pitch and, as well as my ability, he liked my competitive nature. We had to report to the ground, pick up the keys and find out where the club house was – it was part of the signing-on deal that we bought one of their houses for a reduced cost. The house was a tidy little new build, three bedroom terrace that faced the main stand of the Saints rugby stadium at Franklin's Gardens – it wasn't the best view around but a nice little house. We were living out of boxes with a young baby to look after, not ideal, but Sheila being Sheila took it all in her stride. She still missed her friends and family terribly though and, being a coastal girl, she really missed escaping to the beach. Northampton was very different to Exeter, which we both loved, and Sheila was a little homesick with a newborn baby and no network of family and friends. Looking back now, it was a difficult period of upheaval but we had no choice, you just moved with the money. To add to our problems poor little Teresa had been born with her hips out of line and was in a splint from six weeks old which they gradually adjusted over many months, thank God.

Sheila turned the house into a home and nursed Teresa through those difficult times which allowed me to concentrate on my career and the job in hand. For my first day at the club I met Dave at the County Ground, which was a little step up from Exeter's St James Park but still a lower league ground in all honesty. The club shared the facilities with Northants Cricket Club so during the cricket season one side of the football ground was wheeled away and the boundary rope came on to the football pitch. We ended up playing Liverpool, Manchester United and Arsenal on this pitch in 1965-66, I bet they loved it. The meeting with Dave was just the beginning of, what turned out to be, a great relationship between manager and player and then manager and captain. We enjoyed the most successful period of the club to this day in those roles, it just worked based on respect, loyalty and appreciation for each other. You don't always agree but if you have respect at all times you will succeed and, much like Roy Keane for Sir Alex or Tony Adams for George, I'd have run through brick walls for Dave, he was the best manager I ever played under.

Some football men just have an aura of knowledge for the game like Bill Nicholson or George, they have insightful, sharp football brains and get you on board straight away. Dave Bowen was one of those men. A very good player who had been educated in the Arsenal way during the '50s, captained his beloved Wales in the 1958 World Cup, playing the great Pele, no less, and had returned to the County Town where he'd started out. Dave also captained Arsenal in his last two seasons, not bad for a lad from a small mining town in Glamorgan, there were definitely some similarities with my own career path.

Well, I was delighted when he said he wanted to get a side together to challenge for the Third Division title and he had earmarked me from games against Exeter as a key part of what would become a mean defence. There was a particular game that made up Dave's mind. It was a full-blooded encounter at St James Park on Easter Monday 1961 where future teammates Mick Everitt and Terry Branston had been whacking me, and vice versa, all game, all three of us as bad as each other. I wouldn't back down to anyone, on or off the pitch, in my prime but I'd have struggled taking Branst on, Mick was more my size. Terry Branston was a beast of a man from Rugby, carved from granite with the heart of a lion. One game we played together he finished the game after a clash of heads with Tony Hately and his ear was hanging off, I promise you. One tough boy. All three of us were at it all game. I gave Mickey a dig in our box and when the Cobbler's trainer, Jack Jennings, came on he started running in my direction. I set myself steady for some verbals from Jack but he slowed down and said out of the side of his mouth, 'The Boss said if you can do that to those two then we've got to have this lad, he told me to tell you straight away.' Then he was off to treat Mickey.

Only a month later, I'd signed for Dave after Northampton had clinched promotion to the Third Division in a season where Exeter had finished near the bottom under my old mate, Glenn Wilson. Glen was gone the following season while I was the new captain of a side chasing promotion to a league two leagues above – funny how things can turn around in football. At the meeting with Dave he said he had a couple of other signings in mind but the side was nearly there and he wanted me to be the skipper. Now, I was a bit of a hothead at Exeter but Dave felt if I had the added responsibility of the armband then it may help my keep my discipline in check. As ever, Dave was right and it did help me keep my fire under control. If I was meant to set an example to the side I could hardly go around hitting people on the pitch.

After the sour ending at Exeter to hear my new manager say all of this was the gee up I needed, I walked out to take my first session feeling eight feet tall. Dave and Jack Jennings introduced me to the lads including the antagonists of a month previous, Mickey and Branst. They both gave me wry smiles and, in Branst's case, a vice like handshake. It was fate, I guess, that our battle at Exeter had caught Dave's eye, so thank God for those two I say. I picked up my new training gear and met the lads on the pitch, I knew most of them from playing against them the season before so it didn't take long to settle in. It was shaping up to be a very strong side and definitely capable of getting another promotion.

A couple of months later, Dave signed probably the best player ever to pull on a Claret shirt, Cliffy Holton. Dave managed to convince him to sign a few weeks into the season from Watford where he'd scored 84 goals in 120 games, but it was at Arsenal, before Watford, that he'd made his name. What a player Cliff was, how Dave managed to get him to come and play at the County Ground, God only knows. He scored 98 goals in 198 games at Highbury so his scoring record was up there with the best. Cliff was a converted full back, he had the lot, the physique, the skill, a great strike and strong in the air. Added to which he was one good-looking boy, always immaculate, the first player I'd seen turn up with a washbag stocked with grooming products. He was a cut above and, to be honest, he was too good for us. Even on nights out he was a bit different as he didn't drink beer – even I was having the odd beer by now. Cliff would be drinking vodka or gin, far too sophisticated for us. What price would a Cliffy Holton be today? As a modern-day comparison, I'd say he was like Robert Lewandowski, he had that strength, physique and all-round game. How he didn't get a stack of England caps, I'll never know. He was that good. His favourite, when we were under a bit of pressure, was, 'If you want me to help you out back there, let me know, Theo.' I liked Cliffy, you couldn't not like him. He was a loveable rogue who walked the walk and got away with murder.

The side that started that 1961-62 season was the best I'd played in up to that point and, I maintain, especially when Cliff signed, the best one of the lot. The two Third Division sides were better than the Second and First Division sides oddly enough. We had such a strong defence with all four of us on top of our game and well able to handle ourselves, so much so we soon built up a fearsome reputation through the league. We had Mickey playing left back and, as I'd found out in the battle of St James Park, he was fearless and a fine full back. Mick had started at Arsenal too and made it into the Cobbler's team of the Century such was his contribution at that time. Mick was one of the youngest in the squad, at 21, but it never showed. He was a very tidy and compact full back not looking to get past his wide man much but feed him all game and get on top of his opponent. Mick managed the likes of Plymouth, Wimbledon and Brentford when he stopped playing, he knew the game very well.

Then, of course, we had Branst who won everything and anything at centre back. In those days you used any means necessary to stop forwards getting past and Branst was one of those. Forwards hated playing against him and few came off better. I've seen Branst do things on a pitch that made me wince and he didn't care who you were, just ask Greavsie, Denis Law or Ian St. John, all of whom felt the man from Rugby's force.

Terry had a few partners and one was the man who became one of my best friends in football, along with Joe Kiernan who signed later. John Kurila or 'Krunch' as he was known got his nickname for a reason, John was even scarier than Branst. Six foot two with eyes of blue, Johnny was the loveliest man you could wish to meet, but upset him and you had better be quick. A broad Glaswegian from the Gorbals,

John started out at Celtic before joining the Cobblers, he was also in his early 20s that season but never overawed and gave hell to anyone he marked. Opponents would have a pop at him and he'd just give them his steel-eyed Glasgow stare and they soon piped down. He didn't even need to get involved in any verbals. John chinned Tony Hately off the ball without any verbals in the game that Branst tore his ear, so Terry got Johnny's payback that game. He also caught Ian St. John of Liverpool with a stray boot that sliced his forehead open as he stooped to head it. Saint went off to get stitched up and ran back on bandaged up and said to Branst, 'Your pal is a wee bit wild.'

To which Terry replied deadpan, 'You're lucky, they don't normally come back on.'

If I could choose any man to go into battle with in any walk of life, it would by John. A brother in arms. We got very friendly with John and his lovely wife, Nan, despite us being 'far too old to be mates' according to Nancy, a real Scottish character, in fact the only person able to keep Johnny in check. We remained best mates for 55 years right up to very recent times when, sadly, John passed away suddenly. I miss him terribly every day.

Whoever played with Terry, be it John, Derek Leck or Graham Carr, they had a partner that would win everything and he was a dream to play alongside – just a force of nature. I genuinely cannot recall any players giving Branst a tough time, even in the First Division. Derek Leck was our next door neighbour and a fine servant for the club appearing in, what is now, central midfield or at centre back much like Johnny. Tall and athletic with a good all round game, Leckie was a manager's dream, able to adapt as required, a good solid pro. Known to everyone as 'Daisy' he represented the Cobblers in all four divisions.

Then there was me on the right, I was quick then, aggressive in the tackle, good enough in the air and with a good right foot strike that could hit the ball to a forward's feet or in the air. I'd back myself against any winger and was learning the art all the time. If I could get past our winger on the overlap I would do, as Dave and Jack's training had everyone so fit back then. I was on top of my game, playing my best football, and as fit as a fiddle. The sessions were brutal, the like of which you just don't see any more. This was before you had post-training meals at a training ground so we would all go to the local café for a tea and a roll, without exception all present with the chat and mickey-taking flying around. Fans would see us and stop us for autographs or call out from cars, it made us more accessible and visible. This really helped the town get behind you on a Saturday and the fans were great at the County Ground, we punched way above our weight, on and off the pitch.

Dave always said we needed to be the fittest and that would give us an edge and, as usual with Dave, he was right and we were strong throughout 90 minutes and throughout the season. In addition, I was Dave's lieutenant on the pitch as his captain and he knew I would carry out his instructions without question, he would approach me privately about any issues and vice versa. It was a great manager–captain relationship, full of trust and respect.

Cliffy signed in September in that first season and what did Dave do? He gave him the bloody armband. Now, I wasn't best pleased, and Cliff was a very different type of captain leading by his sheer class, but how could I get upset; it was bloody Cliff Holton. When I piped up one day about the armband, only half joking, Cliff replied, quick as a flash, 'You supply the crosses, Theo, and I'll supply the goals.' The lads rolled about and I just had to shrug and smile. That was Cliff, he talked the talk but he also walked the walk, it was a waste of time getting annoyed with the man, he was pure class.

Behind us was Chic Brodie who was, like many goalkeepers, especially those in the lower leagues, one day unbeatable and on others he'd make the odd mistake. The higher we got the more the mistakes were punished so Dave moved to sign a replacement but, in those early seasons, Chic was a key player for us. In midfield we had Johnny Reid playing as a halfback alongside Johnny, Roly Mills or Derek Leck in a classic 4-2-4 formation with Barry Lines on the left wing and Ray Smith usually in front of me on the right. We had a young, talented winger Tommy Robson waiting on his chance to shine. Linesy out wide left was great value in that side, he just delivered great crosses continually like a metronome, the ball out of his feet, shift it a yard and bang, deliver. For a forward what more do you want? None of these four drops of the shoulder or three crossovers, he just played to his strengths. The lads benefiting from Linesy's quality and banging in goals for fun were Cliff and Frank Large, both lethal up front. Barry became the first Cobblers' player to score in all four divisions.

Dave wasn't joking when he said we had to be the fittest around. Jack, the trainer, ran the bollocks off us every day, we didn't see many footballs during the week. Jack used to take us out on the roads for six mile runs and hill climbs while he pedalled along happily on his bike, barking out instructions. I used to let his tyres down or slide off his chain, now and then, which used to make Jack go mental as he pushed it back through town barking, 'I know it was you, Foley.' Then he'd run us even more the next time – so probably not a wise move. There was no way we could moan to the boss about the amount of running as he always joined in and he was always up the front. Dave was some runner and led by example on keeping fit, something I followed when I became a coach, joining in the running right up until I stopped coaching aged 68. Players don't moan as much if they can see you're doing it too.

We were sharper than ever, we had a good collection of players and we had a top player up front. Needless to say, Cliff was excused from the relentless running, in fact he was excused full stop. Dave struck a deal with Cliff, no doubt to persuade him to sign, whereby he gave him two or three days off a week to look after his business interests in London or head off wherever he headed off to. An international man of mystery was our Cliff. One trip away to Coventry he asked the boss if he could drop in and see his relatives on the way so he headed off with the 'keeper, Chic, while we all went on the coach. He was nowhere to be seen for a good half hour after the meet but, thankfully, they turned up in time for kick off. In that same game at Highfield Road our young left back, Tony Claypole, broke his leg, the poor lad. Tony was a former England U21 international and a promising young player who'd only just got married three weeks before and was gearing up for a career in the game.

I can still see him now, he went to play the ball down the line and their centre forward, Ron Hewitt, caught him full on the shin from the side as his leg followed through. His leg cracked like a rifle going off and went like a twig, it was sickening. No footballer ever wants to see an injury like that to a teammate or an opponent but as you run over you can't help but see it, the bottom part of his left leg was at right angles to the rest of it. In those days, that generally signalled the end of your career and, from that moment on, he was finished.

Now, only Hewitt knew if he meant to hurt Tony, okay I'm sure he never wanted to break the poor kid's leg or end his career but he left his leg there and meant to do him in my eyes. I'm on the opposite side of the back four but it looked very nasty and Branst, Derek Leck and I were on the scene quickly. Hewitt was up and half squared up to me, knowing he was going to get some stick. Well, before I knew it, I've hit him sparko with a right hander. Bang, he's gone. I'm not proud of it, but it is pure instinct when you go like that, and it is quite shocking as you are momentarily out of control. Having watched sons Adrian and Paul in non-league football over the years, and a fair few red cards dished out to both, they have the same Dublin fire in their blood all right. All three of us have that trigger switch, I guess. Sean was much calmer on the pitch, so must take after Sheila, and all I can say is it's a good job Teresa didn't play, as she'd have been the worst of the lot.

Bearing in mind this was still early in my first season as the new 'club captain', here I was punching players so maybe Dave was right to toss the armband to Cliffy. The ref saw the punch, everyone in the ground saw it, as I'd made little effort in concealing the fact. The ref came over, didn't even give me a talking to, gave me a look as if to say, 'Okay son, I understand,' and called on both trainers as Hewitt lay flat out on the turf. I guess the ref understood the emotion of it all and turned a blind eye although the home fans weren't best pleased.

Hewitt stayed on though, and they won 1-0 in Jimmy Hill's first game as manager of the Sky Blues. Tony never played again, last I heard he had a B&B in Cornwall. Ever the gentleman, Jimmy Hill admitted after the game that we were by far the better side, I always got on well with Jim, a real gent and complete football man. When he pushed through the maximum wage deal for pro footballers to be scrapped in 1961 and the Fulham legend Johnny Haynes went on to get £100 a week it changed everything for evermore. People forget how important Jim was before he became a figure of fun, unfairly, as a pundit on TV. I was next to Dave Bowen when he gave Jimmy some advice on his new career telling him not to 'listen to anyone and have faith in what you believe in' – which you could never accuse Jimmy of not sticking to. Sage advice from a clever man.

Back to Cliffy, now if he wasn't producing on the pitch and missing training we'd have all been moaning at the boss but his form was incredible. Even though he was 32 when he signed, he still had it all – he cost the club £7,000 and he was worth ten times as much. In his first game away to Crystal Palace in September, he scored a hat-trick just four hours after putting pen to paper. He went on to get a hat-trick in four games that year including a 7-0 hammering of Grimsby Town who, believe it or not, went up and another in a 4-1 spanking of Notts County at their place. By the time he'd scored two in a 4-1 win over Coventry at home with three games still to go, he'd passed the club record of 34 goals in a season which had been held for 23 years by another ex-Arsenal man, Ted Bowen. He ended up with 38 goals that season and he scored all sorts, pile drivers from outside the box, fox in the box tap-ins and powerful headers. When you need someone to pull out a piece of match winning skill, it's the top players that deliver and Cliff was like the Royal Mail, he always delivered. What a player he was for us.

Even with Cliff's amazing contribution we came up short in

that first season, finishing a respectable eighth but a good few points behind champions Portsmouth, and Grimsby in second place. Our poor form without Cliffy at the start, and a bad run at the end of the season, cost us dear. We were good enough to go up that season but it just made Dave even more determined and he got to work straight away on new players for the following season. In the third last game of that season, away to QPR at White City, I had a game I'll never forget. We lost the game 2-0 to Rangers who ended up finishing four places above us in fourth spot. Well, there were a few tackles flying in and, with a few minutes to go, their forward Mark Lazarus ran through on goal but got clattered by Terry Branston as I ran across to cover. We all ended up in a heap having clattered into each other.

While Mark Lazarus was getting treatment on the pitch, a fan ran on and decided to get retaliation on me, for some reason, and he gave me a right hook as I'm on the floor. I didn't even see him coming, well the nose went splat and the blood flowed. Dazed and groggy and before I could launch myself, Chic Brodie had raced out of goal and had him by the throat up against the goalpost. The lad got frogmarched away and arrested while I got treated for a broken nose, which I ended up breaking another three times over the years. The case went to court and it turned out the lad was a bit off the rails and had been in and out of prison over the years. He was a fellow Irishman called John Kennedy – he got banned for life from QPR and tragically killed in some altercation around Shepherds Bush sometime after.

The nose went again when John Crossan of Sunderland punched me in the air as I went to head it from a corner and boy, did that hurt. I'm sprawled on the turf blood pouring out of my nose and Crossan leans over going, 'You all right down there, Theo?' in his thick Northern Ireland brogue. He didn't even get booked. On another occasion, in a game at Millwall, I caught a stray elbow above the eye and it was a right mess so I went off to get sewn up. You didn't have qualified physios or club doctors back then, each club just had to have a first aider on hand. The old boy at Millwall that day was pissed as a newt, obviously counting on no one getting injured. There I am with a drunk old boy with a needle stitching me up around the eye. Well, he starts putting the needle up under my eyebrow bone near the top of my eyeball and I go ballistic, I could have swung for him. I had a go at him and the saucy bugger started swearing at me. It seemed to sober him up a bit though, and he was able to finish it off, to a fashion so I re-joined the game. The eyebrow still has an untidy scar thanks to that drunk first aider.

For a first season with all of the upheaval we'd had as a new family in a new town, it had been great fun. The team spirit was great, all of the lads would meet up with their wives for a meal or we'd go to the Salon dance hall, just a short 7-iron from our house. The lads might get together to play snooker in the local club or skittles in the pub. We all got on great, there were no fallouts and there was a lovely atmosphere around the club. It had been a tough time for us as a family but things had settled down and we were really enjoying life and football in Northampton.

Then on Monday 27th August 1962 we had new arrival number two, a bit inconvenient as we had Bristol Rovers the next night at home. Adrian Paul arrived so I had the textbook girl and boy family and, hopefully, someone to inherit the football genes, but more of that later. Of course, I still played in the night game and we won 2-0 with two goals from Alec Ashworth. Teresa had been much more considerate the year before coming a day after an away game at Peterborough although we'd been spanked 7-1. Maybe the luck on the births was changing for the better but either way I was the luckiest man in the world with two healthy kids.

The craic in the dressing room was great at Northampton. Now, I've been in dressing rooms and on training grounds for over 50 years, they are my places of work, my office if you like. I've been lucky as there is no better way to spend your days, laughing and joking, ribbing and winding each other up – just like being at school really. The characters you meet, the laughs you have together, it's what life is all about and with the Foley wind-up gene very prominent, I loved it.

When I meet up now with old teammates or colleagues it's no different, we just slip into those old types and our roles in the group.

It does make me smile when you hear about dressing room pranks these days as if they'd invented the concept. We used to hook our boots up on nail pegs every day, or your apprentice did after cleaning them religiously, onto a ply panel in the boot room. One of my APs (apprentices) was former Liverpool legend Phil Neal who played right back too obviously so they matched you up to senior positions. Well, it was a well-used wind-up to nail one boot onto the ply so you pull the whole lot down to roaring laughter. Phil was one of the smarter lads though, turning down Spurs to stay and finish his O Levels before signing for Liverpool in the '70s and winning the lot. I always got done while I had treatment too having put my knicks and training gear on the peg, while I was on the treatment bench, usually face down, and the lads would all take it in turns to my wipe their Algipan-covered hands on my knicks. Jack, the trainer, was in on it, definitely, the sneaky old get, and I'd jump off, get changed and head out only to have my bollocks and arse on fire in about five mins. Cue rolls of laughter as I run off to get changed.

Jack was a key part in the atmosphere during training and the lads loved him. When he was working us hard, if someone made a comment that was it, we got the well-worn lecture that soon shut us all up. 'Too bloody hard? I've been in a fucking prisoner of war camp, don't talk to me about hard. I used to shit in my helmet.' Stony silence, how could you argue with that? Five minutes later he's goading and winding someone up having a laugh. Dave just let him get on with it, I think secretly he loved it. You need people like Jack to break the monotony, day in day out, he was a force of nature, I never saw him downbeat. He even had us in the barracks doing what the commando boys were doing, there was no hiding place. One of his favourite wind-ups was to run in with a freezing cold water hose as we were in the bath. I could have killed him, I hated that one. The old bastard knew it too and always made sure I got the most. He loved it when it snowed too, hiding from me like Cato from The Pink

Panther, then pelting me with three or four pre-prepared snowballs.

In the end, you walked around on edge with your wits about you but someone would always get you. One of my favourites was, during a warm up, to crouch on the grass behind someone if we were backwards running and send 'em flying. Once a week that would work. You were careful who you targeted though. Johnny K was usually left out of it just in case he whacked you back but the lads always dug him out about his clothes because he was always a bit different John, a very sharp dresser. Now, anyone who has been in a dressing room environment will know it's best to blend in, not stand out, but not John, he didn't give a monkeys. They'd all hammer him and he just shrugged and smiled, he knew they'd all be wearing the same stuff in a few months. Mess with his stuff though, and you were in trouble, he had to be pulled off long-serving wing half Roly Mills one day, John wanted to kill him, his cobalt blue eyes had 'gone' completely. It took a few to restrain him, I don't think Roly was on John's Christmas card list afterwards.

You get these flare ups every now and then, it is inevitable really being with each other every day every week. Generally though, the atmosphere was great, all good lads together. We signed Graham Moore from Manchester United in 1964, a Welsh international, a big signing for the club. Well, in training one day he striped the back of my legs and made the mistake of laughing after. Now, maybe he thought he was above it all a bit having been at Chelsea, Man Utd and being an established international but the other lads knew what was coming. The game restarted and I chased him then booted him up the backside and in the air. They had to pull me off him. He never kicked me or laughed at me again and we got on fine after that, in fact we played together at Charlton in 1969 and then I managed him. He was a very good player Mooro and, sadly, passed away recently.

Jack did more than train us, at times, and even stepped in on a couple of occasions when Dave had some periods when he'd stepped down, having been told to take some time off under Doctor's orders. Jack left the club at the end of the 1963-64 season after a long stint being a player during the war and a strict sergeant major disciplinarian on the training pitch. He played a huge part in getting the side into shape to compete at the higher levels we were aiming for. We missed him when he left; he was a great old school character. He ended up touring the world with the MCC, he loved his cricket and passed away in 1977. His replacement was another wartime vet hero, ex-pro Joe Payne, who was at the D-Day landings. You can see how the emphasis was on fitness and not coaching in those days with these Army PT types, Dave might offer the odd bit of advice but it was a world away from the coaching Ievels we eventually ended up working to at Arsenal and a world away again from current coaching.

Dave strengthened the side over the summer of '62, and we mounted our charge on the title. 1961-62 had been a good first season for me personally, as I'd played in every game bar an FA Cup win over Millwall, the highest appearance tally along with my neighbour, Leckie. Cliff carried on where he'd left off banging 'em in again and we added a forward called Alec Ashworth from Luton for £10,000. They hit it off up front scoring 21 goals together in only 10 league games, including an unbelievable 8-0 win over Wrexham and a 7-1 mauling of Halifax, Cliff netting another hat-trick. That was to be Cliff's final hat-trick as he bowed out in a 5-1 drubbing at Southend's Roots Hall and bloody Alec Ashworth was given the armband. How can a selfish forward be the captain I ask you? Unfortunately, we had lost our talisman Cliff to Crystal Palace as he wanted to get back to London. That was the last we saw of him in the Claret of Northampton. He continued to score goals for another three years before having his three season journey around the capital to Watford, Charlton and then Leyton Orient retiring at the ripe old age of 38. Sadly, he passed away suddenly on holiday in 1996 – a genuine footballing legend.

We started well that season, then hit the buffers but had an act of God to get our season back on track, a lengthy 45 day cold snap from Boxing Day, and Frank Large took centre stage when we started back. John Kurila got sent off in that final game before the snow, a defeat away at Notts County, which meant he avoided serving any of his six week ban, the lucky bugger. Meanwhile, I had to avoid the grocer every week, who had supplied our Christmas turkey, as we didn't get any appearance money for nearly eight weeks, just the basic wage. We were all skint and my excuses were getting worse every week. He must have known I was lying but he never let on once. People assume you are earning well playing in front of packed grounds but back then you didn't, we lived hand to mouth no different to the majority of people watching on the terraces.

When we started back after the snow Dave was still utilising some of the young talent we had at the club, players like wide man Tommy Robson, who wasn't fazed at all and a match-winner on his day. We had John Reid in the heart of midfield, a classy footballer from Scotland who'd been around and, of course, Frank Large up front who was as game as you like and would always grab a goal. The side had a new look but the defence, which was always the bedrock for the team's success, was the same back four with Chic still in goal. We had cruised to the top of the league before the cold snap but faltered in the lead up to Christmas with a few poor results including a terrible run of four defeats in a row.

The break made us hungry, in more ways than one, without our appearance money, and we went on a good run starting back with a satisfying 3-1 February win over QPR at White City, where I had said goodbye to a straight nose only ten months earlier. We only lost four games after the enforced break all away to Bournemouth, Bristol City, Port Vale and Shrewsbury Town. Four defeats in 22 games is good form and we blew our challengers away finishing in style with three wins, clinching the title, then finished the season with a 3-0 win over Hull at the County Ground, who gave us a guard of honour. I even managed to get on the scoresheet with the last goal of the season, a penalty of course – a perfect day. We only conceded 20 goals in those final 22 games including eight clean sheets. The defence would always say we won the league that season.

We had done it, we'd realised Dave Bowen's dream, as well as our own – we had won the title and were now going to be in the Second Division with some big names. I'm not quite sure what it is to be 'in the zone' but, in that season, I was so focused, every game thinking about the opposition and my opponent. We scored over 100 goals with Alec Ashworth and Frank Large on fire. We were so tuned in as a team and a real unit that was the sum of its parts without the need for a talisman. Those days, like the last game at home in front of a packed home crowd, are ones that stay with you forever and are the best days of your life, the realisation of all that work, all those runs with Jack through town, the injuries, the sacrifices at home, all of it worth it, without question. I will forever be the Northampton Town skipper who lifted the Third Division Championship, always etched in history. At times like that, I used to cast my mind back to Inchicore, to the street kickabouts, to the brutal Keogh Square games, to Mammy and Daddy, Jimmy, Terry, Anita and to my good mates Jimmy and Littler. I'd think about how far I'd come and how much of my upbringing had played a part in it all, made me what I am, a leader on the pitch. They were out of sight but never out of mind and I knew they would be proud too.

The scenes after were brilliant, with the trophy and medals presented on the pitch by the club's president and fans mobbing the lads and Dave. Sheila, Teresa and Adrian were there but this wasn't like now where you bring kids onto the pitch, we ended up all disheveled back in the dressing room drinking beer in our boots and shorts with cigars on the go, unbridled joy, that togetherness can never be matched anywhere else. We sat and chatted for ages, the release of a season – jumped in the bath, no cold hosing down from Jack – then all got changed and headed into town and joined in with the fans, mobbed wherever we went. We met up with our wives at the Salon dance hall all three sheets to the wind, in no fit state to dance. What a day and night, I woke up the next day, late in the afternoon, to find my Hillman Imp with the headlights on and a flat battery – I don't recall if I just moved it or drove it – not big and not clever.

Usually the return after the euphoria is difficult but we just got straight back in the saddle excited by the prospect of the new league and games against the likes of Manchester City, Middlesbrough and Newcastle, Leeds and Sunderland. Added to which, the boss had brought through some players to cope with the higher standard. This will always keep things fresh with honest, hardworking lads and we had a full squad of those. Tommy Robson had come through the ranks and was really pushing himself forward for selection, as well as 19-year-old Don Martin up front who had also been a youth player. Don was as good as he wanted to be, a real talent who could have been a top player but I think influences off the pitch affected him, a real shame. He ended up at Blackburn in 1967 with the club cashing in on his talent for £35,000.

The key addition though, was one of the finest players to put on the Claret of Northampton, Joe Kiernan – the king. Along with John, my best friend in football and life. Another Scots boy from Coatbridge, Glasgow where George Graham also came from, another Catholic but otherwise the polar opposite to John. Joe was a quiet lad, never swore, with a very dry sense of humour but, like John, just a lovely man. Joe never touched alcohol and would say 'fuppin' instead of swear – when he joined from Sunderland with his lovely girlfriend at the time, Pat, the six of us, John and Nan, Sheila and I, were inseparable and remained that way until he sadly passed away in 2005. It broke my heart when he died, still hurts to this day – just a beautiful man Joe, another Scottish brother just like Johnny.

John and Joe called me 'McGint' which is more creative than Paddy, I guess. Joe was the 'King' as he loved Elvis, or 'Fuppin Joe.' On the pitch he was the king too, a class act with a great left foot and eye for a pass. Joe made us tick as soon as he signed, he was the piece we were missing and he was voted the best player by a select poll in the First Division campaign of 1965-66 pipping yours truly but I always told him it was me really. Joe could have easily played for a bigger club and always attracted attention from those clubs but stayed true and loyal to the Cobblers for 10 years.

As ever the work started far away from the pitch on the roads with Joe Payne this time, pounding pavements and striving to be the fittest side in the league, looking for that edge again, sold on it even more now after the previous season. We had a solid enough season after a fine start even without Dave who was on sick leave. We finished in eleventh spot a fair way behind champions Leeds but not a bad first season in the second tier. Take stock of the new league, hold your own and have a push the next year, which is exactly what we did. We did hammer the mighty Sunderland 5-1 that first year who ended up getting promoted so we showed what we were capable of. I missed a stack of games that season due to an Achilles tendon problem which was to become a problem from then on, flaring up on the harder pitches.

In March 1964 I received the news I'd been waiting on since my letter received at Exeter from the FAI with a call up to play Spain in Seville in the Quarter Final of the Nations Cup which they were hosting. The Nations Cup was just another name for what we now call The Euros and this was only the second time it had been staged with the Soviet Union winning it in 1960 beating Yugoslavia in France. I thought I was going to explode with national pride and rang Mammy and Daddy straight away who were delighted for me. I was to line up with fellow Dubs Ray Brady, Johnny Giles, Andy McEvoy and Joe Haverty of QPR, Leeds, Blackburn and Millwall respectively. These were top players along with Cork man Charlie Hurley, the legendary Sunderland centre back. I was more thrilled to be on the pitch with these idols of mine rather than the likes of Pareda, Marcellino and Lapetra for Spain. We got well beat 5-1 though even with our strong side as the Spanish tore us to shreds. It was an eye opener for me and another step in my football development, playing against technically better players, their testing gamesmanship, the difference playing in front of a foreign crowd and so on. Spain were a top side and went on to win the tournament beating the holders, the Soviet Union, 2-1. I felt I did well enough and definitely didn't let myself down but I was not happy to be on the wrong end of five goals. Pleased, proud but a wee bit disappointed at the same time too, I headed back to the nuts and bolts of the Second Division. Generally, the 1963-64 season had been a step up in football levels and I'd coped well I thought, my game was much improved and I'd say, nearing its peak.

The second cap came just two months later in May away to Poland in Krakow in a friendly so I must have done well enough in the Spain drubbing. As was to become the norm back then it was a different Eire side with my old Dub mate and Man Utd star, Tony Dunne at left back and a couple of different League of Ireland players in Paddy Ambrose and Jonny Fullam both from Shamrock Rovers. I knew both from our Dublin days as a kid, Paddy became a Shamrock goalscoring legend and Johnny was yet another of the famous Home Farm products to get full International caps. We got beat 3-1 by another very good side with their little maestro Szoltysik in midfield and their dangerous front man Faber. They were different again to the Spanish side, more direct but even worse with their play acting when you went near them which we found very difficult to stomach. Sure enough, Paddy scored our consolation, he was deadly up top but that was to be his second last cap oddly enough. I always felt these League of Ireland lads were included almost because the selectors had to and they were never really viewed on merit under the assumption that the English Football lads were better. There were some good players at home that's for sure and some just didn't want to move to England, it didn't make them any less talented. Maybe the FAI missed a trick or two there?

In the same month I received another call up to play away again in Oslo against Norway in another friendly. It was a similar side to the one that played Poland with Dunney, Ray Brady, Gilesy, Andy McEvoy, Charlie Hurley and Joe Haverty included again. We had most of the big names playing with Noel Dwyer in goal this time, yet another Dublin lad I knew from games against Stella Maris. We rolled them over easily enough 4-1 with two from the Roker Park legend Charlie Hurley, one from Gilesy and one from Andy McEvoy. Now you'd do well to get three better players on your scoresheet who shone on the world stage. That was a great line up but we just never managed to get the same players out for a run of games. It was great to finally get a win with the Republic and it really helped settle me down playing alongside and against these big names. Unfortunately, I missed the next game against England at Dalymount just after the season had finished in May which was a shame but we got beat 3-1 with Greavsie getting the third in a very different England side that went on to glory two years later.

Back in the league, it was the tried and tested routine again for the 1964-65 season, try to get even fitter, really go for it – those years were the fittest I'd ever been, and the Achilles had finally settled down. As a full back it was a huge asset to feel sharp, I could recover quickly if a winger got past me, I could close down quickly when the ball travelled a long way to that winger, I could snap into tackles and win headers with a better spring. Added to which I could go the other way and get past my midfield partner and overlap to deliver crosses into the box. I loved being fit, I genuinely don't recall wingers giving me a hard time even in the Second Division, I was on top of my game that season and I'd expect wingers to hate playing against me, not the other way around.

Frank Large up front had a great first season in the Second Division in 1963-64, ending up top scorer but moved on to Swindon before the season was out so Dave had brought in Eastender Charlie Livesey for the 1964-65 season, a forward who had been at Chelsea and Southampton. Frank would be missed, he was a straightforward footballer who never got put off his stride, even when a fan threw a dart into his back whilst defending a corner at Leyton Orient midway through the '63 season. He just pulled it out and threw it on the ground, you'd never get under Largey's skin, not even with an East London tungsten tip. In the same game we had a brick thrown through the dressing room at Brisbane Road which I found odd as it was their ground but they were a bit mindless that day. Dave also signed outside right Harry

Walden from Luton Town who would turn out to be my regular and steady partner in front of me on the right side for the next two seasons.

A few different faces, another year older for the young talent, and we were stronger again. Dave was a master at unearthing these gems and improving all of the time. At the back we were the same core, the only unit left untouched with Graham Carr waiting in the wings at centre back if needed – Graham is now in a senior role recruiting players at Newcastle and his comedian son, Alan, is doing great on the box. Forward Bobby Hunt signed late in the 1963-64 season from Colchester United where he'd been prolific but he struggled a wee bit with us in the Second Division.

We flew into the season fighting fit but started with a 1-0 defeat away to Middlesbrough but bounced straight back with a 2-0 win at Manchester City's Maine Road. Two tough away games to start with, we were already racking up the motorway miles. We then drew at home 1-1 with 'Boro, got beat 2-0 away to Southampton before embarking on an unbelievable 17 game unbeaten run with 10 wins including wins over Newcastle, Coventry, Charlton and Crystal Palace. Again, our defence was on top form with only 17 goals conceded in that run with seven clean sheets. That set us up perfectly to mount a serious challenge.

Towards the end of 1964 I picked up my fourth cap in a home game at Dalymount on 25th October versus Poland against a different side with no fewer than seven changes from the side that beat us five months earlier. We had four League of Ireland lads this time with winger Frank O'Neill, inside right Jackie Mooney and left half Liam Hennessy, all from the famous South Dublin club, Shamrock Rovers. The reason I'm mentioning these lads is that they were all Dub lads that, again, I knew well from junior days at Home Farm and both Frank and Jackie were another two to play for the Farm. It really was and still is an amazing club. It was my second win and back to back too as we came out 3-2 winners with one goal from Jackie and two from the wonderful Andy McEvoy. I felt as though I finally belonged at this level now, having learned so much over the four games.

In the League, young Billy Best and Brian Etheridge, both local lads, were brought into the side for Tommy Martin and Bobby Hunt at the start of that run and both played their part. The run was to prove the sizeable springboard for the season. We had 12 single goal victories that season, Dave being an exponent of the Arsenal way that George and I cultivated many years later. The unbeaten run was ended by a thumping 5-0 defeat at the hands of Newcastle with little Tommy Robson on the end of an assault that saw him suffer a broken jaw, lost teeth and concussion. We swotted that one off as a blip and just went on another run of four wins and four draws with three clean sheets again. We were now all set approaching the last two months, just eight games to clinch promotion – we were nip and tuck with Newcastle with a fair gap to third and fourth spot with Bolton, Southampton, Ipswich and Norwich all on similar points. Little old Northampton not only up there with these clubs but ahead of them, shockwaves were being felt around the league.

In the spring of 1965 I got another call up by Eire to play in a friendly at Dalymount Park against the talented Belgian side. Now I was totally focused on the promotion charge but you never turn down the chance to wear the green jersey. I reported to Dublin in March to line up alongside a different side to the other games I'd played with the likes of Alan Kelly of Preston back between the sticks. Alan's son (also called Alan) played in goal for The Republic in the '90s and we had Shay Brennan of Man Utd making his debut. Andy McAvoy of Blackburn was up front again, but he didn't play many more in green and we had four League of Ireland players again in Neil, Mooney and Tuohy of Shamrock and Liam Hennessey again, having moved to Shelbourne. A few of the bigger names obviously dropped out and Paul Van Himst and co were too good for us, winning 2-0. It was another proud night for me though as family and friends were all there cheering me on and I did well enough to stay in I thought with the big World Cup qualifiers coming up. I travelled back to Northampton feeling good about my game and where my career was heading. Life was good.

Back in the league we stumbled a little, probably realising the enormity of what we were on the cusp of doing, winning four, drawing two and losing two. We ended with a disappointing 1-1 draw at home to Portsmouth whilst Newcastle won so we finished one point behind them in second place. Okay, we should have won it that season but what an achievement, the promotion was the key thing. The big time, the world famous First Division, the Holy Grail, what I had wanted my whole life, I had made it. The celebrations were even longer and larger than the Second Division championship win and why not, this was an unbelievable achievement for a small club like Northampton.

This time the club pushed the boat out as we knew promotion was guaranteed before the last game and laid on a night out to The Talk of the Town in Leicester Square, now called The Hippodrome. Coincidentally, this was where my eldest son, Adrian, met his American wife, Lisa, many years later. It was all very different to the Salon dance hall, this place was huge and the drinks were expensive compared to what we were used to but the board covered all of the cost as a thank you gesture. We had a blast and danced the night away – a night to remember to cap off a remarkable season and I carried on drinking for far too long, my pledge to Mammy but a distant memory.

CHAPTER 5
One Night in Paris
1965 – 1968

Mid-1960s The Beach Boys introduced their new California surf pop sound and the fabulous Dusty Springfield introduced herself – my favourite Stevie Wonder bursts onto the scene with Uptight in 1965 and Van the man released the brilliant Brown Eyed Girl. On the Silver Screen we get the era defining 'Graduate' with Bancroft and Hoffman, and Beatty and Dunaway light up the screen as 'Bonnie and Clyde'.

The whole country was ablaze in '66 when the football team achieved the impossible of winning the World Cup. The USA were planning their moon landing looking to pip Russia, anything seemed possible. Martin Luther King took on JFK's baton pioneering the change to Civil Rights and Racial Equality but he was also assassinated in 1968. Unfortunately, not everyone shared his 'dream'.

I picked up a lovely new cream coloured Hillman Imp, well I thought so at the time. Local car dealer and former rally driver Andre Boulde gave me a decent deal on it as I guess it helped sales of the car if the captain was driving one around the town. It wasn't free, unfortunately, just a few quid cheaper.

In Northampton Town, Val Doonican, who I loved, was a regular performer. Val sang my favourite singalong track, Danny O'Rafferty's motor car – he used to perform in the 101 Club and someone stole his car one night so I lent him my car to get around which didn't run on a 'gallon o'stout' – a lovely man and his wife Lynn was the same despite personal tragedy with their little boy.

When the dust settled on our amazing achievement we reported back for the most important preseason of our careers, everyone so eager to get our teeth into the First Division and Man United, Liverpool, Leeds, West Ham and so on. We felt we were more than good enough and had earned the right to dine at this table, the town was ablaze with euphoria everyone getting excited for the season ahead.

We had a preseason tour to Czechoslovakia in '65 where we played a couple of games including one against FK Dukla Prague who were playing in the top league out there. Well, the Stadion Juliska Stadium made the County Ground look like Wembley. The pitch was like a ploughed field and the ground was open on four sides with a track around it. The game wasn't worthy of note, a 1-1 draw from memory but the Czechs were very cute, go near them and they went flying, but if you had the ball you got little shirt pulls and nudges. It was an education in European football again, that's for sure, that stood me in good stead for later in the season, they were all technically better too, every player was that bit better on the ball.

In our free time after the Dukla game, we'd headed into the heart of Prague and had a few of their famous slurps that were so cheap it was unreal – we were walking through the Old Town Square and Johnny Kurila decided he wanted one of the flags off a pole and he ran off down the street with it. He was pie eyed laughing away while we egged him on but the patrolling army saw him nick it so gave chase. Now, upsetting the army in 1960s' Czechoslovakia was not a smart move and we were all rolled up watching this mad Scotsman trying to outrun the army through the famous old square. We were cheering him on until we saw them draw guns and we shouted at him to stop. Now, even JK had to stop himself from flying after one of them with a gun pointed at him, but you could see he wanted to; the eyes were set back ready to go. After a fair amount of persuading and begging, they let him go and we laughed about it later but he nearly caused a diplomatic incident. I still don't know why he nicked the flag, maybe it was a Lithuanian one to reflect the family name. Never a dull moment with JK.

We went into the season on a wave of emotion, the whole

town was buzzing, we were mobbed wherever we went – no one could believe it. I'd called home as usual and talked it through with Mammy and Daddy, he couldn't take it all in, his lad set to be playing the likes of Best, Moore, Charlton, Greaves in front of full and famous grounds. Our first five games were away to Everton, home to Arsenal and Man Utd then away to Newcastle and Burnley. Welcome to the top flight!

The big day came, in front of 48,489 fans at Goodison Park I led out the side for the club's first ever top flight game, with my chest puffed out with pride, swelled with the achievement of finally making it to the summit of football. I was 27 years old, it had been over 11 years since I'd headed over on the ferry to make the grade. I'd always hoped I'd make it but even I probably didn't expect to get there, least of all with little old Northampton Town. Well, the Toffees blasted away all of that warm glow with a thumping 5-2 win, their side included England left back Ray Wilson, the best full back in the league and the excellent Colin Harvey, known to his fans as the 'White Pele'. We were taught a lesson that day but managed to score through Bobby Brown and Bobby Hunt and actually played okay which was a positive. Everton had no fewer than eight England U23 players in their side and they were just too good on the day.

As a footballer, after a defeat, you get straight back in the saddle and look at who's up next? It was only Arsenal at the County Ground with Frank McClintock, George Armstrong and Bob Wilson in their ranks. We drew 1-1, a fine result after the opening day spanking with Browny scoring again cancelling out Baldwin's early goal. We were without Branst which set the tone for the season as he struggled for fitness and Mick Everitt also had to go off injured, to be replaced by Northampton's first ever substitute, Vic Cockcroft. The rock that was our base to build on in games at the back was beginning to show signs of wear and tear. Next up was only Man Utd, with the full complement of Charlton, Stiles, Law, Best and my full back peer and fellow Eire international, Tony Dunne. Another fine result, 1-1 with Hunty equalising Connelly's early goal, with ten minutes to play. On inspecting the pitch before the game, Dennis Law was not impressed with the County Ground and was heard to say, 'How can you possibly play football in a place like this?'

We had gained confidence from those two good results against two of the biggest teams and we'd answered a few question marks hanging over us. We went into the next game away to Newcastle with a bit more belief and looking for more points to post – sure enough we were punished for a Bryan Harvey mistake just after half-time and we ended up losing 2-0 in front of 28,051 at St James Park. Three days later, at my old stomping ground, Turf Moor, we got spanked 4-1 but I managed to score my first goal in the top flight but, sadly, it was an own goal to set Burnley on their way, Charlie Livesey getting our consolation. This wasn't the top flight goal for Burnley I had in mind when I set sail 11 years earlier. With five games down, we had lost three and drawn two, so not the best start.

That pattern continued for another eight games of a draw or a defeat with not a win in sight. The defeats to West Brom, Burnley again and Sheffield Utd were all by one goal so we were tightening up but still no wins. Big Branst was still missing and Graham Carr, who was a different type of centre back, was playing. Terry was a big miss to the back four and a key part of the last four years of success. We drew more games away with Notts Forest, home to Sheffield Weds, away to Arsenal at a packed Highbury and away to Leicester in front of 27,484 where I scored my first penalty of the season past the England 'keeper Banks to earn a point. This was the game that I scored two against Banksy and I've dined out on that story for years skimming over the fact it was a retaken penalty.

There were flashes of a return to form and solid results away in packed opponent's grounds but then we got a real football lesson at the hands of Don Revie's famous Leeds side getting humiliated 6-1 at Elland Road in front of 33,748. With Billy Bremner, Jackie Charlton, Norman Hunter, Peter Lorimer and fellow Dub Johnny Giles in their side they tore us apart. At the end of the game, Billy Bremner was telling me that Johnny wasn't happy about a tackle I'd put in on him – I was probably getting frustrated and caught him late but Gilesy was well able for it, I saw him catch a fair few players over the years.

Finally, we recorded our first win in late October, beating West Ham with the likes of Bobby Moore, Geoff Hurst and Martin Peters at home, 2-1. I scored my second penalty of the season sending Jim Standen the wrong way to put us 1-0 up and the packed County Ground went wild. Ken Leek popped up late to score the winner. I have always been very proud of my penalty record having never missed one, even the great penalty taker Matt Le Tissier had one saved. I used to show the best penalty takers at each club I coached, how I took them which always drew a bit of stick, be it Razor Ruddock at Millwall or Kevin Campbell at Arsenal. I used to wipe my boot on the back of my other leg, take a straight run up and usually open out my body and strike it to the right. They always took the piss but I never missed one when it mattered so who's the fool?

It had taken 14 games to get a win to go with our six draws and seven defeats which was nowhere near good enough. We were not used to runs like this, Dave wasn't used to it. We were definitely missing Terry at the heart of defence, no offence to Carry, and Micky Everitt was in and out with injury so Vic Cockcroft was deputising. The regular, solid backbone of previous seasons had been destabilised and it showed, I felt. I was starting to struggle myself having missed a few the season before with some knee cartilage trouble as well as an inflamed Achilles, both probably from the countless road runs we went on.

Now, at the start of the season I had negotiated a bonus for the lads based on the crowds at home as we were obviously going to be playing in front of full houses with the bigger sides coming down. From memory it was an additional £5 a man when it went over 18,000. Well, lo and behold, the times that attendance was just under 18,000, the crafty buggers. Only for the odd gold label fixtures like Man Utd, Chelsea, Leeds or Liverpool did it creep over into the 20s when they erected temporary scaffold, which was definitely not in line with current safety standards. We got the bonus a handful of times but nowhere near as much as we should have, so an early lesson learned, don't trust a director when it comes to money at a football club.

We managed to get a fine second win, two games after our first against Aston Villa, winning 2-1 with two goals from the exciting young talent that was Jim Hall. Straight after the Villa win I had to play midweek in the biggest game of my career for Eire in the World Cup against Spain. The following game was away to the mighty Liverpool at Anfield just three days after the Spain game which was being played in Paris. What a run of difficult games. I ended up playing with stitches in my cheek and eyebrow at Anfield after getting done by a Spanish Archer (El Bow) in the Paris game which split my face wide open. It was a World Cup qualifier play-off held at a neutral venue in Paris, all as agreed by the FAI in their infinite wisdom.

This was the critical play-off game to reach the finals being held in England obviously and, looking back, one of the biggest games ever for Eire. What the FAI decided in the run up to the game though still riles me to this day. Following the withdrawal of Syria on protest grounds due to allegations from the African section, we had to play Spain on a two-legged home and away basis and, after home wins for both teams – I missed the 1-0 home win at Dalymount Park but picked up my sixth cap in the 4-1 defeat at Seville where Pereda ran amok and scored a hat-trick – we were due to play each other again in a one-off game. The 4-1 defeat was a big disappointment as we had some big guns playing with Old Trafford legend Noel Cantwell making a rare appearance to no avail.

After the home and away fixtures, we had to play at a neutral ground for this one-off game. Where was it planned to be? In London, most probably Wembley, not far from the huge Irish communities that would have swamped the place. What did the FAI negotiate? It was agreed to play the game at the Stade Olympic in Paris where Spain would outnumber our support by thousands, all in return for a 'contribution' towards the FAI taking both sets of gate receipts, allegedly £25,000, three times the annual FAI income at the time. The players could not believe why they had made it harder than it could have been with the chance to play in a 'home' World Cup – the general comment was they were worse than Al Capone. Who knows how we'd have fared, the Republic had some great players back then. Johnny Giles, Tony Dunne, Noel Cantwell, Charlie Hurley, Joe Haverty, Andy McAvoy. I don't care what anyone says, they were huge names playing in the top league. They were heavyweights of the game and they could have been playing in front of their own pretty much, what a short-sighted view. What price legacy and glory?

As for Tony Dunne, it's funny how paths cross, especially in the smaller world of Irish football. When we were kids back home playing on the streets in Drimnagh, I used to pick this young lad Tony, about four years younger, for my team who was a game little bugger. Little did I know I would be lining up with Dunney some 15 years later in a packed Paris stadium in a crucial World Cup qualifier. He was a top full back, one of the best. In many ways, the side was picked in a similar way for this qualifier as it was back on the streets of Dublin. These squads, at that time, were all chosen by a committee of five, who'd never played the game by the way. The management role was so vague back then with 'Johnny' Carey in charge for the previous games and Noel Cantwell drafted in to help out as a senior player.

Back then, when you reported for international duty, the journey and organisation was all very different, players headed in from all over, none of this meeting up as a team and going together, it's a wonder we all got there at all. We were to head to Dublin for the flight over. I got there to find out I was playing in midfield and marking Luis Suarez, the original one, who was one of the best players in the world at the time. On the one hand, daunting as hell, on the other, I was flattered they thought I could suppress him. I don't know if this was the committee's decision or the 'manager' Jackie Carey. It was par for the course, all very disorganised, not Johnny's or Noel's fault they were just answering the call of their country. If Roy Keane thought Saipan was bad, all I can say is it's a good job he didn't play in the '60s.

Now, I hadn't played midfield for many a year and, although I always fancied myself as one when I was younger, I'd rather not have jumped back in for such an important game against a top side and one of the best players in the world. What do you do though? Who am I to start calling the odds? If they'd stuck me in goal I'd have given it my all, I'd have the green jersey on and the shamrock on my chest, that was the main thing. They played Man Utd's Shay Brennan right back who actually could play midfield but they wanted Suarez marked out of the game and obviously felt I was the man for the job. Talking it through with Gilesy recently, neither of us could understand it for a game of this importance and had Carey more of a say, I'm sure he'd have switched me with Shay. Johnny quite rightly made a comment about the selection switch with Shay, in his book, being a strange one. I lined up alongside Johnny that night and we just got on with it but I bet he was pleased I was in there after a few minutes tracking bloody Suarez all over the place. If Suarez had left the pitch for a pee I reckon I could have kept lookout for him I was that close. The bottom line is I played where I was told, I didn't demand to play there regardless of what Johnny or I felt. I even delivered a free kick in the first half to Gilesy which he headed close so maybe I was a midfielder after all?

It nearly paid off too as I felt I did a good job on Suarez, I managed to frustrate him and get a fair few tackles in when I could to try and unsettle him. Obviously, the idea was to then allow Johnny to get on the ball and do what he did best. Gilesy was probably the best I played with, a wonderful footballer but he could also handle himself all right, us Dubs are just made that way. I remember thinking during the game that I wouldn't fancy marking Suarez every week, he had unbelievable feet, vision and ability but pure endeavour and graft can suppress that for one game if you're lucky. Back home, Dad and Sheila's dad, Sam, were both listening to coverage on the BBC World Service along with my Dub pals,

Jim and Littler. They all heard the commentator say at one point, 'I don't think the Spanish fans are saying Ole Foley as he sends another tackle in on Suarez.'

What you often got in these games back then, against continental countries, were the dark arts and, unfortunately, the inexcusable act of spitting. Over here that is one of the lowest things you can do on a football pitch but, in Spain, they seemed to do it freely in those days. The back of my shirt was covered in phlegm at the end, disgusting. I didn't bite though as that would have played into their hands, although it was tough at times. The game was a choker, we were so unlucky going down 1-0 to a solitary Ufarte goal that was a loose ball that he followed up, other than that it was like my front room, there was nothing in it. We could have nicked it definitely, it was very close and, maybe, if we had played in London, it would have swung the game. We'll never know that thanks to the powers that be at the time at the FAI. The noise all the way through the game was deafening, constant whistling from the Spanish fans and plenty of handkerchief waving, the small Irish contingent were well drowned out. We were playing away, not on supposed neutral territory.

I got one back from whoever late in the game with a stray elbow whilst going up for a header in their box which split my cheek and eyebrow. It was no different to when a lad whacked me back home in Dublin as a kid and I spat my teeth out, just a Spanish elbow this time. It was a bit of a mess though, so I had to leave the pitch to get it patched up with Vaseline, basically, as it couldn't be stitched. Sod's law, they scored while I was off getting tended to, but I made it back on, kept it swabbed and played out the game spilling some blood for the cause. The whistle blew and I remember crouching down, completely spent after running myself into the ground, we had left nothing out there. The dream finished.

The Spanish lads all shook hands, sporting enough now after spitting on me for 90 minutes, all part of the game, I guess. It was one of Noel Cantwell's last games for Eire and his last chance to reach the World Cup Finals so he'd given his all, Andy McAvoy was the same; this would be the last chance for the free scoring Dub to show his skills on the world stage. Dunney was young enough to go on and play for another 10 years and Gilesy would go on and play for Eire for many years and manage them too as player-manager. Shay played in the 1970 WC qualifiers after making his debut that night in Paris. Another young Dub made his debut that night, Eamon Dunphy, who I ended up managing years later at Charlton. Little did I know at the time that, with a troublesome left knee getting worse, it would be one of my last games in my beloved green jersey.

After the game it was clear I needed stitches to my face. The suits came in having a break from their sherry and sandwiches and then told us all we were unlucky and so on. It meant nothing to the lads and you can imagine the comments as they left the room. They assured me they would send someone to the hospital to accompany me, collect me and make sure I got home okay. Did they bollocks, I was left in the hospital trying to explain to non-English speaking Parisians what had happened. It was a long night, spent on my own as the suits attended a big civic reception, more interested in a few vol-au-vents than one of their players in hospital having spilt blood for the cause. That did hurt, and still does to be honest. In the Irish press I got some glowing reviews in what many felt was my best display in a green shirt, with the reports filling Mammy and Daddy with pride.

The Irish Times singled out Mick Meagan of Huddersfield who didn't give their danger man Pereda a kick all game and The Irish Independent said I was one of the 'outstanding figures' in the match, playing with 'whole-hearted endeavour' and that my second half header where I took a whack from Olivera was 'Ireland's best effort in the second half'. Mammy read all this out to me on the phone before sending over to me as usual, bless her. In the build up to the game, in The Independent the reporter had asked about me playing either as a sweeper behind the captain Noel Cantwell or in midfield marking Suarez. Even back then, it seemed like the press would get to know about the side before the players. I can only speculate but I would not be surprised if money for information was in full swing back then. We had played without Charlie Hurley which was a blow as it would have been interesting to see him up front with Andy McEvoy unsettling the Spanish defence. The Independent felt that my injury was a key point as they scored with 11 minutes to go as I 'was just coming back on'. They would never have let me back on these days, I looked like I'd gone 10 rounds with Marvin Hagler, swollen and bloodied with two weeping wounds.

The Irish Times referred to me as the 'tough, uncompromising Foley who covered a vast amount of ground' and 'gave the Spaniards plenty to think about by the vigour and determination of his tackling' which is a polite way of saying I got well fired into them. It mentions some 'heavy and vicious tackling by both sides' late on and I recall Gilesey and I sending in a couple of extra heavy ones. It did turn a bit sour at the end, my blood was up, literally, and caked on my jersey. The press generally felt that it was a valiant effort in defeat, small consolation but let's say the Irish press were not always so supportive. This time though, all of the articles were complimentary and balanced, and to read positive comments about me personally meant a lot, this was my own people and in a huge game too. This is why I kept the clippings which I never did normally. These articles made my parents, family and friends all proud of me, and that meant a lot. Saying that, one of Dad's favourite things when I played for the Republic was when I received my match fee of £40 cheque and £20 cash which I gave to him, he would be made up, I don't think he told Mammy though.

Now, in their defence, The FAI have since done some great things and have improved a great deal celebrating their old international players like the lovely day we all had at Croke Park collecting a commemorative gold cap. I have dealt with them personally over the years having been in the running as manager and assistant. I managed to get shortlisted back in '75 and once as assistant with George Burley more recently. When I was up in '75 it must have been close because two representatives turned up at my house at quarter to 12 at night. Again, it was just another example of the poor organisational qualities of the FAI, why didn't they just turn up the following day? Sheila was not impressed no matter what the job offer was, I wouldn't mind but I didn't even get the bloody job. I was on the shortlist of three after I'd left Charlton and they seemed very interested but they gave it to Eoin Hand who also managed my local Inchicore side (Dad's beloved St. Pats) at the same time. Eoin had a tough time missing out on three qualifications for three consecutive major tournaments and was sacked. I'd have loved a crack at the job. When I applied with George Burley in 2005, he felt convinced he had the job but he lost out to Brian Kerr.

Having made it out of Paris unaccompanied and trekked to the airport, I got on to a flight looking pretty bashed up with the disappointment of the result sinking in. Like every sportsman alive – don't believe any tripe that players don't care – I took defeats badly and needed some space. Sheila was great, she knew how to read my moods and when the coast was clear. This one stayed a little longer though, probably a mix of the enormity of the game and the FAI's role in the outcome and also to me personally, after the game. But I needed to get my head back on for the day to day challenge of the First Division, and quick. I made it back home by the following afternoon, worn out and all bet up. I stayed in bed and spoke to Dave agreeing to report to the ground on Friday for a light jog and rub down. Sheila looked after me and the kids were a welcome distraction, they just always act the same no matter what result you've had.

Who did we have next game? Let's get back mentally into the total focus needed as captain, time to get the fixture list out. Liverpool at Anfield, oh shit. There would be fewer tougher games all season – Ron Yeats, Ian Callaghan, Roger Hunt, Ian St. John, Tommy Smith and the player who was probably my toughest opponent, Peter Thompson. If you've never heard of Peter Thompson, look him up, what a player. Over 500 league games for Preston, Liverpool and Bolton but over 400 of those at Liverpool and 16 caps for England which would have been more had Sir Alf not jettisoned playing with wingers. He was with Bobby Moore when he got arrested for the infamous set-up that was the 'Bogota bracelet' incident at the 1970 World Cup. He had pace to burn, tricks to stand you up then explode and he had the stamina to run all game. A full back's nightmare and all of this three days after a physically and mentally draining game abroad. He played on the left but was right-footed so cut inside but it made no difference if you knew it was coming or not, he still went past you. Not what I needed. There are videos posted online of that wonderful side and you will find the 1965 European first leg semi against Inter Milan in May 1965, which also features the classy Suarez who I man marked literally in Paris playing for Inter. He'd cost £142,000 in 1961 making him the world's most expensive footballer at the time.

We were well beaten 5-0, they were 3-0 up at half-time and if it wasn't for Norman Coe in goal it could have been worse. Thompson scored the second and kept saying to me, 'Come on, Theo, let's go for a run,' as he motored down the wing, he knew I was bollocksed from the Spain game. I managed to get through the game but there wasn't much in the tank. However, had I been fresh as a daisy it wouldn't have mattered, they were just too good for us. They wound up winning the league that year by five points, in the days when you received two for a win, so they walked it really.

We were reeling and lost the next game at home to Spurs even without Jimmy Greaves, with Dave Mackay and Frank Saul getting their goals without reply. Unsurprisingly, the crowd had been just under the bonus sweet spot again with our new signing from Ipswich, Joe Broadfoot, making his debut. Then we had a great win away at Fulham, like the Northampton of old, running out 4-1 winners with a Bobby Brown hat-trick against his old club and Bobby Hunt getting the fourth. The legendary Johnny Haynes got the equaliser before their goalkeeper Macedo got injured and a young Rodney Marsh had to go in goal. The boss played Tommy Robson instead of Barry Lines that day as he knew Chelsea were tracking him and, sure enough, he was off to Stamford Bridge two days later for £30,000.

The result at Fulham gave us a boost, makeshift 'keeper or

not, and we achieved back to back wins with a 2-1 home win over Blackpool, the goals coming from Linesy and Joe Broadfoot, Fulham and Blackburn both losing so we jumped two places up the table. We followed this with a disastrous result against fellow strugglers, Blackburn going down 6-1 at Ewood Park. If ever a result told a story this was it, the second half of the season would be a long old slog as we battled it out with Blackburn who were the worst side by some distance, despite that result, and Fulham, Sunderland and Notts Forest. Dave strengthened the squad with the signing of Graham Moore from Man Utd for £15,000. Graham was a good signing but possibly still too late as we'd had a poor first half to the season only winning four games from 21 played. It was nowhere near good enough, we were second bottom at the turn of the year and two sides relegated.

Christmas came and went but I was only thinking about the league not my new sweater or slippers. It was with me all the time, I've always been like that and this was worse than ever as I knew this was the most important season of my career. It had taken 11 years to get here and I wanted to stay, this was the real deal. I tried to enjoy Christmas with the kids, and Sheila was heavily pregnant with our third, but I just couldn't separate football from the everyday. The day after Boxing Day we played Chelsea at a packed County Ground in, what is believed to be, one of the largest Cobblers' gates ever of 23,325 but probably more knowing the club. The gate on Wantage Road broke allowing plenty of happy punters in for nothing. I had to watch from the stands injured, we were 1-0 up in the second half through Bobby Brown before Bobby Tambling equalised for the Blues within nine minutes then scored another two minutes later. Debutant Graham Moore scored our second only two minutes later so a flurry of three goals in only four minutes and heading for a good point against one of the best sides in the league and who pops up on 84 minutes to snatch the win? Bloody George 'Stroller' Graham. At the end of the game there was an almighty scrap between Terry Branston and Tambling both rolling around as tempers flared.

Believe it or not, we played them the following day at Stamford Bridge as you did in those days after a week of eating and drinking over Christmas. I made it on to the pitch for this one with only two changes to our 11 from the day before while they only made one change, amazing really. Our former teammate, Tommy Robson, was making his debut for the absent Tambling who had sadly lost his father so couldn't play. I had to mark Tommy, and kept him quiet enough but we lost 1-0 so were sick of the sight of them over the two days. That Chelsea team were a very good outfit with Peter Bonetti, 'Chopper' Harris, Johnny Hollins, George the Stroller, the mercurial Peter Osgood, Terry Venables and Bobby Tambling. They finished fifth that season.

We had a mini run of a draw, win, draw against Sheffield, Blackburn and West Ham away, home and away respectively. We'd managed a win and a draw in the two games against the Hammers who were a very good side with their famous England trio and we got some payback on Blackburn for the thumping defeat only four weeks earlier. I missed the Sheffield game through injury, a sign of things to come for my troublesome left knee. Four points from a possible six was miles better and, on that form, we would be fine if we could maintain it. Two days after tossing the coin with the great Bobby Moore at Upton Park in January '66, Sheila gave birth to Sean Anthony who was a bonny baby weighing in at 9 pounds 6, so no surprise he now stands 6 feet 4.5 inches tall. Added to which, he was two weeks late, he's always been laid-back has Seanie boy. The family was expanding, with three kids under five years old, which was great, I loved them to bits but I couldn't help thinking we'd better stay in the top flight to keep earning and fending for them as the knee and Achilles were a concern by now.

Before the season had started I'd ventured into the retail catering world with Foley's Bake 'n' Take pie shop which was a joint venture with singer Ruby Murray's manager, Tony Hepworth. We knew Ruby and her husband, Bernie Burgess, very well as they were local and on the scene around town. Tony had a few business interests and had two cafés in town so he knew the business. We used to mix socially with Ruby, Bernie and Tony and also my favourite Irish crooner, Val Doonican, as they all lived locally. Quite the celebrity socialites we were!

Val was a lovely fella, sadly no longer with us, and he sang one of my favourites 'Danny O'Rafferty's Motor Car' which the kids liked to sing along to on the old eight track tape cassettes. He used to come to the 101 Club at Northampton and we got to know him well. They had a personal tragedy when their infant son passed away but they had a saying that always stuck with us 'you can't worry about kids getting mud on the carpet, Theo' as if to say small things really didn't matter. With regards to the pie shop, Tony approached me to see if I was interested in taking on his unit opposite the Post Office in Town and starting a takeaway business. We would get Ruby to open it and get plenty of coverage in the press, so I thought, why not? Ruby was a lovely Belfast girl with the voice of an angel, 'Softly, Softly' was a huge hit in the '50s, and nowadays her legacy is probably more for her name which is used as rhyming slang for a curry. She too passed away many years ago, in Torquay, as the years in showbiz probably caught up with her.

I managed to pull together enough money to go in with Tony and we converted the café he'd found into a pie and chip shop easily enough so I was a restaurateur of sorts whilst captaining a First Division football side. We did it all properly, researched the pies at Peter's Pie factory then secured a good deal with another local company, Fleur-De-Lys, who made cracking chicken and mushroom pies still talked about to this day. Let's just say the kids had a fair few pies growing up. I used to help out the young lad and his wife who worked there from time to time and, if it helped shift a bit of grub, I was happy to muck in. I can't see Yaya Toure dishing up chips around the Etihad Stadium though can you? It did all right, it was never going to replace the football income but it was a welcome top up at times, and the pies were lovely, packed with meat, so it was good wholesome grub. As far as I'm aware, the shop is still there in some form as a food outlet.

Whilst the pie shop helped the revenue, I would have traded it in if it could help our league position, as the games kept coming with no let up. We lost at home to Nottingham Forest 2-1 in the FA Cup, Browny scoring for the third consecutive game. I missed the Everton defeat the week after, at home, because of injury again with the attendance once more just below the bonus threshold. I'd even taken to guessing the crowd to see if the lads were due their bonus.

Then I was back available for one of the gold riband games, away to United at Old Trafford, which was up there with the visits to Anfield and Highbury. In front of over 35,000 we were clearly overawed and 4-1 down by half-time with two from Bobby Charlton, one from John Connelly and one from Dennis Law. Graham Moore getting our reply against his old club. They completed the rout in the second half with Bobby getting his third and Dennis his second while Don Martin pulled one back to make it 5-2 briefly in between their two goals. This was the same week that United defeated Benfica in the European Cup Quarter Final, one of the best sides around, so no shame in being beaten, but shipping six stung. Once again, we were missing the big man Terry Branston as we had against Leeds back in October when we also leaked six. The regular back four was continually disrupted that season along with the GK Brian Harvey and it definitely affected us. Brian, Terry, Micky and I all missed games through the season and that isn't being overly critical of Norman Coe, Graham Carr, Vic Cockcroft or John Mackin, who all deputised admirably when asked to, but it just wasn't the same as we knew each other's games so well.

It got worse with a repeat 6-2 defeat away to Stoke which is another game I missed, Johnny Mackin coming in and Terry missing again, our season was in tatters with two heavy defeats back to back. We bounced back though with a good 3-1 win over Newcastle at home, notable for the fact we had Brian in goal and Branst, Micky Everett, Johnny Kurila and I all back in the defensive line up again. The talented Don Martin bagged two with another from Graham Moore who was proving to be a good buy. We had a steady 1-1 draw away to West Brom, with the same defence and Don getting on the scoresheet again. In a burst of the Cobblers of old we had a great 2-1 home win over the mighty Leeds with debut signing George Hudson getting the winner and setting up the other, followed by a six-goal thriller sharing the spoils at Notts Forest with the same defensive line up for the fourth consecutive game. Johnny Kurila popped up with a last-minute equaliser after a goalmouth scramble. In that run of four games we ended up with six points from a possible eight. That was so much better and was top of the table form, if only we could all stay fit, maybe we could avoid relegation.

We fell off the chariot though at Sheffield Wednesday going down 3-1 with George Hudson grabbing his second in three games since signing. Maybe it was one game too many for the same creaking defence for the fifth consecutive game. Then we were back in the saddle with three draws and two wins from the next five games, again seven points from a possible 10 is top of the table form. I got injured in the first of those games a 2-2 draw at home to Leicester with George Hudson getting his third goal in four games and Mooro getting another. I had to come off and that was my season over as I didn't play again, missing the last seven games.

The left knee was really struggling, flaring up after games and catching me something rotten during games, I was genuinely concerned about my future as a footballer. I was forced to watch the run in as a spectator, pure torture for someone like me, unable to help the lads other than offer moral support. The run of six wins and seven draws from the last 21 games had given us a great chance of staying up but Fulham had been on a remarkable run too and it was all gearing up to a four-pointer at home on 23 April 1966. Thankfully, the rest of the regular defence were fit for the run in and we recorded some fine results with a 2-1 win at Villa, Tony Hately et al, dragging them into the dogfight too. Mooro scored again and we had a crucial home win against Stoke, the enigmatic Don Martin getting the only goal of the game. Possibly the result of the season was a 0-0 against eventual winners Liverpool after their 5-0 mauling back in November. This was the game that Ian St. John got cut by JK and Saint always blamed me but I wasn't even playing.

We drew 1-1 with Spurs at the Lane with Jimmy Greaves getting a late equaliser from the penalty spot cancelling out yet another George Hudson goal, a result made even more impressive as John Mackin went between the sticks with Bryan Harvey off injured. Good news for the lads was the fact that all three home games in that run were well over the bonus threshold gate so they would get an extra £15 in their pay packs. Recently, I attended a sports evening where Greavsie was the after dinner speaker, before Jimmy had his stroke, obviously, and he was on great form telling some cracking stories. He spotted me outside and we had a good catch up before he went up to talk. Well, he slaughtered me when everyone was sat down, said I always kicked him and anything that moved basically but I never actually played against him in 1965-66! He missed the game at the County Ground and I missed the return at the Lane. Not only did his partner say I cut his head open, Jimmy says I kicked him all over the park, both of them bloody making it up! Sometimes you just can't escape reputations but I didn't spoil his fun and just kept quiet.

Back in the '70s and '80s I used to get Jimmy to play for my celebrity sides in various charity games, he was always so generous with his time and a real diamond. He was in the throes of his drink battle then though, and one game I took him off after about five minutes and he wasn't happy swearing away, 'Why have you fucking taken me off?'

To which I replied, 'Jim, you were running the wrong fucking way, you're pissed as a fart.' He didn't even try to argue, just smiled and nodded walking off to have a sobering shower. I really hope he is on the mend now as he is a lovely, genuine man.

The other famous footballer who lost his battle with his demons was Bestie and he was the same, nothing was ever a problem. Brian Moore the commentator did loads of work for charity and when we moved to London, he often asked me to help out getting stars to visit hospitals, hospices, you name it. Well, we were headed to a disabled centre in Tunbridge Wells and the player we had lined up dropped out the same day so I took a punt and tried Bestie on the phone, 'No problem, Theo, meet me at Blackheath train station at 1.00pm.' He turns up looking a million dollars, like the fifth Beatle in an expensive suit, probably been up all night, but sober. He could not have gone down better, he got changed and he was in one of the wheelchairs playing games in the gym and spending so much time with everyone. He was first class and was there all day. I dropped him back to Blackheath in the evening and he persuaded me to go in to The Railway Tavern for a few beers but I had to duck out before closing as he was getting bedded in for the evening, with strangers buying him drinks just because he was 'Bestie'. I offered him a few quid for his time and he was so offended I soon put the notes away, he didn't want a penny, God only knows what or who he had planned that day but he dropped everything to be there. Another lovely man, he just couldn't shake off his demons, unfortunately.

Back to the crucial Fulham game in April, this was huge, with the winners of the game being in charge of their own destiny. The whole town was involved, everyone was chatting about it and the drive to the ground was busier than normal with thousands heading to the game. I parked up and got the usual from passing fans, 'We going to win today, Theo?' or 'Two points needed today, skip' or the more hopeful 'You fit today, Theo?' The usual replies of 'Course we will,' and 'Let's hope so,' seemed more nervous than normal and the final reply of 'Not fit no, unfortunately,' even more distressing than usual.

We were at home, one spot above them and two points ahead of them, but we were the favourites as we were much better at home. In front of the official attendance of 24,523, we had a dream start and went one up through George Hudson again his fourth in seven games, before Bobby Robson equalised for the Lilywhites. Joe the King struck a typically sweet strike to put us 2-1 up just past the half hour mark and then, midway through the second half, came not one, but two huge turning points, which were to prove critical to our whole season and our First Division status. First we had a free kick from John Mackin that sailed over

McClelland in the Fulham goal and over the line but was disallowed for a phantom foul on the 'keeper.

Then George Hudson had a great strike that crashed off the bar and bounced over the line before being hacked away. It was obvious to everyone except the infamous World Cup referee, Jack Taylor, who glanced over to the linesman who, can you believe it, had slipped and fallen over at the critical moment. Joe and George chased Taylor who said to the King, 'Sorry Joe, I didn't see it, I can't give it.' Our First Division status which had been hard fought over 42 games, as it turned out now, boiled down to a split second when a clumsy linesman missed one of the key things he was there to officiate on. Typical. Now I know there are hundreds of variables that go into the outcome of a season but I go back to the comment about that great night at Anfield in '89, some things are just written down and destined by fate.

We had gone from potentially going 3-1 up and undoubtedly going on to win, to seeing Fulham grow in confidence and inevitably they scored an equaliser through Steve Earle and, in an instant, the mood in the ground changed to one of fear, including the lads on the pitch. We pushed for a winner and, sure enough, we played into their hands with Earle scoring two late goals in the last three minutes. Game over, beaten 4-2 in a crucial dogfight game at home which we should have won had it not been for bloody Bambi the linesman and his flag. The mood after was funereal in the dressing room, both Dave and I trying to raise spirits as we had two games left to play, there was still a lot to play for. However, we both knew that it was a hammer blow despite our words of positivity.

We had two games left, at home to Sunderland and away to Blackpool. In front of just under 18,000 we went 1-0 down to Sunderland around the half hour mark with the Wearsiders needing just a point to stay up. We owed Sunderland for the 3-0 drubbing at Roker Park though, and dug deep to equalise with 20 minutes to go thanks to a Mickey Everitt 20 yarder that rifled in off the post. Within two minutes George Hudson scored the winner, his sixth goal in ten games since signing. We had kept the escape alive and headed to

Blackpool for the final game hoping for a slip up by Aston Villa who had Arsenal at home.

We stopped over at Blackpool and Dave took us all to the cinema on the Friday to see The Sound of Music of all films. It was a strange choice at the time and even stranger now, maybe a Western may have been more rousing. I was a coiled spring again, completely helpless watching from the stands as we toiled in the searing heat. We made it to half-time with the score 0-0 so it was all set up with news of the Villa game coming through as a draw also. Then it all unravelled as Blackpool raced into a 2-0 lead midway through the second half before Alan Ball sealed our fate with a late penalty. At Villa Park news came in of a 3-0 win with Tony Hately grabbing two. It was over, the dream finished in a one season cameo. Dave somehow dug deep to give a post-match pep talk stating we would be back and thanking everyone for their efforts and so on. In the middle of the doom, it was Dave's attempt to raise spirits when he must have been crestfallen too, it marks out the man really as he must have been beside himself with frustration.

There were tears in the dressing room that day, some tough fellas sobbing away. It hurt like hell, after all the graft, all the sweat, to get there and back in a season. A taste of it all, some great days and then bang, the door slammed in our face. We might not have wanted to admit it then but we probably all knew the chance to play in the top flight wasn't coming again. How do you lift yourself from that to go and compete in a league you were promoted from two seasons ago? With great difficulty is the short answer and we struggled across the board that following season. For me, personally, I just wanted to get back on the pitch and playing again. It was killing me not to be playing and I wanted to be back doing the only thing I knew. I'd had my knee looked at, the surgeon had removed all of the cartilage which is what they did then and I was told to give it a go. It had been a difficult year with the game in Paris still stinging and then to go and lose top flight status so marginally, added to which the cloud of a serious injury was hanging over me.

Only a matter of weeks after the Blackpool game, I'd been

called up to play for Eire against West Germany in Dublin and, looking back now, I shouldn't have played as the knee still wasn't right. We were well beaten 4-0 by a top side even with our big names of McGrath, Hurley and Haverty making what would be their last hurrahs. The Kaiser, Franz Beckenbauer, scored the fourth as the Germans cruised into top gear for the World Cup Finals. I came off the pitch having nursed myself through the game but in a lot of pain, I knew I was in trouble.

Preseason was different definitely in the summer of 1966, there was plenty of talk of this and that as for other years but it just felt hollow as we'd been relegated for the first time. The club had only known success for four years so this was new territory. We did the same routines, the same runs and drills but they felt different without that wave of success. I felt pain in the troublesome knee after the road runs so ice and rest just became the norm in our house as I was desperate to get fit enough to play, a vicious circle that any injured sportsman will know all too well. We looked okay in the friendlies, Dave still seemed positive and we had more or less the same squad as we'd had in the First Division, so it was a case of let's get back in that league.

Those plans were dashed for me almost immediately as my knee would flare up between sessions and friendlies, so I told Dave that I wasn't available to play. We both agreed on getting it right before coming back and risking it so I embarked on plenty of 'bodies' and bike work to keep fitness levels up without aggravating the knee. As it turned out I waited and watched, for months unfortunately. That German game had really done some damage, I think.

We started the season terribly and carried on until Christmas in that vein, we were losing games at a rate we'd never witnessed even dropping points at our beloved County Ground. We had the false dawn of a record 8-0 win over Brighton at home in the League Cup which turned out to be a one-off as we hurtled to the bottom losing every other game pretty much. Every time I tried to make a return the knee flared up and, with each passing week, I grew more concerned about my career, the mortgage, the kids, not to mention the club. I'd discussed it openly with Dave, and we'd spoken about a possible coaching role, which really appealed to me as I couldn't see a long future in my playing career. On the back of those talks, I signed up to do my preliminary coaching badge with the F.A in preparation for a new role at the club.

The League position stayed as it was and we scrapped for survival in a league we'd been promoted from only two seasons before. January and February came and we limped along still, not even talisman forward Frank Large's return before Christmas gave us a shot in the arm. I could take no more, I had a long chat with Dave and we agreed to give it a go on a return to the side and if it was no good we'd revert to plan B and a coaching role. In January 1967, I returned for the away game to Plymouth some 10 months after my final game against Leicester in the First Division.

It wasn't a huge success, I played 17 games in that period of January to May and we won four, drew five and lost eight so my return made little difference to our points per game ratio really. We lost Joe Kiernan to injury in February for the rest of the season which was a hammer blow as Joe supplied the flair and created the chances for the front boys. We had gone through the leagues as a team bound by a great team spirit and work ethic yet we slumped with a whimper despite attempting to behave in the same way. When you spiral like that in sport, sometimes you just cannot halt it. Dave tried to bring in players, he shipped some out like Micky Everitt to Plymouth, brought in young players like Billy Best but the old magic touch had gone. He started to look a beaten man and you could see he was beginning to doubt himself, the death knell for a manager.

The final game that season was away to Charlton, a game we lost 3-0 with two goals from the future Addicks manager, Eddie Firmani, a man who, little did I know, would feature heavily in the next part of my career. The club had suffered back to back relegations, the whole season had been a disaster and the master Dave Bowen looked unrecognisable. The years of joy and success were getting tarnished. To make matters worse, I think Dave neglected our 'deal' as he just had other worries, I guess, but it's fair to say my performance levels were not as they once were, I was struggling through games so the offer of a coaching role definitely appealed. Dave had brought ex-player Roly Mills into the fold though, and he explained that was the plan for next season too. We never really fell out as such, but I told him I was disappointed he'd gone back on the agreement. He knew full well I had the club's interests at heart and I would be there for him in whatever role required the following season.

As a final bookend to all the good times I also played, what turned out to be, my last ever game in the emerald green of Eire. I was at a low point after the season we'd had, my worst since turning professional, and I knew my knee was on the way out. I didn't have many games left in me so when I got the call from the FAI at the end of the season, I jumped at it knowing there might not be many more. Little did I know it would be my last. We were playing Czechoslovakia at Dalymount Park, so I made sure everyone came along just in case it was to be the last. The Czechs were always a tough challenge, runners-up in 1962 World Cup, technically excellent and they'd go down at the slightest touch so a real change from the hustle and bustle of our league. Up front they had Josef Adamec, a prolific goalscorer who became famous for scoring a hat-trick the following year against the brilliant 1968 Brazil side. Well, I reported with a mixture of enjoyment and sorrow but just wanted to take it all in.

Our side that day was a new look team as the set-up was looking to make changes top to bottom and have a real manager in place and move away from the daft FAI selector's committee. We had the Preston North End goalkeeper, Alan Kelly, back in for Man United's Pat Dunne. It was a position we never really nailed down which didn't help as a defender playing top level opposition. I played in front of three different goalkeepers, Pat, Alan and Swansea's Noel Dwyer. We had Fulham's John Dempsey in at left back, again my fifth 'partner' in the full back spot, which is never a good thing, and Limerick's centre back 'Al' Finucane. John went on to have great success with Chelsea in the FA Cup against

Leeds Utd in 1970 and then in the Cup Winners' Cup the following season against the mighty Real Madrid scoring the first in a 2-1 win with a volleyed finish. Michael, or 'Al' as he was known, holds the record as the oldest player to appear in any European competition beating the legendary Dino Zoff. Al was nearly 44 when he played for Limerick in the Cup Winners' Cup against Girondins de Bordeaux in 1982. By then I was at QPR coaching them having stopped playing some 23 years before.

We also had Celtic's Charlie Gallagher up front who was part of the Lisbon Lions squad that won the European Cup that year but he only ended up playing two games for Eire, this being his second. It was a groundbreaking move when he got called up as he was the first player born in Scotland to play for Eire. It's fair to say it was an experimental side playing alongside the old guard of Hurley and McEvoy and the 'new' regulars of Eamon Dunphy, Mick Meagan and Ray Treacy. This slight shift in the set-up may have been a backlash to the debacle of the Paris game against Spain but it was necessary as the squad needed some new blood. By 1969 the set-up had finally caught up and we had an actual manager in place as Mick Meagan became the first of his kind having stepping up from playing. Mick was followed soon after by the likes of Liam Tuohy in '71 and then my old Dub teammate, Johnny Giles, in '73. We were still miles too late and you can't help feeling that, if some stories are to be believed, we've been catching up ever since.

Charlie Hurley was the 'manager' for the Czech game and we ended up losing 2-0, a goal in each half and, unfortunately, an own goal for poor old Al Finucane on his debut. Masny scored their second just after half-time and we had a bit of a go back and, in truth, we played well against a very good side. I was nursing my stiff and painful knee through another 90 minutes and really not doing myself any justice. I made sure I got my opponent Kabat's shirt at the end of the game, clapped off the fans and waved at Mammy and Da in the stand. The crowd that day wasn't the best so I picked them out all right. I knew at the end of the game as I trudged off that, barring a miracle, that was it. I'd achieved more than I could ever have hoped for but it still stung like hell.

I'd played nine games more than I could have dreamed of for my country, played against Juan Lapetra and Luis Suarez of Spain, Wlodek Lubanski of Poland, the brilliant Paul Van Himst of Belgium and the entire West Germany '66 side including der Kaiser, Franz Bekenbauer. I'd also had the ultimate honour of leading out my country in my home town as captain for the Czech game. Now if you'd told me all of this when I played 'soccer' in my wellies on the streets of Inchicore I'd have said you were as mad a March hare. Aside from all that, it still stung because I loved my country and I loved wearing the green jersey. I should never have played in the '66 West Germany game, it probably did lasting damage that I never got over but can you blame me risking it? West Germany and Beckenbauer in my home town? It had been great while it lasted, my souvenir shirts from those games are still prized possessions.

Well, after the dust had settled back home, I received a phone call in the close season saying Bobby Stokoe, the manager of Charlton, wanted to sign me and would I meet him. We were heading for a short break to Margate the following weekend so, on the way back, I met Bobby at The Clarendon Hotel overlooking Blackheath, one of the best spots in London. Bobby quickly convinced me to sign, Charlton were a big club with a lovely ground and some very good players and had plans to get into the First Division. Bobby's leg was in plaster that day from a fracture but he was so pleased I was signing he jumped up to shake my hand. Had he known how many games I would play he might have jumped up and hit me instead. Northampton allowed me to go on a free on 9 August 1967 as recognition of my time there but I don't think Bobby or myself quite knew just how bad the knee was.

We were off again, it was less a case of deserting my beloved Northampton, more a case of feeling wanted again as Dave had gone lukewarm on me. Charlton agreed on what was a similar financial deal to the one I was on, no big money increase but I'd get a discounted house from the chairman, Michael Gliksten, who owned a lot of property locally. We didn't know it then but the house deal would last much longer than the playing deal. We were heading to the bright lights of London. We were off to pastures new once more, have boots will travel. We tied up all of the loose ends, like putting the house on the market – we'd had some great times there with the kids, and we settled up coming out of the pie shop, telling Tony to sell it on. The incredible Northampton story brought to an end including my brief foray into catering.

CHAPTER 6
Whistle and Stopwatch
1968 – 1970

Neil Armstrong walks on the moon, the first jumbo jet flight takes place and things can never be the same again,
Concorde goes supersonic, Robert Kennedy was assassinated just a month after Martin Luther King in unsettling times. North Korea is a serious nuclear threat and captures a US ship that had strayed into Korean waters. North Vietnam launches their surprise offensive against the US, signalling the beginning of the end of the war for the US as support back home subsides considerably. Lulu ties the Eurovision Song Contest and Monty Python airs for the first time as colour TV begins to feature. The Beatles are still getting airtime, The Jacksons hit the charts and my old favourites, Frank Sinatra and Elvis, still look to be part of the scene. Andy Williams is on my eight track regularly.
Steve McQueen races his green Mustang through San Francisco in 'Bullitt' while Jack Lemmon and Walter Matthau are 'The Odd Couple'. Redford and Newman spark off each other in the iconic 'Butch Cassidy and The Sundance Kid'.
I didn't have McQueen's muscle Mustang but I did have a lovely red Mark II Cortina that I used to push to the limits around the streets of South East London thinking I was in 'Z Cars'.

As ever, Sheila prepared everything to load up the car again with a young family of three children, this time with eight-year-old Teresa, six-year-old Adrian and two-year-old Sean. We were leaving behind great memories of a great time in our lives and my football career. We had been carried along on the wave of success at the football club and the general good times of the 1960s. My good mates John and

Joe were shocked we were going but fully understood the situation. We knew we'd always stay in touch as the bond we had was so strong and sure enough we did. Along with their wives Nan and Pat, you would not find more loyal friends anywhere. They knew we had to pay the bills though, so getting a wage secured was essential. This was a new adventure, a new city and a new football club, the biggest club yet, but it didn't feel quite right. With concerns over my knee which was still playing up, it wasn't with the spring in my step I had going from Exeter to Northampton six years ago but with a cloud of doubt for my career hanging over me.

We knew nothing of the area, heading to South East London which was all very different to Northampton. We drove through London on the way down, snaking down the Embankment, taking in the sights before heading south through Elephant and Castle, New Cross, Deptford and Lewisham until we reached the oasis of Blackheath. The house was between Blackheath and Charlton so not far from the desirable areas of the Heath and Greenwich with its wonderful Park. New Cross and Lewisham were very edgy back then and not like the shiny new areas they are now. The journey would become very familiar over the years as we headed back regularly to Northampton to meet John and Joe. That first trip down was an eye opener though, as the city was so large, busy and intimidating in many ways. The house we were placed in was lovely, much bigger than we'd been used to, and we liked it so much we are still there now. We looked to settle down in our new home, not always easy with a young family, and I tried to get myself fit for preseason.

In no time, Sheila had Teresa and Adrian accepted in the local Catholic Primary School and I was reporting for training at The Valley. I was introduced to the squad by Bobby Stokoe, many of whom I knew anyway from playing against them in the last game of last season. My old teammate from Northampton, Graham Moore, was well known to me, obviously. Centre back Paul Went was an impressive strong fella in the flesh and Keith Peacock was a bubbly character straight from the start. Experienced midfielder Harry

Gregory was a warm and friendly guy, defender Peter Reeves seemed a quiet lad while the young full back Bobby Curtis had boundless energy. I made an instant connection with forward Matt Tees who was a similar age and yet another canny Scot. The other lads seemed friendly and it appeared to be a strong squad made up of seasoned pros and some promising young lads.

The atmosphere at the club seemed good as it is at most clubs, never mind what you read in the papers about this or that. As I've said before, you are doing what you love, keeping fit, laughing and joking every day with like-minded colleagues and getting paid for it. Okay you get the odd bad egg but they soon get found out and told, don't worry about that, and you might even have the odd 'incident' as I did with Mooro at Northampton that day but it's all soon forgotten about. Much like that famous John Hartson incident with Eyal Berkovic, that would be forgotten about in a day or two, I guarantee. I've seen much worse than that over the years. Johnny Kurila at Northampton straightened out one of the team one day and the gentle giant, Bobby Hazell at QPR, went for another player on one occasion in the car park at Greenford Training ground. Bobby didn't take kindly to continual goading and his face changed, his eyes went wild and, with a face like steel, he chased this lad around parked cars. He caught him and it took about five people to get him off. The player at Northampton kept well clear of Johnny afterwards as did the prankster at QPR from Bobby, lessons learnt, the laws of the dressing room. It works, fairly basic and brutal but always effective.

With introductions made, and the new boy paraded to the squad, we steamed into preseason with a tough schedule split across training at the ground in the car park on the old Redgra hard surface and road runs for hill work at nearby Maryon Wilson or Greenwich Park. Both lovely, picturesque London parks, you would struggle to find a better park anywhere than Greenwich Park, beautiful place and I still head up there regularly with Sheila for a stroll. There are great views across London and the Thames, the Isle of Dogs, the Naval College and Maritime Museum and the famous

Observatory. A beautiful spot at any time of the year but when you have to run up the killer slopes and hills to the point of fainting and throwing up you soon hate the place. You always get one lad who has eaten before, had a drink the previous night, or heads off too quick then he's throwing up by the side getting plenty of stick. Ours was Bobby Curtis; he shot off one day, we were all cursing him so he's giving verbals back and laughing at the old boys. Half an hour later, he's saying hello to his breakfast again and not chirping so much in between wretches and spews. Well, he got some stick all right.

The knee wasn't holding up well though, it would be okay on the grass up the park, and I'd always use the grass rather than run on the hard paths, but we'd run along the roads and pavements to get there and it sent shudders up my leg as my foot hit the pavement. I would suffer in silence, get through the session, get home and do the familiar routine known to every sportsman or woman in the land, RICE. Rest, Ice, Compression and Elevation. I'd be necking painkillers on the way to training, the swelling would flare up by the time I made it home, the knee stiff from the driving position. I needed to train to keep fit, I needed to show I was fit or I was in trouble and I wanted to be available for the start of the season but I just couldn't get over that hump with the knee. I was in trouble and a few of the lads probably knew it thinking, what have we signed here? I bet young Bobby Curtis, who played right back and was a great prospect, spotted it. I had come full circle some 12 years after watching the wily old pro Brian Doyle at Exeter and his chest problem but still making it out onto the pitch every week. The difference here was I was only 29, Brian had been 35. From being a principled young lad to a wily old pro in the space of just 12 years, it's sad what happens really, when money becomes more important due to bills and family.

I just about made it through preseason, kept quiet only telling Sheila and my old mates at Northampton who I knew I could trust. Sheila was great, reassured me that we'd cope somehow if I was forced to retire, we'd find another way. She was never fazed that woman and has been my strongest ally for 60 years now, I'd be lost without her that's for sure. The only problem now was the friendlies were coming up so there would be no place to hide out on the pitch. Amazingly, I came through the first one alright. dosed up on painkillers, and Bobby seemed pleased enough. After the game though, the knee flared up and yet another Sunday was spent on the sofa save for a limped journey to the local church in Charlton, being driven by Sheila. I used to keep a low profile on the back pews as the church was full of Charlton fans.

Come Monday morning, I was still limping badly and the knee was swollen, there was no way I would be able to train. I had to declare it to the boss and headed off to see the physio, Charlie Hall. I explained the history behind the knee, I think he knew anyway, and I told him it had been gradually getting worse through preseason, which was sort of true. Well, Charlie was a wily old bugger and I think he knew this had been a problem for a while. There were no magic cures though, and I was off training and restricted to only doing exercise that wouldn't aggravate the knee, so it was countless abdominal exercises, straight leg exercises and so on. I knew the drill and I also knew that overall fitness goes very quickly if you can't run. This was a big blow and I knew it could be serious for my Charlton career never mind my playing career full stop. I spoke to Bobby as honestly as I could and, no doubt, Charlie did too. Bobby was as good as gold, he told me to just get it right and take my time. I bet inside he was thinking, what a bloody mistake he was.

I rested, then rested some more while the friendlies came and went with young Bobby Curtis playing in my position at right back and playing well. I did endless bodies, worked hard on my abdominal muscles, pushed countless press ups and did straight leg raises with a metal boot weight the club had bought me. You strapped this red metal boot on your bad foot and put the loose weights either side then did straight leg raises to work your quadricep muscles. I'd do these for hours until my thighs burned and seized up. You could add weights to the boot to work the muscles even more but, after a while, the muscles would say enough is enough.

The legs were as strong as they could be, the left was now as strong as the right but running and kicking would still aggravate the knee no matter how hard I worked the leg. I used a bike all the time, I spent every available minute working at it, as this was my last shot at getting back on the pitch I felt.

I missed the final friendly and was not fit for the start of the 67-68 season so, for the first time in 12 years, I would not be involved on the first day of the season. Like every other sportsman, I'm sure, I am a terrible spectator. This was a new club, fans were asking why their new experienced Irish international signing wasn't playing. While I'm sat watching, there's a young lad playing in my position who looked a real prospect too, just to finish me off. What did I have to be positive about? I was a worried pro and not very old either which is not a good place to be. I wasn't giving up just yet though, as anyone will tell you, I've never been a quitter. The steel shoe was used more and more, I was continually on the bike and the quads were as hard as rock, so I thought I'd be okay. I slowly built it up the intensity on the training ground and the games came and went. We'd started the season terribly which, I'll be honest, part of me was quietly pleased about as if I came back and we started winning, it would be good for everyone, or so I thought with my twisted logic. This is what happens to you when you are in the last chance saloon of your career; you become very self-centred, even so-called 'team players' like me.

It was now the end of September and the side had only won one out of eight matches, drawn three and lost four. I was itching to get back and Bobby was under a bit of early pressure. I spoke to him although, to be fair, he had been in constant contact with me since I'd joined and declared myself ready to play again. We agreed to target a couple of weeks after a practice game or two and I came through those okay without too much pain, still necking painkillers before as a precaution then icing after all training sessions. The planned game was at home to Carlisle United on 21 October, at last my debut for the club. As someone who never really suffered with nerves, here I was nervous at the age of 29 because I'd put so much into getting back on the pitch and I didn't want to let anyone down. To make matters worse the side had picked up in the last three games with two wins and a draw all at home to Plymouth, Portsmouth and Middlesbrough. A bit of pressure then, just what I needed.

It was the fourth home game on the bounce and finally I made my debut in front of 13,645 watching eyes with a suspect knee and a barrel full of worry. I don't remember much about the game but I got through it okay, dosed up again on painkillers, we drew 2-2 with goals from Alan Campbell and Harry Gregory inside the first five minutes so it should have been a comfortable win really. The fact the side had picked up six points from a possible eight helped smooth over that fact. Although it was only a point, I'd finally contributed to the season and made it through 90 minutes so I felt better about everything even if I hadn't set the world alight.

Well, I didn't know at the time but that was about as good as my Charlton playing career got. In the next three games we were beaten by Ipswich Town, Blackpool and then Bolton Wanderers. Out of a possible eight points the side had picked up one point while I had been playing. Added to which, after that fourth game away to Bolton, my knee flared up again. I was distraught, I went through the same processes after the game of ice, rest and elevation but I had to declare it on the Monday, so I was out of the side again. I was out for the next four months still doing the steel boot, the cycling, the icing, basically flogging the proverbial horse.

Once again, the side seemed to do better without me, winning the next two after the Bolton game just to add to my personal woe. There was even a rare win over local rivals Millwall at the turn of the year and, in the 17 games I missed after the Bolton game, the side had a good run, winning six and drawing six, which was an improvement on the early season form. I came back for the Ipswich Town game at home but we lost 1-0 with my old Cobblers' teammate, Bobby Hunt, on the bench for Town. My knee was hurting again, I was desperate, beside myself now with worry. I told myself I'd give it one more go and stop kidding myself if it flared up again.

I spent the whole week nursing it through training and we headed to Huddersfield Town with a fair side that included Paul Went, Alan Campbell, Peter Reeves, Matt Tees, Ray Treacy, Tony Booth and Keith Peacock. All good players and good enough to win most games in the Second Division, let alone Huddersfield Town who were not the top tier side they are now. Well, we got spanked 4-1 and even the goal we scored came from one of their players. I struggled all game until I got substituted with about 20 minutes to go. This was to be my last professional game as it turned out, a real whimper of an exit to my career, finished at 29 years of age. What happens now?

I'd played only six games for Charlton over six months, we'd drawn one and lost five, what a signing I was. Looking back a little further, I'd only played a total of 56 games in the last three seasons with 33 in the 65-66 First Division Cobbler's campaign, only 17 in the Second Division in 66-67 with Northampton and then just the six for Charlton in the 67-68 campaign. It was a drawn-out conclusion to what now is blindingly obvious, but I just wanted to carry on doing what I loved, the only thing I knew, plus I needed the bloody money. Saturday, 20 March 1968 was to be my last ever proper football game, a very sad day for me. All my childhood dreams, finished. I knew it too. I'd managed nigh on 400 games and played at every ground (at that time) bar one, Chesterfield Town, so in many ways I'd exceeded my wildest dreams but it still hurt me, even now it still stings as I should have been at my peak. I do feel for lads like Dean Ashton who have to finish playing so young when they have the world at their feet, it must really hit hard and affect your personality. I've never been one to suffer with depression or mental illness, thank God, but looking back I'd been low for a long time trying to hold it all together so if ever there was a time I came close it would have to be then.

The side went on to have mixed fortunes in the last eight games of the season, either winning or losing high. This attacking philosophy was to become the Charlton trademark over the next few years as the sides were always good to watch, if not always successful. We finished 15th which was a big underachievement given the players in that side, Bobby Robson's impressive Ipswich Town just pipping QPR to the title. The boss paid the price for our poor league position and Eddie Firmani, who had returned as a player for his third spell at the club, was appointed manager and hung up his boots, a really talented player with Italian caps to prove it.

It was an all-time low for me not really knowing what the next few weeks would bring never mind the years ahead. It could have all gone downhill fast as it does with some lads who are finished early but, as I've found throughout my career, if you look forward and say the right things something generally crops up as long as you aren't too choosy. Stay in the game. Eddie knew I was keen to coach, he knew I was doing the full FA badge and he knew I got on with the lads and could help him in his first job. I'd been to Lilleshall to do my full badge with a golden generation of future coaches and managers. Looking at the photo recently, in that class of '68 you had a golden crop with Dave Sexton taking the course and top coaches galore. That year Don Howe, Jackie Charlton, Lawrie McMenemy, Bobby Robson, Ronnie Moran, Jim Smith, Bobby Campbell and Malcolm Allison all took their first steps towards illustrious coaching and management careers. I was in exalted company and we had some great bonding sessions in the bar, what people may call networking now.

Eddie asked me to step up to player-coach, as Malcolm Musgrove had moved on in December 1967 while I was still trying to play, but we both knew it wouldn't be long before I would hang up the boots. We actually dropped the player part eventually after my registration with the PFA was terminated in August 1969 and I became the assistant manager in January 1970 without anyone really noticing, apart from a bit of mickey-taking from the lads. My wages were a princely £37/week which had been retained to match my playing wage. I really got the bug, I was a man reborn, I threw myself into the new role and kitted myself out in the full uniform including the obligatory whistle and stopwatch. As someone who had always been a strong runner and seen the merits of high fitness levels at Northampton under Dave Bowen, I have always been keen on improving your chances, to be as fit as you can be, not just fit enough, to have that edge. This did not always make you very popular, especially with lads with whom you'd previously shared the pitch, a dressing room, a team bath and nights out.

That transition from player to coach, or manager, is never easy as you need to assert some authority and, even more so as a manager, keep some distance from the players. We had both gone from teammates to the enemy overnight together, so not easy. I got plenty of stick alright, and often got told to 'fucking put that stopwatch away' and stop being 'busy'. Well I carried on until they got the message, I wasn't one of the lads anymore and after a few stern looks they realised. It's not easy though, as I love the craic of the dressing room, but you have to strike a balance. I'll admit it was very difficult in those early days.

Eddie was a classy fella, on and off the pitch, not unlike George Graham in later years I found out. As a player he'd turned out for Sampdoria, Inter and Genoa in between spells at Charlton and the far less glamorous Southend. Even now old Addicks fans will put him in their all-time favourite player lists, a Charlton legend with a scoring ratio better than a goal every other game. At Sampdoria it was nearly a goal a game and that takes some doing in Serie A against the best defenders in the world. He had that air about him and the lads respected him straight away, his career and ability commanded respect. That will only get you so far but there was substance to Eddie too. We both made some mistakes, as you'd expect in our first jobs, and tactically we were both a little naive at times, but it worked well generally. We even looked alike as a pair and a few called us the Italian brothers which I was quite pleased about as Eddie was one good-looking man, always immaculate.

We had a great season really and played in some high scoring games where Eddie's view was you are just as well to lose three nil as one nil so we became an entertaining side to watch with players like Alan Campbell, Graham Moore,

Harry Gregory, Dennis Booth and Keith Peacock in midfield. Up front we had Ray Treacy, Matt Tees and Paul Hince supporting now and then. At the back we had my replacement, Bobby Curtis, and the impressive Paul Went at centre back. Bobby was different class, he could have been as good as he wanted to be that lad. He used to get up and bring balls down on his chest that others would head, a really talented footballer who combined well with Harry Gregory on the right side. Wenty was the same, a very good player who should really have played at the top level. He stood out in games, caught the eye, I'm amazed a big club didn't sign him. Maybe they'd seen him and Bobby Curtis after a pint or two in the British Oak and been put off, but they were excellent on the pitch. Alongside Paul was Peter Reeves who really was our best kept secret. Reevesy was a rarity, not especially tall for a centre back, not what some might say technically superior but what a player to have in your side. Peter was a manager's dream, like a James Milner or similar, completely selfless and a seven or eight out of 10 every week. Reevesy was an ever-present that season, steady as you like, read the game better than anyone I know and never seemed to lose out in the air. Brian Kinsey and young Phil Warman shared the left back position in a back four that had really good footballing ability.

We still leaked too many goals though, keeping Charlie Wright busy between the sticks, but that was probably more to do with Eddie's wishes to always have a go at sides rather than the defence. We still kept goals conceded at just over a goal a game, which isn't bad, whilst we scored a goal and a half a game on average including a few games where we scored four or five. Our home record that season was great, with 30 points from a possible 42 which is up there with league title tallies and The Valley was a real fortress with the fans starting to roll in once more. Unfortunately, the away form was a little below what was needed and we shipped a few goals on the road. It was the year Brian Clough's resurgent Derby won the league some distance ahead of Crystal Palace, who were seven points behind in the days of two points for a win. A couple of seasons later it was the First

Division title for Cloughie and Peter Taylor. All of the stories of Cloughie ring true with me. We played in a preseason tournament years later with Arsenal and Brian was there with Forest. We got chatting in the hotel and I mentioned that daughter Teresa was getting married soon and he made a note of it then sent a huge bouquet of flowers. He really was a great old stick.

The future looked bright and even the chairman, Michael Gliksten, seemed happy but not enough to open his chequebook for us. Mr Michael, as I called him, was real old school plum in the mouth posh and was ferried around in a Roller which he'd let me drive now and then if we were going somewhere together. I got on grand with Michael, his brother was a bit more outspoken after a few liveners in the boardroom during the game though. He became a little chatty shall we say, in the old wood panelled room under the main West Stand. The offices and boardrooms in the old stand were all clad in stylish timber panelling as the chairman owned a huge timber supplier. He was a very wealthy man and good as gold really. He didn't stick his oar in much at all, he knew his football knowledge was limited which is more than can be said for most directors and chairmen in the game. I was lucky really, I have been fortunate to have worked with some great chairmen over the years. As Len Shackleton famously demonstrated with his blank page in his book entitled The Average Director's Knowledge of Football, it's fair to say directors aren't on the board to develop the football strategies. The club was run as a tight ship with secretary Ken Calver involved in all administrative duties including contract negotiations. If you needed travel sorted for an away trip, Ken would find the cheapest deal, if you needed 24 bog rolls for the changing rooms he'd find a deal on a gross for 2p less. Ken was a handy man to have around for the club, if a little thrifty.

I'm not entirely sure what went wrong the following season, but it was the exact opposite yet still the same squad, same routines but a really poor season. We started okay then had a heavy 5-0 defeat away to Swindon Town which was a warning sign of things to come. In September I lost my rag away to Norwich when we were awarded a late penalty with the scores 0-0. We jumped up happy to have won the penalty and the fans near the dugout were giving us some stick. Unwisely, I told a couple to piss off and that was it, the cushions they sat on at Carrow Road started raining down on us. Well, I threw a few back and then all hell broke loose. We scored the penalty to go 1-0 up so I gave the Canary fans some stick and then what happens, they go and score in the last minute so I got it back tenfold. You live and learn, or maybe not as it turned out.

A few games later we lost heavy again, 6-0 away to Bristol City and we were becoming prone to leaking large numbers. It happened again away to Huddersfield, 4-0 this time, Eddie's 'have a go' approach was failing especially on the road. Eddie was not the type to change his ways but it was becoming too commonplace, another heavy one away to Birmingham then Preston North End, who were both down the bottom. We looked a soft touch on the road and the atmosphere was changing but the final nail in the coffin came with a terrible 5-0 defeat at home to Leicester City. Now a heavy defeat at home is less of an issue when it's clearly a one-off, or you've had someone sent off early, but after a few heavy defeats and being near the bottom of the league, it heaps pressure on everyone.

Sure enough, at the end of March 1970, Eddie was sacked after a topsy-turvy two year reign where we just missed out on promotion to the First Division but were now perched just above the trapdoor to the Third Division. Eddie said his goodbyes, he wasn't one for any emotional gestures and he was gone, my Italian brother. The easy choice, I guess, was for me to take the reins for the last four games and, sure enough, Mr Michael asked me to keep us up and it would put me in the driving seat for next season. No pressure then, safety was no way guaranteed as we were in the hat with Watford, Birmingham and Aston Villa. We managed to get two draws and a win which was enough to see us home by two points, Villa and Preston going down. Huddersfield and Blackpool went up that year as we stayed in the Second

Division just about.

The four game interview had gone well, we'd stayed in the Second Division and Mr Gliksten was true to his word. In May 1970, I was appointed the new manager of Charlton Athletic at the age of 33, some two seasons after hanging up my boots. I was very proud to have been appointed as manager of a club steeped in tradition like Charlton. It was a quick transition, pushed along by injury and then a bad season, maybe too quick as it turned out having only just got comfortable in my tracksuit on the training ground. I was going to need a coach to help me out so I enlisted FA coach Colin Murphy who I didn't know too well but he was fairly active in coaching circles at the time. The announcements were made and it was a fairly easy progression for everyone as we all knew each other. It was the usual drill from me, hard work in preseason so plenty of running, plenty of hill work and loads of the usual moaning from the cynical old pros. The chairman told me there would be no money available, despite the poor league placing the previous season, so it was a case of work with what you had or balance the books, it was a tight old ship. It had been a quick transition from player to coach and now manager. It was time to ditch the tracksuit and pull on a kipper tie.

CHAPTER 7
Bobby Moore's Leather Coat
1970 – 1974

The largest ever music festival is held on the Isle of Wight as flower power takes over. Sixties stylised mods, rockers and Teddy Boys all make way for long hair, moustaches, loose clothes and flares. Terrorism exposure at Munich Olympics and tragedy occurs on 'Bloody Sunday' in Derry, Northern Ireland. Inflation goes sky high and VAT introduced. The positivity of the '60s changes swiftly to become an atmosphere of uncertainty. Muhammad Ali loses his title fight with Joe Frazier after an enforced lay-off in a brutal fight at Madison Square Gardens, then beats George Foreman to regain his belt in Kinshasa before beating Frazier, this time in Manilla. The Golden Age of Heavyweight Boxing. In football, Brazil win the 1970 World Cup in Mexico, beating Italy in the Final while West Germany beat the brilliant Dutch on German soil in '74.

The Beatles split up, Sheila's favourite, Neil Diamond, breaks through and Rod Stewart comes to the fore while Michael Jackson releases solo work. Elton John and Stevie Wonder hit their peaks with some great songs. 'Dirty Harry' loads his magnum for the first time and 'The Godfather' redefines cinema and raises the bar permanently. Gene Hackman puts in career defining performance in 'The French Connection'. One of my favourite films of all-time, 'The Sting', sees Paul Newman and Robert Redford team up again in an all-time classic.

I drove a lovely red BMW 2002 for a while which I threw around like Jackie Stewart back then. It shifted along nicely, how I wished I'd kept that as an investment. This followed the Mark II Cortina, so fast and red was the order of the day back then.

It didn't go unnoticed by me that I had been given the job with zero experience and hardly any time as I coach but here I was, the manager of a fairly big London club with plenty of history. It was both daunting and exciting at the same time but, if nothing else, I was going to look the part thanks to a lovely leather jacket I'd bought off the legend that was Bobby Moore. I'd bumped into Bobby in a café called Dirty Micks off Fleet Street one day and, having chatted over old times with a fry up, he said he had a few leather coats to sell if I was interested. He got up and went out to his car to get one, a lovely three quarter, double-breasted, dark brown, thick leather coat. It was really good quality which was no surprise coming from someone with Bobby's style. A true gentleman was Bobby, poorly treated by the FA despite his class as a player and a man. I told him the coat was lovely but I didn't have that sort of money on me (£100 from memory). He wouldn't take no for an answer, just waved me away saying, 'Don't worry, Theo, pay me whenever you can.' Well I didn't pay him for a good few weeks but he never asked for it once and that coat was an eye-catching purchase long before Jose or Pep's touchline fashions. The whole transaction sums up Bobby, just one lovely man.

Years later, a couple of years before he sadly passed away, I saw him at the old Wembley trying to get into the private bar after an England game and some arsehole on the door wouldn't let him in without a pass. 'Can you get me in here, Theo?' he said, as I walked past. He had to ask me if I could get him in, the captain of the England World Cup winning side at the home of English football. What a joke. I pulled the doorman aside and gave him one hell of a bollocking as Bobby was just too modest to have a go. Ironically, there is now a bar at the New Wembley named after him as well as a restaurant and a statue outside. All correct and only right but all too late, unfortunately. Many have said the same but his treatment by the FA was scandalous, Harry Redknapp is 100 per cent right, Bobby should be knighted posthumously.

Now, I've always felt I could spot a player and I pride myself on the signings I made, or was involved with, over the years but the early years at Charlton were tough. The club had made it very clear that they didn't want to spend a penny so I had to balance the books and try to reduce wage bills. It was an eye opener alright and, looking back, you can see why they gave me the job as I was the cheap option and maybe a little green with naive enthusiasm. At the time though, I tried to make a fist of it, looking to get cheaper players in from lower leagues or the reserve sides of the bigger clubs. I'd also be pushing certain players to see if other clubs wanted the more saleable 'senior' lads who were on a bit more money. I was learning fast and getting used to the tricks of the trade.

I raided Yeovil down on the south west coast for Dickie Plum and Cyril Davies. I signed Dickie for about £7,000, but things never really took off for him and he left after a couple of seasons having only scored 10 goals up front despite being prolific down in the West Country. I eventually sold him to my old club, Exeter City, for £5,000 where he played for a couple of seasons but still never recreated his Yeovil form. Some players are like Guinness, they just don't travel very well. Cyril Davies, on the other hand, was a real find having picked him up for £5,000.

He'd had a couple of brief spells at Swansea and Carlisle but hadn't really gone on from there. 'Squirrel' probably had one leg shorter than the other from playing wide on Yeovil's old Huish Ground slope which had an eight feet slope side to side, long since gone. Dealing with an end to end slope is bad enough but side to side is even worse as it's just so noticeable like a wonky snooker table. You just hope you didn't draw those sides with slopes like Yeovil or Wycombe away back then in the FA Cup. Cyril was a real find and flying before a freak injury where he kicked the corner flag resulting in knee ligament damage – he was never the same again. He even managed to get capped by Wales, just the once mind but I'm proud to have played a part in that and get him away from that Yeovil slope. He dropped into local non-league at Tonbridge Angels before becoming a local groundsman. I met up with him recently and he looked exactly the same even though he must be in his late 60s now. A promising career cut short, these are the flip sides to the nice lifestyle getting paid to do something you love, the stories of those careers cut short by injury.

I signed a German lad, Dietmar Bruck, from Coventry City where he'd played nearly 200 games, in an attempt to steady the ship at the back. Dietmar cost just over £11,000 because he was more of a seasoned pro. I met Dietmar recently for a meal, and we chatted about old times. He is a lovely fella who has an interesting background coming from Germany as a very young boy in a remarkable story of escape during World War II. Dietmar was born in Danzig to German parents, during the war. While his father was fighting in Russia, his mother was taken seriously ill after childbirth so Dietmar's father was given special leave to come home. Tragically, the train he was travelling on was blown up and Dietmar's father was killed. Thankfully, his mother recovered just in time to escape Polish occupation of Danzig, now known as Gdansk, and make it to Osnabrueck where she met a Royal Navy based Midlander from Coventry. The family then moved to Coventry and Dietmar became a Sky Blue where we played against each other in local derbies a fair few times. Dietmar's story is a unique and remarkable tale, that's for sure.

I jumped at the chance to sign my old Cobblers' teammate, Bobby Hunt, from Ipswich Town, also for just over £11,000 as I knew that he could bring to the side a steady and stable influence. He was okay for us but, as he was nearly 30 when he signed, we probably didn't see the best of him over the two seasons he was at The Valley. He drifted back to Northampton on loan and then we sold him to Reading for £5,000 before he ended up at a regular post-Charlton haunt, Maidstone United, who were a big non-league club at the time. The Foleys have strong links with the 'Stones as eldest son, Adrian, and youngest, Paul, both played for them some 20 years apart and it's great to see them back pushing for league football again.

The biggest money signing we made was for Dennis Bond who I paid £25,000 for from Tottenham Hotspur. Bondy was a tidy midfielder who had even played in Europe for Spurs but it never really worked for him at The Valley over the two seasons we had him, although he played in plenty of games from 70-72. We lost a few quid on him when he went back to Watford where he'd started for £13,500 in 1972. Who knows why some players just don't fit into a side? They may look great somewhere else, look the part in training, have great ability but, for some reason, they just don't work out. We all know a few of those types.

One of the main problem areas I had was between the sticks and I ended up letting Charlie Wright go in 1971 as I felt we weren't right in goal but, with hindsight, we never really improved it until a very good young prospect came along in Graham Tutt. This young lad had the lot, the stature, presence, he was brave as a lion but he was just too young to throw into the tough situations we often found ourselves in. I signed him as pro at 17 and gave him his debut six months later in my last season in 1974. Tutty could have gone on to be a Charlton legend but he suffered a horrendous injury whilst playing for my successor, Andy Nelson, away at Sunderland, virtually losing the sight in one eye from a boot from their forward. Sadly, the injury ended his career here forcing him to head out to play in South Africa and the States. Every now and then he comes back to the club on match days, still a lovely lad, so unlucky but never bitter about it, I think he went into coaching.

Before we released Charlie in 1971, I signed Derek Bellotti in October 1970, who was an East Londoner and had been playing in goal for Gillingham. He cost next to nothing, five grand, and truth be told I should have probably spent more on a 'keeper than the money spent on Bondy and Hunty but I was a young manager still learning my trade. Derek hardly played, as it turned out, he was a quiet and nervous lad and he struggled with being thrown in at a bigger club I think. After 14 games he went to Southend for a couple of years, then on to Swansea for a short spell before dropping into non-league and settling in my beloved West Country. It was a punt that didn't work which was a disappointment as I always felt I had a good eye for a 'keeper having played in front of so many over the years, a view that would come to a head at Highbury many years later.

With all of these outgoings, I had to recoup the money and more by selling our best players and I had to let the main creative player, Alan Campbell, go for a large fee of £70,000 to Birmingham City. Alan was to be a big loss but with his transfer fee we could sign six or seven players with money to spare and I'd hoped Bondy would plug that gap but we never really replaced Alan. The British Oak drinking club had lost a key member too so it may have shifted the 'culture' at the club a little. I also sold Harry Gregory for £7,000 to Aston Villa in October 1970 as I felt we had plenty of cover in his position. Up until Harry got ill recently and sadly passed away we had got on great working together in the hospitality suites at The Valley so thankfully there were no hard feelings between us.

Harry and Alan were popular players so it was a bold move to sell them both but it had to be done to free up funds. I made one other sale letting George Riddick go across the Thames to Leyton Orient for nearly £8,000 which was a good bit of business. George was never likely to feature in the side having signed from Gillingham before Eddie was sacked. We also released a couple of young lads, Minnock and Crawford, for a total fee of £3,000 so I'd generated nearly £88,000 in transfers and spent £64,000 leaving £24,000 in the kitty so Mr Gliksten was happy. These numbers look tiny by today's standards but back then, this was Charlton's market and I'd done as I was told, for good or for bad. It's always a risk selling key players but is no different now just bigger numbers for the 'selling' clubs like Southampton who have cashed in on their assets and survived well in the top flight.

On the training ground I threw myself into it as I was so keen to make this opportunity work, my first job in management in the second tier of the Football League and a big club in Charlton. We looked well prepared and ready in the friendlies but I knew from years of playing, friendlies are no guarantee. I hated them as a player but it was all change now I was a manager looking for different things and I was looking forward to the challenge. There was a sense of the unknown with all the new signings and we'd also just got

Mike Kenning back from two seasons at Norwich having been with us before in 1968. It's fair to say the transfer dealing was bloody hard work and something completely new to me so all part of a very steep learning curve.

We started okay, not pulling up trees but steady enough, then a defeat away to Sunderland was followed by the obligatory defeat to Millwall at The Valley. For some reason, Millwall's record over their nearest rivals has always been a good one to this very day. This run of defeats carried on for two more games and, all of a sudden, we were in the middle of a mini slump. We steadied the ship before going on a poor run again which was a pattern that followed all season. We never got out of the blocks and limped to the end of the season finishing again just above the drop zone in 20th spot, three points above Blackburn and six points above bottom side Bolton. Leicester went up as champions with Sheffield that year. We'd pocketed a bit of money from transfers, moved the bigger wages on, brought a few new players in but, unfortunately, there was no real improvement on the pitch. My first season of management, learning on the job, I'd made a fair few mistakes, but I'd enjoyed it and felt better for it. I wanted us to be more difficult to break down and less 'open' in games without losing our attacking flair going forward but with Alan Campbell, the main creative outlet gone, it was always going to be tough.

Focusing on the positives, as I've always done, we did cut down on goals conceded and we scored more than the season before so in that sense it was an improvement, but still not good enough. The new signings were a mixed bag but I had little option really other than to play the ones I'd signed. I soon realised how it all shifts when you become manager and the lads you shared a dressing room with as a player stop telling you the stories about so and so getting three sheets to the wind or where he'd stayed the other night or a big bet that had come in. They were extra wary too as I knew the ones to look out for, and who was up to no good, as they say you can't kid a kidder. I knew if I stopped by the British Oak on Old Dover Road most nights I'd find Bobby Curtis or Alan Campbell before we sold him, or Graham Moore and

Dennis Booth propping up the bar. I even had a deal with the landlord in there who rang me when they turned up so I could drop in by 'chance' while they were all in there.

This was how football was in the early '70s, players weren't paid a heap of money but they had plenty of time on their hands and saw nothing wrong in a having a good drink in the week. It was more acceptable back then but as a manager when it's your bollocks on the line on a Saturday, I'd be lying if I said it didn't piss me off sometimes. As someone who'd never been a big drinker, as I never wanted it to affect my game, I never understood it anyway but these lads loved it. I couldn't stop them as long as they complied with the 'two days before a game' rule but I wanted them all to know I was on to them so standards on the pitch had to be maintained. It didn't go down too well with some of these big characters.

It soon became apparent too that you were expected to do it all at a club like Charlton. I'd developed a real interest in the coaching side but that was really suffering from looking at sides we were due to play, scouting for players, sorting out travel arrangements, dealing with players' gripes, wages and so on. I had no time to prepare sessions to work on the specific areas that needed it, game to game, so I was forced to rely on the coach, Colin Murphy, who was competent enough but I had ideas for the training ground that were just strangled by a lack of hours in the day. It was miles away from the separate coaches for defenders, forwards and goalkeepers you have now with a network of scouts and a general manager for backup. If they could have found a broom they'd have stuck it up my arse, I'm sure, to sweep up as I went. I doubt Charlton were any different to any other clubs at that level and below. It meant I had to spread myself too thin though, and that was something I definitely underestimated. Throw into the mix a wife and a young family at home and it was a juggling act that was very difficult at times. Don't get me wrong, I wasn't complaining as this was my new career and my choice but it was a lonely place sometimes and you were always disappointing someone. Some good news came from the board as our house was finally purchased from the club at a cost of £6,400 which gave some welcome stability at home. At the same board meeting though, I was told by a director, Mr Law, that the 'greatest service Mr Foley could do for the club would be to produce a team that would make money through increased gate receipts'. Not win games, make money. In black and white in boardroom minutes.

Despite the fairly poor showing in my first season as manager, and the dawning realisation of the scope of the task, I threw myself into it again for the 1971-72 season. That's the beauty of football, there's always next week, next season, another chance to put it right, at least until you get the sack that is. In February 1971 I'd signed a lad called Barry Endean from Watford for just over £11,000 who always looked the part for them whenever I'd scouted him. He was an intelligent player, strong, he scored more than enough goals and I thought he would be a success at The Valley. He ended up playing 27 games, scoring just one goal, so I quickly sold him to Blackburn in October later that same year in an exchange plus cash deal for Eamonn Rogers. Eamonn was a fellow Dub who'd played a rake of league games and was an international to boot. He hardly played in the three years he was at the club so it was good money after bad and neither signing ranks very high on my list of successes.

To rub salt in the wounds, Barry Endean actually started scoring goals again when he couldn't hit the proverbial cow with a banjo with us. Sometimes you just don't fit into a side that doesn't have the players that complement your strengths and as a forward it is more noticeable as goals dry up. Look at Fernando Torres, he was one of the best forwards in the world at Liverpool with Steven Gerrard picking his early runs from anywhere with his fantastic range of passing. Then he signed for Chelsea but didn't look the same player without that Gerrard connection. Added to which, Barry was definitely no Torres and we didn't have any Stevie Gerrards either, so you can imagine how it went.

I was expecting someone to steal Bobby Curtis, who was one of our best players, so I signed Mick Jones, a full back from Orient for £7,000 where he'd won the Third Division a year before in 1970. Mick had plenty of aggression and knew the game so I hoped he would add some steel to the side. I'd let Mike Kenning go to Watford for £9,000 so it was one in, one out with a bit of cash in the kitty again. I'd also moved on Dennis Booth for £7,000 to Blackpool and my old teammate Graham Moore to Doncaster for £4,000 so we were in credit with a lower wage bill too, should we need a player or two over the season.

In July 1971 I made one of my best signings ever in Mike Flanagan on a free from Tottenham. I'd gone to watch a reserves game at White Hart Lane after a tip-off from our scout, Les Gore, and they had a young lad in midfield who looked the part until the manager Eddie Baily decided to take him off. This lad pulled his shirt off and threw his shirt down, swearing at the bench in a broad Scottish accent as he stormed off down the tunnel. Not long after he signed for Middlesbrough before carving out a fairly successful career at Liverpool, Sampdoria and Rangers. It was none other than a young, angry Graeme Souness that vented his spleen that day and what a career he went on to have. Bet Eddie wishes he'd never taken him off.

Well, Mick stood out too, in that same game, as a player with bags of ability, a lovely touch and plenty of skill, so I'd seen enough. The great Bill Nicholson was an absolute gent to do business with and, because Mick was a non-contract player on about £20 a week from memory, we got him for nothing, with the club eventually selling him for £650,000 to Crystal Palace years later. We were giving him £17/week and £4/week expenses. Flan always reminds me of this wage when I see him and is still unhappy I dropped him for breaking a curfew on a preseason tour. It was a good bit of business which I remind anyone at the club to this day whenever I can. I was always on at him to shave his beard, the scruffy bugger, but his girlfriend told me in no uncertain terms it was staying.

He started life as a left midfielder but didn't really have a winger's pace and maybe played within himself a wee bit back then but what he did have was great skill and he was always likely to score a goal. We ended up playing him up front and the rest as they say is Charlton folklore. Flan went on to become a Valley legend as well as picking up England B caps, a real class act, so I earned my wages that night. Bill Nicholson, who was a far better manager than I ever was, didn't fancy him for some reason so Mick was dead keen on signing for us as he knew he was surplus at Spurs, I think. We hit the training even harder for the 1971-72 season, working on tightening things at the back without restricting our forward play. With the slight changes to playing staff and a few young lads coming through, we set off again looking to improve on last year's finish. At home, Sheila was pregnant again and due in October which caught us out a bit with a good six years' gap since Sean's birth, in Northampton, but it felt better with some security this time post injury.

We started the 1971-72 season well with two wins from three before the regulation defeat at The Den preceded three more defeats on the bounce and a similar pattern followed throughout the season. Another boy arrived on Wednesday 6th October with Paul James joining the family, the only Londoner in the family. He was very accommodating, turning up on a Wednesday in a week when we didn't have a game. However, this was the last time he proved to be accommodating as he is definitely someone who loves a challenge shall we say.

Back on the pitch we didn't draw many, we shipped a few when we got beat and we just couldn't get a run going to get safe. The league was so tight in the bottom half for the closing weeks with only four points between the ten teams above Watford who were dead and buried at the bottom of the table. As we neared the end of the season we just needed to get a win or two and we'd be okay. With 13 games to go we looked fine. We'd beaten Luton 2-0 then Swindon 3-1 two games later at The Valley followed by a draw away to Middlesbrough. Five points from eight was the type of form we needed to stay up but we had a terrible run over the last nine games of the season getting just two points from a possible 18. As I'd gone through as a player back in '66, the side had come up short in the closing weeks and, once again, it was my voodoo sides Fulham and Blackpool doing the damage. We lost 5-0 on the final day to Blackpool and went down by a single point below Fulham, even giving local rivals Millwall the satisfaction of beating us 2-0 at The Valley the week before. It was all too similar to the pain of 1966, the only difference being I had spared the lads the delights of Julie Andrews in the Sound of Music unlike Dave Bowen six years before.

It's no secret that key points in a season can have a major impact and it could have been a different story had we won in an important FA Cup round that year. We had been very close to getting a bumper payout from an Arsenal cup tie at home having drawn with First Division side Sheffield United twice at home and then away over 90 minutes, eventually going down 1-0 in extra time at Bramall Lane. The players had played out of their skins over 270 minutes before the referee cruelly overruled the linesman to award the winner. We obviously deserved to go down as it was over 42 games but had we gone through to play Arsenal in a big Derby game, we'd have picked up big gate receipts. That would have signed a player or two which could have made all the difference. The three games had pulled in nearly 40,000 fans as it was but I didn't get my hands on any of that for new players. All ifs and buts I know, but that's how it is in football when you have no money to spend.

If anything, relegation hurt even more this time than as a player from the First Division, as I was in charge so I was the one to blame. At least that's what I thought then. I have won and lost enough over 50+ years to know now that a number of people are responsible for both success and failure on a football pitch. On 29 April 1972, having been stuffed 5-0 at Bloomfield Road, I felt like I'd let everyone down but I genuinely could not have done more to avoid relegation. I knew how Dave Bowen felt in 1966 at the same ground but at least Dave had enjoyed great success before. I felt a little let down by some of the lads but I'd bought them and picked them so the buck stopped with me.

We had the obligatory dressing room post-mortem and

views were exchanged on what, how and why. Footballers are generally smart in these situations, say all the right things 'next year we'll get it right boss' and if you're sacked then you're an arsehole, bet your bottom dollar. Generally speaking though, I always felt the lads were with me, especially as I'd given most of them their big chance in the Second Division. Someone new would probably change it all around so I bet they did want me to stay, for their own self-preservation. We just weren't good enough and had a terrible run in so we deserved it. When you go on a run like that any manager will tell you that you try everything. Personnel changes, different training, varied warm-ups, even your matchday routine to get to the ground. Anything to give you that change of luck. I've never been too superstitious but even I started to act irrationally. Driving a certain way to the ground, playing a particular song on the eight track, wearing lucky clothes, you name it. It made bugger all difference though, we were down, I'd managed a relegation in only my second season as a manager. To be fair to the chairman he was great about it, I didn't feel any excess pressure and he assured me I would be kept on to get us back up. I think he just liked the way I kept the books balanced!

Same old drill, back to the drawing board and do the only thing I've ever known, more hard work and improvement. Who could I let go, who could I get in, how do we improve? I took a bold decision over my good mate and Eire team mate, Ray Treacy. Swindon Town wanted him and I'd been offered Arthur Horsfield in a swap plus £20,000 for Ray. Both good players but different types, Arthur was very strong with a great eye for a goal. 'Treace' was a top player, no great height but a bright and clever forward who pitched in with a fair few goals. Added to which, he was a good friend and ally in the dressing room. He was a Dub like me and he'd played for Home Farm although he was a fair bit younger than me. Well, he didn't take it well at all when I told him and we fell out big time, which was a real shame, but such is life. He used to have a tiny pair of leather Adidas boots as a car mascot hanging from his rear-view mirror and he gave me one for my car as a gesture of friendship. After I'd sold him

I bet he threw his one in the bin.

Dave Mackay was the manager at Swindon and he wanted Ray to replace Arthur, and I knew Arthur well and felt he would be good for us especially in the Third Division. It turned out to be that way, as he scored plenty of goals and he hardly missed a game in all the time I was there, he was a manager's dream. He turned out to be even more prolific than Ray and we got some money in Michael's beloved kitty too so, all in all, a good bit of business. Thankfully, I managed to heal the rift with Ray before he sadly passed away in 2015 and we used to laugh about it all especially his miniature Adidas boot mascot, which I kept hold of for years.

The following month, in July 1972, I experienced my first offer of a transfer bung when we were talking to Fulham and Alec Stock who was their manager over the sale of Paul Went. I knew it went on but it still took me by surprise when it happened to me. Wenty was one of our jewels when I took over, along with Alan Campbell, who I'd already sold, and a few clubs were after him. We were talking around £80,000 for him which was a good return for a young lad even though we'd miss him at the back. Alec mentioned a payment for me if we agreed a lower fee and I was taken aback. It was the first time anyone had ever mentioned cash 'off the books' as I'd only signed for three clubs in my playing career. I didn't know what to say, at first, but turned Alec down politely, before agreeing on the £80,000 fee. Alec brushed it off as if to say 'silly boy' but I couldn't rob the club that were already paying me, it just seemed wrong. I'd never have been able to look Mammy and Daddy in the eye had I taken it.

This sum kept the board happy but I needed to get some quality back into the side. I signed a young forward from Arsenal, Paul Davies, who was the younger brother of Welsh international Ron. We paid £7,000 for him after having a look at him on loan. He was a nice lad who had some ability but he never kicked on really scoring only a handful of goals over two seasons before dropping out of the pro game altogether to play for Romford. If only it had been Paul Davis from the Arsenal '89 side who I had the pleasure of working with, now he was a player. We did a couple more deals selling Dickie Plumb to my old club Exeter and Dietmar Bruck to my other old club Northampton for £5,000 and £4,000 respectively so we'd more than covered the Davies fee. I'd made a point of keeping in touch with both of my old clubs to offer players to them first and everyone seemed happy enough.

Another season started, this time with less chopping and changing but a healthy sum available for players if they came up. We may have been missing Wenty and Treace's class but this was a lower league and I had high hopes for Arthur up front. Well it didn't start well with two defeats but we then won five from six with a 6-0 and a 6-1 in that run. At last, we'd put together a good run of results and, for once, things looked rosy. We carried on with a mixed bag of wins and defeats up to Christmas but were sitting nicely in the League with 27 points from a possible 50 which put us in the top spots. I was optimistic for the first time as manager going into games. We headed into 1973 starting the year well so I persuaded the board to part with some of the kitty to get an exciting wide lad from Barnet in by the name of Colin Powell.

I'd seen Powelly in a non-league game at Dartford, along with Les Gore, as we liked Barnet's centre back, Gordon Ferry, and this tricky wide lad caught the eye so we kept tabs on him. He had loads of ability, was a great runner with the ball with a trick or two and delivered great crosses into dangerous areas. What more could you want from a wide man and Arthur Horsfield up front would definitely reap the rewards from his crosses. 'Paddy', as Colin was known, was working in a wood yard in Stevenage at the time and he still moans to this day that he earned more with both wages combined with his part time football and in the wood yard than I gave him but, as I always told him, you can't put a price on being a professional footballer. He wasn't especially young at 24 for someone getting their break in the game but he went on to be a Charlton legend and he's still many a fan's favourite from that time or in their all-time team. He wanted a signing-on fee so I told him we don't do those, which we didn't, so just sign the form and, thankfully, he put pen to paper. He cost the club £10,000 and he was one of the best signings I made along with Mick Flanagan and Derek Hales in my time at Charlton. Paddy was a real character too, just a great lad to have around and he's exactly the same today, still tending to pitches as a local groundsman after years performing the role at The Valley.

I'd signed him at the end of January and told him I'd let him get used to training every day and probably blood him in over a month. Well, he travelled away, for his first week with us, to Bolton midweek and we got well beat 3-0 so I told him on the Thursday that he was in for the next game, no time to blood him in. He made no difference though, as we lost the next two games including a 5-0 spanking at Brentford. Welcome to pro football, Paddy. Now anyone who knows Powelly will tell you he has always been partial to a bet or two. I got wind of this pretty soon and used to trawl the bookies around the area to drag him out and try all sorts of things to keep him away from the betting shops. One day, after training, I told him to come back in the afternoon to The Valley for some extra work and when he turned up you could see him thinking, where's the other lads? I put some cones out on the pitch and he spent over an hour working up and down crossing balls into the box, over and over again. Bless him, he kept at it but I could see he was getting the hump, more and more, until he got a right cob on. He then gave me dirty looks and was getting well pissed off till he finally piped up, 'Boss, why am I doing all of this work on my own? If there's one thing I can do it's cross the ball.'

I told him, quick as a flash, 'Yes, I know, Powelly, but it's kept you out of the bloody bookies all afternoon.' He wasn't best pleased but eventually saw the funny side.

That was Paddy and that was me, I didn't understand why he'd always want a bet but he wasn't going to change no matter how many times I fished him out of our local bookies down the road on Shooters Hill Road and the false sessions made no difference. You couldn't help but like Powelly and all the time he delivered on the pitch you ended up turning a blind eye to any distractions off the pitch. The second half of the season, even with Paddy doing the business out wide, we were nowhere near the form of the first half as we only picked up 18 points from a possible 42 eventually finishing in 11th place. We should have been pushing for promotion but the old problem of conceding goals came back and cost us dearly. Bolton and Notts County went up that year and it's fair to say we were a bigger club than most of the sides in the league so we expected more.

Fourth season looming as manager and I still wasn't happy with the goalkeeper situation. We had signed John Dunn, yet another East Londoner from Aston Villa having cut his teeth down at Torquay. John was never going to set the world alight but he was a steady enough pro and he was cheap, which made the chairman happy. As it turned out, he stayed four years until young Tutty was old enough to take the jersey which always seemed inevitable. John was another who dropped out of the pro game racking up 100 games for The Addicks before going into local non-league, I just wish Graham had been a year or two older as he may have been the difference for us.

Added to Tutty, in the 73-74 season we had a young lad coming through the reserves who was only 15 years old and he stood out a mile, what a talent he was. Mark Penfold was the best young player I'd seen at the time and I knew he would be a first team regular very soon, some lads are just special. Mark was a local lad with the club at heart, he had great ability and could play at full back or in midfield no problem, he never looked under pressure or fazed. I signed him on pro forms at 16 years of age in 1973 and gave him his debut in the 73-74 season. My successor, Andy Nelson, had the best of him for three years before a terrible double fracture of his leg by Tottenham's Don McCallister at The Valley ended his pro career. He went on after a long lay-off to play non-league locally for Maidstone where he actually played alongside my eldest son, Adrian. 'Penny' eventually ended up plying his trade at Gravesend when he really should have played at the very top level, he was that good.

In the middle of 1973 I made, what was to be, my final

major signing, and some may say the best, in Derek Hales from Luton. We'd seen Halesy play a few times for Dartford the season before when we were really trying to sign John Mitchell who was playing against him. Derek caught the eye though and I liked him straight away but Les Gore, who was a great judge of player, didn't really fancy him, funnily enough. Derek's dad was in the bar that night and he was a character alright, telling me how good his lad was and that he was going to be a real player. Dartford allowed me to speak to him but he was to be signed by Luton who were doing well in the Second Division above, but they only really had plans to play him in the reserves. We kept tracking him and eventually got him on loan for a few games at the end of the 72-73 season before stealing him from The Hatters for £4,000 in July. Only four grand for a young goalscoring prospect like Halesy, what a bit of business that was. He'd be worth an absolute fortune nowadays, he was quick in and around the box, brave and lethal in front of goal. He'd had a taste of first team football with us and wanted more, which we promised him, so he didn't take much persuading.

The discussions with Luton manager, Harry Haslam, got a little bit lively after I'd made a lower offer which Harry and Luton director Reg Burr said they couldn't accept. I told them that was all we had and I couldn't offer any more, which wasn't a bluff. Derek's dad had already spoken to Harry on the phone and said that he wasn't going back so I think Halesy was worried that it would all fall through. Derek said that if they didn't let him go he was off anyway, or some industrial words to that effect. The deal nearly fell through but they must have felt satisfied with the forwards they had and wanted to cash in on what was an unknown prospect at the time. Halesy makes no secret of how he got his point across in any transfer talks that followed so he was not naive even at that age. Derek preferred to receive some cash in hand rather than a few quid spread across his wages and he struck his own deal with Mr Gliksten separately.

He was eventually sold for £333,333.00 to Derby County three years later so, all in all, it was great business for the club. Luton had no sell on clause either so they obviously never thought he'd go on to bigger things. Derek is still Charlton's record goalscorer with around 150 goals for the club and a cult icon of those exciting sides. The money made on Derek's transfer along with Flan and Powelly who were sold for a £650,000 and £70,000 profit respectively meant the club made over a million pound profit from just three signings. Back then it was a lot of money too, so I still try to remind people of this down at The Valley, especially when I need a favour or two.

Leading up to the 1973 – 74 season I genuinely felt we were on the verge of something good with Flan, Powelly, Arthur Horsfield, Peter Reeves, Bobby Curtis and a young Halesy up front. There were six players there who were too good for the Third Division and I had high hopes. It was finally taking shape and we looked really good going forward in the warm up games. If I could have pulled in an established goalkeeper I'd have been happier but we just didn't have the money to spend, so you cut your cloth accordingly and hope you've got enough. We started well, winning seven and drawing two from the first 13 then we went patchy again winning or losing with a few draws up to the end of the year. With the usual Boxing Day, end of December and New Year's Day fixture congestion it was all hands on deck and our big tough defender, Dave Shipperley, reported injured after Christmas. What big Ship didn't realise was I'd heard him laughing and talking about this drink and that he'd had over Christmas so I was on to him. I pulled him to one side and called his bluff on it and said outright that he was fannying, which is a heavy accusation against a pro as I mentioned in the Exeter chapter. He didn't like it one bit, denied it but I knew he wasn't being honest. I was fuming but what could I do, he was declaring himself unfit. He let me down at a time when I needed everyone pulling together.

It all came to a head a few weeks later training on the Redgra training pitch in the car park, in one of our Friday small sided games, which I invariably joined in. Dave had been dropped after our difference of opinion and didn't like it, obviously, as he decided to whack me from behind in the game. Now, I'm not sure what he thought it would achieve or if I'd back down but, just like Graham Moore at Northampton years before, I went wild and went for him. I don't remember much but I believe Keith Peacock managed to pull me away but I wanted to have it out with him, never mind how much bigger he was. Well, Dave didn't play much after that and was sold to Gillingham that same season. It's never a wise move to kick the manager in training especially one that never really rated you as a player anyway. It's just as well it didn't escalate any more that day, thanks to Keith, as I was the manager but my blood was up alright and I wasn't going to let it go unchallenged.

It was a tough time for me looking back which may explain my reaction as I lost my dear old dad in mid-January and that had really affected me. I loved my dad desperately, he was a wonderful peaceful, contented man who I hardly ever saw down in the dumps, swear or raise his voice. It still makes me laugh how he'd escape out to the outside loo and pick his horses by candlelight in the toilet. Thankfully, he saw me play and make the grade and was the proudest man in Ireland watching me wear the famous green jersey. For that I'm truly thankful but it would have been great if he'd seen my success as a coach later on. Dad suffered a stroke a few years before falling out of his bed, one day, and only really survived as he was so strong mentally and physically. Sadly though, he was never the same again, dying at the age of 67. His strength of character and great attitude to life shaped me as a man and definitely made me the successful player and coach I became.

There was little time to mourn back then and you were soon expected back to the grindstone. We carried on our indifferent form for the second half of the season and were a real Jekyll and Hyde side with solid enough form at home but some poor defeats away. We had a heavy 5-0 defeat at Grimsby in mid-April which probably made the board's mind up and I was sacked two weeks later, a couple of days after a 3-1 home defeat to Watford with the club around mid-table. The irony being I'd been presented with a Crystal Rose Bowl before the Watford game by the Supporter's Association for four years as Charlton manager, knowing that I was already out the door.

There were no big bust ups and I had no animosity towards the club who had given me a good go at it but I did feel we were very close to having success. The players were generally supportive and it was much more 'my' team now with the majority of the 11 being signed by me. The club eventually finished 14th that season having leaked a number of goals more than the clubs around them. Given the chance again, I would make more noise to the board to buy a goalkeeper, unfortunately Tutty was just too young. Powelly reminded me recently that when I went to the club to clear my belongings and say goodbye to all the lads, I only shook hands with those I felt hadn't let me down. He said he must have done alright as I shook his hand.

I had been called up to see Mr Gliksten, in his offices in London, the night before it was announced on 23 April 1974, knowing deep down it was going to be bad news. I took it on the chin, went home and went over it all with Sheila before doing what we had always done and planned out what we would do next. This time there was a finality to it all as I'd given it my best shot but been unsuccessful, where would I go from here? I'd never been short on confidence in my ability but I did feel vulnerable and I began to doubt if I was up to the task. Trusty aide Les Gore was put in place for the rest of the season and, in June, Charlton appointed Andy Nelson. With hardly any changes to the playing staff they were promoted the following season in third place back to the Second Division where they went on to become a solid mid-table side. Would we have been promoted had I been kept on? Who knows but the signings were definitely getting better and better and I was getting more used to the role, that's for sure. As a young manager having just turned 37 years of age I was on the managerial scrapheap, not having set the world alight shall we say.

I began to wonder if maybe I was a better coach and should concentrate on being a good no. 2. I had been appointed chairman of the Kent Soccer Coaches Association in 1969, and again in 1970, so I was making the right noises as a coach even if the management had scarred me a little. If nothing else I had left my mark with a post-match comment after a defeat that, 'If there was one person to blame it would have to be the team.' A quote which made it into David Coleman's book of sporting cock-ups, Colemanballs. Perhaps it was time to ditch the ties, suits and Mooro's leather jacket and put my tracksuit back on.

Hurling, a brutal game – I was better at soccer and didn't much like getting the hurley stick in the face but a great game all the same – back left aged 12.

Grafton Street, Dublin circa 1954 Me and Mammy in our Sunday Best.

My dear old Dad sat in his chair with his pipe, with my sister Terry behind circa 1965….a real gas character.

Portmarnock Beach, Ireland circa 1967 – Dad reclining with my wife Sheila back left with our daughter Teresa, my youngest sister Anita with our Adrian on the right.

Exeter 24th August 1959 away to Southport shorts rolled over my knicks and puffing my chest out, what a good looking boy.

The best result I have had – marrying Exeter belle Sheila Smith at The Sacred Heart Church in Exeter on Easter Monday 1960 – we married in the morning so I could play in the afternoon – Sheila gets a kiss from a couple of the lads.

Exeter Team Photo 1958-59 season – away to Southport 24th August 1958 – look at the footballs and the boots My great friend Arnold Mitchell seated third from left with the ball and yours truly far right trying to stand tall.

My adopted family – The Smiths of Exeter – my gorgeous wife Sheila front right with her mum Violet next to her and dad Sam looking uninterested next to Sheila's brother Alan and wife Yvonne, back right Sheila's sister Audrey and sister-in-law Peggy next to brothers Gordon and Derek with Audrey's husband Colin who was a good local footballer in his day.

Northampton Town New Year's Day 1963, The County Ground – 3rd Division Championship Squad – Manager and master tactician Dave Bowen standing far left, John 'Krunch' Kurila fourth from right back row and yours truly seated with the ball between my legs - Despite the league we were in, ironically this was the best Cobblers side in my view.

Never missed one, which is one better than Matt Le Tissier – Home to West Ham 1965-66 in the First Division - sent Jim Standen the wrong way in front of a capacity County Ground crowd, World Cup winner Martin Peters fourth from right for the Hammers

The 1965-66 First Division Northampton Squad – our one and only season in the sun with the big boys - Dave Bowen seated with the ball and my great friends Joe Kiernan second from right middle row and Johnny Kurila 3rd from the right back row. I'm back row far left next to Graham Carr now chief scout at Newcastle and father of TV chat show host Alan.

Checking the pies in Foley's Take n' Bake Shop - Captain of a First Division side but running a pie shop – bit different back then.

January 15th 1966 Upton Park – tossing the coin with Bobby Moore. Look at Bobby's boots and look at mine. Later in the year he was lifting the World Cup. Two days after this game my second son Sean was born.

Easter Sunday 1965 at Exeter Airport for a Northampton game away to Plymouth Argyle – our first flight for a game; me crouching with a fetching overcoat and a smart Adidas holdall – it was the 60's after all.

Training on the pitch at the County Ground – not easy to look at the camera and strike the ball.

Getting the keys to my sponsored Hillman Imp – I thought I had arrived. Not quite a Bentley or an Aston but it was brand new – still had to pay but I got a good deal – the Cobbler's clubwear was hardly Jermyn St.

With singer Ruby Murray at the opening of the Take n' Bake long before she became rhyming slang for an Indian meal.

The 1972-73 squad in front of the old West Stand at The Valley - we were getting there with a young Mike Flanagan back left, Arthur Horsfield second from right middle and Cyril Davies second from right front.

From Player to Manager in the blink of an eye – I look happy enough but management was tough at Charlton. Even so the club did make a £1m profit from players I signed.

This was my place of work for over 30 years – the training ground. This is at Charlton's training ground, Unilever Sports Ground in Eltham. Kitted out in Hummel boots overseeing straight leg raises back when they were still allowed.

A 2-1 Charlton win away at Luton, Keith Peacock scored the winner and gets a leather clad hug – the coat was from the great Bobby Moore – this is the photo Charlton fan and acclaimed artist Ray Richardson painted for the back cover.

The best laid plans – Goalkeeper John Dunn gets sent off 16th March 1974 away to Rochdale – the beginning of the end for me and the leather coat.

I love this photo – how cramped does it look in there? Charlton stalwart Charlie Hall (physio) far left. Not sure what ground it is – blocked it out.

Young Manager - swapped the training ground for the office and the stopwatch for a pen it took some getting used to.

Off to the Den as assistant to Gordon Jago, Gordon was very forward thinking and I learned alot from him.

Happy & relaxed at The Den I loved it there - good people.

My other love, at a Pro-Am at Sudbury 1977, the cat is unimpressed, if only I'd bought right handed clubs.

Millwall Squad 1977 – Gordon Jago far left middle and Nicky Johns fourth from right middle – Nicky lived with us for a few months as he had nowhere to stay coming up from the West Country as a kid - big 'Kitch' front centre with ball to his right with my good friend Bryan Hamilton to his right, John Seasman and Tony Hazell far left front, Terry Brisley far left back and Phil Walker back right - this side beat Chelsea 3-0 at the Den 1977 with a Barry Salvage left foot, a Ray Evans thunderbolt and a great move ending with a Bris' header – look it up on You Tube.

At QPR's training ground, Greenford- we had a great youth system, so many went on to play for the 1st team, like Clive Allen and Paul Goddard.

The QPR backroom team who brought the excellent young players through. From left to right George Graham who managed the Youths then myself who looked after the Reserves, Terry Venables the First Team manager. Pitchside Loftus Rd getting respective league trophies.

Broken nose again and at QPR again - this time by my own player not a fan – Big Alan Mac swore it was an accident.

Back to the Lion's Den – Millwall v Bristol Rovers 20th April 1985 – me ready to bark something out while George studies the game – we made a good team at The Den and Highbury – different personalities that combined well as a winning pair – it started at QPR through friendship and love of the game and youth development, blossomed at Millwall and peaked at Arsenal in that unbelievable night at Anfield.

Same game at The Den with George behind – I am giving a player or official the scowl – when you are wrapped up in a game you lose yourself – worse as coach than player.

We turned it around with this team with a host of key signings, players like Steve Lovell, Steve Lowndes, Anton Outalokowski, Dave Cusack and Les Briley who George still considers to be one of his best ever signings – Millwall squad 1984-85 at the Old Den – an intimidating ground.

Nothing sweeter than success – on the pitch at the Den with Kevin Bremner and skipper Les Briley after winning promotion to the 2nd Division in 1985.'

The start of it all, the day the Ian Rush 1st goal legend was laid to rest - beating mighty Liverpool, Wembley Littlewoods Cup 5/4/87 3 days after my 50th birthday. Grovesy changed the game, Charlie got winner deflected off my pal Ronnie Whelan. Viv Anderson giving me a hug, Kenny Sansom like a Pearly King.

The 1988-89 squad that pulled off the unbelievable. A team with plenty of ability and unbelievable work ethic/team spirit that formed the bedrock for the club's success to follow. My 'Stepson' David Rocastle third from right front – what a lovely boy and top player. I'm next to the effervescent Grovesy far left on back.

What a night, 26th May 1989 Liverpool 0 Arsenal 2, the most dramatic climax ever to a season. Look at the joy on my face. Dicko, David and Hayesy at the front with Smudger behind grappling with the League Trophy with Nigel. The hero goalscorer Mickey Thomas just out of picture on the left. O'Leary looks in shock stood behind me alongside Kevin Campbell. I am lucky to have had so many days and nights like this and they are just as sweet on the coaching side.

One of my favourite football photos, warm embrace for the man who delivered when it mattered. Making of a legend, Mickey is one lovely lad - he could do the lot and to think I had to talk him into staying at the club. Anfield 26th May 1989 on the pitch, the Kop stayed to clap and sing to us, touch of class from LFC.

The pinnacle of my career – from Inchicore to Anfield winning the Football League. This is in front of Liverpool fans believe it or not, they were brilliant. This was up in our living room and Ronnie Whelan couldn't walk in the room when he visited.

Even the dugouts were nice at Highbury, this time George is the one ready for a ruck while I chew on a pack of Wrigleys – Arsenal v Chelsea 17th March 1990. At the end of the season I was at The County Ground, Northampton as Manager, a very different club.

ARSENAL STADIUM
LONDON, N.5

1st June,

Dear Theo,

I expect Ken Friar will have informed you of the Board's decision regarding your contract. I hope you find this a satisfactory outcome.

I would like to say again how much we appreciate the contribution that you have made during your stay with us. Arsenal has been transformed over the past few years and I and the other Directors know that your work and influence has played no small part in this success.

I know that everyone at Highbury joins me in wishing you all the very best of good fortune at Northampton. I am sure you will do a great job and perhaps we will meet in the 1st Division again in a few years.

Yours Sincerely
Peter Hill-Wood

Chairman Peter Hill Wood's handwritten letter 1st June 1991 – it's these sorts of things that sets The Arsenal apart – taking the time to handwrite a note out and put some kind sentiments and good wishes in the note – a gent and a scholar.

The backroom staff with trophy haul. A close knit group orchestrated by George. From left Pat Rice (youth team), Stewart Houston (reserves), Gary Lewin (Physio), George and myself, Steve Burtenshaw (Chief Scout) and Terry Murphy (Youth Scout).

Back to the Cobblers with my dear friend Joe Kiernan as my Assistant. Joe was delighted to be back in football and back at Northampton. It was an emotional return to our beloved club and for a while it worked until the club hit the buffers.

Northampton Town squad 1991-92 – some of the old magic was still there – we managed to pluck a few players from lower leagues who went on to be successful like Kevin Wilkin third from right back row and Terry Angus third from left middle row.

Before it all turned sour – recognition from League sponsors Barclays with a bottle of bubbly and a decorative plate for Manager of the Month. Won two awards that season so did something right before the money dried up & I didn't get paid.

This never happened at The Arsenal – all hands on deck as from right Joe Kiernan, coach Billy Best and I clear the pitch of snow to try and get a game on, never one to shirk a bit of work. The training kit has gone from Adidas to Brooks or Umbro. Even the changing rooms at Arsenal had underfloor heating....the opposite end of the football league.

Southend v Oldham 3rd
September 1994
at Roots Hall – I'm not pleased about
something and look ready to launch
while manager Peter Taylor looks like
a coiled spring too. Glass dugouts
of Highbury are a distant memory,
even my kit is ill fitting.

The old routine – thanks to a late Alan Neilson winner
the oldpartnership picked up another trophy and the
last one for us both.Tottenham Hotspur 1 Leicester City 0 Worthington Cup
Final, Wembley 1999.
You never get tired of winning. Sir Les Ferdinand, David Ginola,
Darren Anderton and Sol Campbell in very strong Spurs squad.
George at back joining in, me far right.

Back together at Wembley, this time in the blue colours
of Tottenham Hotspur not the red of Arsenal 21st March
1999. Spurs v Leicester City Worthington Cup Final.

Just two 'foreign' lads who have adopted England as
their home. If Mammy could see me now – meeting HRH
The Prince Philip Duke Of Edinburgh at The Theo Foley
Soccer School, Coldharbour SE9.

2017 Coaching Staff Christmas Meal – every year we meet up in a lovely London restaurant and discuss old times, wind each other up and put the world to rights; L-R David Pleat, Pat Rice, yours truly, George Graham, Stewart Houston, Terry Murphy, Vic Akers.

Still great mates – with George at my 80th birthday.

Over 28 years after he made history me with the man, the legend, Michael Thomas - at the premiere of the fantastic 89 Film.

Back in my hands again 28 years later - the trophy that changed everything.

The Dublin Foley Clan 2014 – always laughing and giving out - My Sisters Anita and Terry with me 'back home' in Dublin.

My lovely family in Dublin for my golden cap presentation at Croke Park. In a bar in Dublin enjoying the city life. L-R Adrian, yours truly, Teresa, Sheila, Sean and Paul. They all came to support me on a proud day back home.

CHAPTER 8
Into the Lion's Den
1974-1978

Richard Nixon gets embroiled in the Watergate scandal, we have a miner's strike in response to a three-day week in the UK, 'Happy Days' and The 'Six Million Dollar Man' both start airing on the box and the IRA/UVF step up their terror campaigns as 'The Troubles' worsen. Serial killer Ted Bundy strikes fear into heart of America and there's a kidnap attempt on Princess Anne at Pall Mall. '74 was a good year for dictators as Ceausescu comes to power in Romania and Pinochet in Chile. Red Rum wins the Grand National at home. Everyone seems to be testing their nuclear weapons until Ford and Brezhnev sign a treaty to reduce nuclear arsenals. Abba win the Eurovision Song Contest and Holland reach the World Cup Final playing the best football never to win a World Cup, losing out to West Germany 2-1. Pele retires from football as the other Greatest, Muhammad Ali, beats Foreman using the 'rope-a-dope' technique in the Rumble in the Jungle. Lord Lucan does a runner back home after a grisly murder in Belgravia.

The music has gone all glam rock but Stevie Wonder with the peerless album 'Innervisions' and Gladys Knight are still flying the Motown flag and Barry White is going down well at our house. The Hollies were on the record player regularly with the brilliant 'Air That I Breathe' and it was around this time that I fell in love with sound of The Carpenters. Paul McCartney grew Wings with a new sound and Elton was in full flow releasing hits, Barbara Streisand too. Local lad David Bowie released 'Diamond Dogs' which eldest son Adrian was into before drifting into the California sound of the Eagles.

Francis Ford Coppola does the impossible and releases an even better film as a sequel in 'Godfather II' whilst Jack

*Nicholson and Faye Dunaway shine in the stylish
'Chinatown'. Robert Redford and Mia Farrow do the same in
the equally stylish 'Great Gatsby' in what was another golden
period for cinema. It is the year that the incomparable
comedy to top all comedies, 'Blazing Saddles', is released.
I drove a fairly nasty Mark IV Cortina, nowhere near as nice
as the old red Mark II, and, to make matters worse, it was
beige. Not a car highlight but I redeemed myself with a
lovely cream VW Variant Fastback. It was air cooled like the
old Beetles so made the same whistling noise, a lovely looking
car. Be worth a fair few bob now.*

Unemployed at the age of 37, it was time to find some work
and pay the bills with four kids and a wife to feed. Ideally
back in football, even though my confidence had taken a
bashing, but I'd have taken anything to get some money in.
I took a job for a short while at a local secondary school,
Eaglesfield, which was only five minutes up the road from
our home on Shooters Hill, taking PE lessons just to get some
cash through the door. I found dealing with the young lads
very rewarding trying to help them through school in some
small way but, on occasion, I've got to say, it was tougher than
managing professional footballers. Out of the blue, Dulwich
Hamlet FC chairman Jimmy Rose asked me down to help out
with the coaching and I jumped at the opportunity. Dulwich
were an amateur side and Jimmy was a popular local
publican, landlord at the Plume of Feathers right next to
Greenwich Park. He was a big Charlton fan and a lovely fella
so I was only too pleased to help out on a temporary basis. I
stayed until September as my radio duties at LBC were
increased and I had a regular slot predicting the scores on a
Saturday and regular phone-ins with Steve Tongue, Andrew
Gidley and a young Jeff Stelling.

This small step back into football, in turn, led to Dartford
FC asking me to help out their manager, Ernie Morgan, in
February 1975. Dartford were one of the biggest non-league
clubs around at that time having recently won the Southern
League and reached the FA Trophy Final at Wembley. Many

years later my sons, Adrian and Paul, both played for the Darts so there has definitely been a family link at various times. Adrian had the longest spell there in a very good side that included Andy Hessenthaler and Peter Taylor, who I ended up working with much later on at Southend. It was only to be a short term, limited role helping on the coaching side but, if nothing else, it gave me some comfort that football clubs, albeit two non-league ones, thought I still had something to offer. Both jobs kept me involved in the game in some way at a time when I was beginning to doubt myself. What you realise very quickly is that footballers are the same no matter what the level, the same ribbing, the same pranks just less ability maybe and less money in non-league. The toughest thing I found was trying to cram a week's worth of fitness and coaching into a couple of sessions a week after they've all done a day's work.

No sooner had I flitted between school teaching and non-league football than the call from Millwall came in April 1975 and the start of my first real managerial partnership began. The manager at the time was Gordon Jago who I knew from various coaching and scouting networks as a very forward-thinking football man. Having played for Charlton for years and managed QPR at the time I was in charge at The Valley he was well known around the London football scene. Gordon has since become a key figure in the development of football in North America and is still active in the States to this day. When he asked me to help him on the coaching side I didn't need to be asked twice. I knew the club well enough from my teenage days at Exeter being warned off retrieving the ball by Arnold Mitchell to managing the grudge matches between Charlton and Millwall. They had good players, the intimidating crowd and ground were an advantage at home and it was a club where you felt you could make a difference. It had soul and not every club has, believe you me. After meeting with Gordon, he didn't need to sell the club and he had some good ideas on ways to improve both on and off the field.

As it turned out, I was only out of the pro game for a few months and in place as coach for a club that were playing in the League above the club I'd just been sacked at, Charlton. Football can be a strange back to front world and sometimes you have to grab those opportunities when they come along. I got a few spiky comments from people I bumped into around the area as I still lived in Charlton territory but I was well able for all that, I've never had any qualms about taking a job no matter who their rivals are. If I'm with a team, and employed by them, then that's my team, be it Charlton followed by Millwall or Arsenal followed by Tottenham. It's my job and it has to pay the bills, that's it pure and simple. It's not for everyone but I've never gone in for that old bollocks to be honest.

As I familiarised myself with the players in the squad studying programmes at home I was encouraged by the quality we had already at the club before we thought about improving any areas. We had the likes of Ray Evans once of Tottenham, Tony Hazell who'd played plenty at QPR, an exciting young winger called Gordon Hill, a prolific front man in Phil Summerill and the ultimate Lion's legend that was Barry Kitchener. Some very good players, playing expansive attacking football in front of a passionate crowd, no matter what anyone says about Millwall fans, they are the best in the land when they're on your side. I loved the feeling of belonging and the unity straight away. Real people, real football fans.

So instead of Maryon Wilson and Greenwich Park, we were working in Southwark Park or Deptford Park sometimes having to clear off the dog shit before we could train. In deepest South East London you'd usually find a few young lads having a kick about and they didn't care who you were, they'd tell you to piss off out of it. I lost count of the times we had to give them a few bob so we could use the pitch. That's how it was back then, no fancy training grounds and private sessions, anyone or anything could scupper your plans. We seemed to work well though, as a pair, as Gordon was less keen to coach and, after getting burnt at Charlton, I was equally pleased to just focus on the coaching side. The old Second Division had some big clubs in it that season, like Man

Utd, Sunderland and Aston Villa and, sure enough, we struggled to compete financially. We generally pulled in around 10,000 for home games but just couldn't compete with the big gate clubs at the top of the league.

The Den was the key to any sort of survival, it always has been. The season started much as they had during my Charlton days with patchy form for the first couple of months followed by a terrible run up to Christmas. We had a spell of eight games from October to December where we didn't win a solitary game. We pulled it around again briefly only to have an even worse run over the last six games with four defeats that sent us down to Division 3. We went down with Cardiff and Sheffield Wednesday both below us, but three points adrift of Bristol Rovers. I thought, here we go again, maybe it's me, as once more a side I'd been involved with ended up relegated when they really should have been safe. Northampton in '66, Charlton in '72 and now Millwall in '75. At least the usual bogey sides Fulham and Blackpool weren't involved this time.

Gordon, to his credit, didn't panic and really showed his mettle by asking for money to improve the squad and bounce back to the Second Division. When I think back to Charlton, I'd tried to keep the budget in check when we'd gone down, as I'd been instructed, but Gordon just went in and asked in a direct way. He went out and made a bold statement for a club like Millwall with the signings of Phil Walker and Trevor Lee who were the first black players to play for a club that had really struggled for some time with terrace racism. That was Gordon, he was way ahead of his time and both Phil and Trevor really helped the club both on and off the pitch. Don't get me wrong, it wasn't a change of mindset overnight but they blazed a trail that hadn't been travelled before and turned people's opinions on their head. Both very different characters and players, Gordon plucked them out of non-league football from Epsom and Ewell for a combined fee of £40,000. Always watching football, Gordon saw them feature in the famous old FA Vase final.

Phil was a confident lad who had a real swagger about him, you'd never get him on the back foot whereas Trevor was a little more introverted but still a strong enough character for the Lion's Den. Phil christened himself 'The Dude' which tells you he wasn't short on confidence and he played his football that way, a very talented midfielder, comfortable on the ball. Trevor, like many forwards, would drift in and out of some games but he was always capable of winning a game for you. Both lovely lads and they shook up the club and dressing room in a positive way during a time when football really needed to be shaken up. Thankfully, Gordon didn't give it a second thought, he knew they'd improve the side and they cost the club bugger all. Both Walks and Trevor went on to have successful careers after Millwall, Phil even playing in Portugal for the likes of Boavista, where he still lives to this day. Trevor is the same today, just a lovely, laid-back fella sometimes seen down the New Den not far from his birthplace of Lewisham.

We also signed a key player in Millwall's history, Terry Brisley from Leyton Orient. Bris was, in many ways, the missing link between defence and attack enabling us to really get at sides. I got on great with Bris, a little dynamo of a player with a huge heart, a typical Millwall type player much like Les Briley many years later. The transfer fee was zero as we swapped him for Doug Allder, which was a good bit of business for the club. We'd lost the talented winger Gordon Hill a couple of months in to the big boys of Man Utd for a £70,000 fee which was far too low in my opinion. 'Merlin' as he was known was one of the best young wingers around which he proved operating on the other flank to Steve Coppell at Old Trafford to good effect reaching two FA Cup finals in '76 and '77, winning the second 2-1 against Liverpool. Gordon was a chirpy, confident lad always destined for bigger things you felt.

With these few tweaks we just clicked and had a really good season, improving as it wore on with the new lads making a real difference. In February we made another key signing in John Seasman from Luton, another steal from the Hatters to follow my raid for Halesy three years earlier. As with Derek, we borrowed him on loan at first and managed to get him for a bargain at £10,000 before an increase based on appearances, that Luton were desperate to avoid, kicked in. Seasy was a very clever forward link up player who was probably ahead of his time, he'd be great operating behind a forward like many sides set up with now. He was just the spark we needed and we went on a great run winning ten out of the last 16 games to see us promoted in third spot behind Hereford and Cardiff. We secured third spot with three points to spare over fourth placed Brighton effectively sealed by a 3-1 win over the Seagulls at The Den with three games to play. We were back in the Second Division and, at last, I had another promotion under my belt to counter the more recent relegations.

I met up with Seasy and full back Jonny Moore recently for a charity golf day and we had a laugh about some of the old times, notably a big fight that occurred between John and our centre back, Tony Hazell, after a game at home. Tony was a confident lad, shall we say, an acquired taste and not everyone's cup of tea but I always liked him. He wasn't shy or retiring and he'd played at a good level so he was a key player for us, but he did rub some people up the wrong way. We had a game at The Den, on one occasion, and Seasy was dropping off and showing to receive the ball to feet as he always would and Haze is just drilling it long behind the defence which John was never going to chase. I can still see Seasy on the pitch now chirping away getting more and more 'Scouse' as it went on but it made no difference to Tony, he was still hitting it long. I think it ended in a draw and they came in after 90 minutes still chundering away at each other, Seasy cleaning his boots moaning about 'effing this and effing that' as Haze strut past him, completely bollock naked, and said, 'You're just a lazy bastard,' before easing himself into the bath. Well John, who was not an aggressive type, just flipped and threw his boot at Haze before launching himself, in full kit, into the bath as they knocked the shite out of each other. They were pulled apart by the lads and it was a wee bit of an icy atmosphere for a few weeks between them both but we all just got on with it. Haze was never going to change and still carried on hitting his favourite pass, showing off his sweet right foot to full effect. To this day though, it will still get Seasy spitting feathers but Tony was a strong boy so it's probably just as well he got pulled away.

Gordon had pulled it round and bounced straight back to the Second Division with some shrewd signings and fine football. At last, I felt a big part of success once more, as it becomes a worry when it starts to became a run of bad luck. We were back among the bigger clubs like Wolves, Chelsea, Forest and Sheffield United not to mention Charlton, who had gone up with what was effectively 'my team', but like the Murphys, I'm not bitter. I was looking forward to playing against my old employers especially given Millwall's superior record over them but we drew 1-1 at home and lost 3-2 at The Valley. I got some stick that day make no mistake.

We kept the same squad for the league above with just a couple of new lads added. The youth side had some excellent players coming through expertly managed by Bob Pearson. Two years later the youth side won the FA Cup beating Man City 2-0 over two games which was a great achievement for a smaller club like Millwall. Every single player went on to play first team football from that side which was the lifeblood for clubs like Millwall back then, producing homegrown talent at no cost. Bob was excellent at spotting the best local talent. Players like Dave Mehmet, Kevin O'Callaghan, Tony Kinsella, Paul Sansome and Andy Massey all played plenty of games for the first team and Cally even got to play with the great Pele in Escape to Victory!

Jokes aside, Kevin actually ended up having the most success playing in a very good Ipswich side that won the UEFA Cup in '81 and winning plenty of caps for Eire as a winger of real talent and ability. We gave Mehm his debut in the 1976-77 season as a young 16 year old in the last game of the season at home to Burnley. Now, if ever a player should have played at the top it was Dave, with a range of passing like Glenn Hoddle. He played plenty of games for Millwall, Charlton and Gillingham but he really had the ability to play higher. My son, Paul, played in the same side as Mehm at Fisher Athletic where he used to get taped up to both knees apparently just so they could get him onto the pitch.

Then there was Mass, a great lad with bags of heart and a great attitude. We always laugh about how I refereed one of his school games (God knows why) and then saw him later in the evening for a game at The Den where he used to sell snacks around the pitch as an usher. From then on, as I came out of the tunnel, I'd grab him and tell everyone nearby that 'this kid will be a player one day' and I was right. His dad was from Dublin so he had a head start straight away and he was determined to play for Millwall from a young age. He was clearly upset when he ended up getting swapped with Les Briley of Aldershot years later but he knew that was just how football is sometimes.

We signed a young goalkeeper too, Nicky Johns, from non-league who I'd seen playing for Minehead against Dartford on a wet, freezing night without any gloves. Not for the first time I'd gone to watch someone else at Dartford and come away wanting to sign another. There was this tall, gangly kid holding onto a wet ball with bare hands between the sticks for Minehead and I thought, he'll do. Get him some gloves and sort out his suspect kicking and we may have found one. He was a shy and quiet West Country boy who'd never been away from home so he ended up staying at our house for six months before he'd sorted out his digs and brought his girlfriend, as she was then, Alison, up to the smoke. Nicky doesn't remember one incident at our house but he's probably blanked it out.

Nicky used to get up, quiet as a mouse, and have his breakfast, usually his favourite 'pokie egg' or poached egg to you and me. One morning he's sat there and Teresa, my eldest, comes down half dressed in a dressing gown that I felt was far too short, she must have only been about 17. I told her, in no uncertain terms, to get upstairs and put some clothes on as I was little embarrassed shall we say. Teresa had a sharp tongue in those days and from memory told me to 'piss off' or something similar, which made me go wild. She was pouring out the milk on her cereal but I told her again to get changed, following her into the hall, where she swore at me again and after a push she ran upstairs and locked herself in the bathroom, for what seemed like hours, until it was safe. Poor Nicky just sat there in silence embarrassed to witness it all. Happy families.

Nicky went on to take the more experienced Ray Goddard's place before going to the States and then signing for Charlton and QPR, playing well over 300 league games. I spent hours and hours after training working with Nicky especially on his kicking which was the weakest part of his game. We managed to improve it even if he still fell on one side as he kicked it now and then. I'm still in touch with Nicky, Alison and their lovely family so cereal-gate didn't scare him off, thankfully. We signed Roger Cross from Brentford halfway through the season and, although he didn't play much for Millwall, Roger was a key part in the success that followed in later years helping Bob Pearson produce player after player via the youth system.

The youth system produced players like Teddy Sheringham and Neil Ruddock, not to mention cult Millwall legends like Keith Stevens and Alan McCleary. The players produced by a club with the limited resources it had available was incredible, getting talent from under the noses of Arsenal, Tottenham or Chelsea. The incentive for these lads was that they would get a chance sooner at a club like Millwall and, sure enough, they all played at a young age. Other than Roger in '77 we made a couple of loan signings but that was it, we coped well and were much better equipped for the Second Division than two seasons before.

If you want to see how times have changed look up Millwall v Chelsea from September 1976 at a packed Den on YouTube with goals from Barry Salvage, Ray Evans and Terry Brisley. Three excellent goals past Peter Bonetti and a world away from the current wealth of Chelsea in front of a full house. The goals sum up how we sent out the side to play in an attacking way with the talent we had going forward. We more than held our own and finished in 10th place with Wolves, Chelsea and Forest going up. Hereford and Cardiff, who came up with us in first and second spot the season before, finished bottom and fifth bottom respectively so we had fared much better than they had. In fact, we were only nine points away from third spot and promotion to the top flight. Gordon had proved himself again and I was just happy to be a part of it.

That season saw the last of Ray Evans who deserves a special mention. We had Ray from February 1975 for the second half of that relegation and he'd been a key player in the following promotion season. He then played up to March of the 76-77 season before heading off to the States. For the life of me, I can't recall why he ended up going as he was a class apart, maybe he fell out with Gordon. Ray had played for Spurs for seven years and even had UEFA Cup experience. He liked to let his hair down and have a few drinks so maybe that's why he left and why we ended up having someone with his quality in the first place. I never remember it affecting his levels of performance though, he was a top player.

We decided, for the following season, that to stand still would be to slip back so we looked at getting new players in. We signed Brian Chambers from Luton for a few quid and got Northern Ireland international Bryan Hamilton from Everton on a free. Hammy was a really bubbly character full of confidence and chat, in fact I'm still in touch with him now. He'd come to the house and leave notes everywhere just saying 'I'm brilliant me,' and sign them Bryan Hamilton. He was an experienced pro who had played for two good Ipswich and Everton sides, he obviously liked blue and white kits! You don't get 50 caps for nothing and it was no surprise when he went on to have a long management career, even managing Northern Ireland in the '90s.

We also signed Les Barratt from Fulham for £12,000 which wasn't the best bit of business we made. Les was a wide player who'd played over 400 games for Fulham and was the wrong side of 30 but we'd hoped to get more than eight games out of him. There are shades of my 'playing career' at Charlton there. We picked up a young centre back on loan from Colchester, called Lindsay Smith, who we eventually signed many years later from Plymouth Argyle when I returned to the club with George Graham. We also signed Tony Tagg, another centre back from QPR, as Barry Kitchener was 30 years old now and, unfortunately, he was beginning to suffer a bit with injuries.

Kitch was irreplaceable though, a Rolls Royce at the back. He has this cult status at Millwall which will always be the case, but people who didn't see him play assume that's because he was a tough, hard player. That's not to say he wasn't as tough as teak and a pure winner, but he had great ability too, lovely feet for a big lad and was always comfortable on the ball. Kitch is another who should have really played at the top level but decided to stay at the club he loved and the fans adored him for that. He was a big, loveable, gentle giant too, a leader on the pitch and a gentleman off it, sadly taken far too young at 64. What price would a Barry Kitchener be today?

For me personally it was more of the same as we were now doing what I'd call real coaching, at last, and Gordon was happy to just let me get on with it. Now, when I started coaching at Charlton, I was no fool and well used to the players' tricks but I probably was still a little naive in some ways. In a dressing room, as in a class room, one lad at least will be the mouthpiece, the troublemaker who will try to drive you mad. If you get two like that you're in trouble and, more than two, you've had it. You'll plan your session out and it would get continually disrupted if they wanted to no matter how much control you think you have.

What happens is you walk out with a bag of balls, put them down and do some running, then all they ask is when are the balls are coming out. Then you think I'll leave them in the dressing room so then they think they're in for non-stop running and have a moan up, sulk you name it. You wear a stopwatch and whistle round your neck and they give out non-stop, moan and whinge telling you to 'fucking put that stopwatch away'. After a while it just becomes a noise and you block it out, you have to remain upbeat and positive no matter how much you want to give them a bollocking. You have to develop a thick skin and pipe up when needed as otherwise you'll just get walked over. I've lost count of the times I'd have to stop a session with, 'Right, anyone wants to carry on fucking about and generally taking the piss, we can put the balls away and just run all session.' It soon does the trick.

The favourite little try-ons usually relate to any physically demanding work, obviously, such as shuttle work or 'doggies' as they were known in my day. Let's say you were going to do five lots of shuttles all timed on a stopwatch and record the times for each player so you can monitor progress. Well, any seasoned pro will know that their times have to improve to prove they are getting fitter so they'll do the first one at a canter the slippery bastards. There was a whispered phrase or two if one of the group, usually a keen young lad, was going a bit quick. 'Plenty of arm movement' or 'don't be a hero' were two commonly heard comments. Similarly, players always want to know 'how many of these are we doing, Theo?' – always a courteous 'Theo' when they're after information, otherwise it's 'you wanker' or similar. If you're doing say five runs they will slowly improve over the five. You have two options and it all depended on how I felt. You can say 'never you mind busy bollix, just get on with it' or you lie, say three and do five. Either way they didn't like it.

Then you'd get the lads who actually enjoyed working. They were a dream. I wouldn't say I always enjoyed training as a player but I knew I had to be as fit as I could be to be at my best, as I wasn't good enough to cheat. I would always say I was what you'd call a good trainer. I often found that the lads who'd come from lower or non-league appreciated the opportunity more, not always as I found out maybe with Powelly though! Lads like Cyril Davies were keen as mustard, Nicky Johns always wanted to work on things and so on. Then you had the old pros like Graham Moore, Ray Treacy who knew the games at Charlton or Tony Hazell, Harry Cripps and the like at Millwall. If you want a broad sweeping statement too it could be said that forwards as a group were generally lazier always at the back in the running, moaning and cursing as they ran. 'Why do I have to do these long runs, I only do quick sharp ones in a game,' that sort of thing. Now that may be true but you must have a good 'base' fitness and then tailor it but try telling a bollocksed forward that after an hour's work. If they did the business on a Saturday, I might just might cut them some slack but it was unlikely.

Then you had the goalkeepers, a weird old lot. These were the days before designated goalkeeping coaches so they had to join in and, back then, they weren't the fittest shall we say, usually carrying some timber. I was fortunate to work with two top class keepers in Phil Parkes at QPR and John Lukic at Arsenal who had great ability but they still needed to be fit so they'd join in sessions. Neither were made for running but kept a good level of fitness. You would have to work into your sessions drills that involved some shooting or crossing to make sure they weren't standing around. Specialist coaches were very rare then. I've always worked with 'keepers as part of my coaching role and they're not a bad bunch when you get used to them.

At Millwall we had the experienced Ray Goddard and young Nicky Johns, two 'keepers at opposite ends of their careers. Ray was a steady 'keeper and thick set lad so was never going to enjoy running while Nicky was stick thin, tall and had natural agility and fitness but, again, not made for running. He may as well have worn his leather slip on moccasins which the lads used to slaughter him for. Ray knew the drill, knew what he needed to work on and where he may have been weaker. He lacked a little height so we'd work on crosses, where to take the ball and when to come maybe a bit more but he was a good 'keeper, brave and steady which is exactly what you want. Nicky was a bit more fragile back then and developing his game all the time. A very good shot stopper, good on crosses with his height but he did struggle terribly with his kicking. We worked over and over on his place kicking for hours at a time and he manufactured a way around it. He improved, over time, and became a very good 'keeper even if he never filled out especially or really sorted his bloody kicking out.

1977-78 turned out to be a tough season right from the start as we chopped and changed the side trying to find the right blend. We lost three on the bounce straight from the off and didn't win a match until the sixth game. Nicky came into the side and pretty much made the no 1 shirt his own from Ray Goddard who had a couple of injuries that season. Nicky was in and out at first and, by his own admission, had some stinkers early on in his Millwall career but he really settled in over time. One game away at Halifax he was so poor I didn't talk to him all the way home but we've always been close and I even helped him with parts of his game when we were at different clubs dropping in wherever he was on the odd afternoon. One of the strangest goalkeeping incidents I've seen on a pitch, though not at the time, involved Ray Goddard in one of his last games when he thought a shot was going over so he swung round the post to retrieve the ball only to see it sail into an empty net. Ray was a great servant to the club though, and another taken far too young at 58.

Dave Donaldson and Jonny Moore were our regular steady full backs that season as Ray Evans had gone to Fulham. I always spent hours and hours with the full backs as it was my position, even with Ray when he was there to make sure they worked as a pair, when to show, when to tuck in, when to overlap and so on. Up front we had our key link up man Seasy alongside a lad we picked up from Wycombe Wanderers, Ian Pearson. Hammy played most games in midfield and Kitch played a good number even with his injuries sharing duties with Tony Tagg. The model pro Haze played almost every game and was as steady as ever, still pinging long balls over Seasy's head. Then Gordon Jago dropped his bombshell that he was off to manage and develop 'soccer' in the States. It was a real bolt from the blue but I think Gordon felt disillusioned when his plans to rebrand the club fell through. We lost key player Terry Brisley also who left in January for rivals Charlton which was another big loss for the club.

Gordon was always seeking to change the image of the club which was not great in terms of the hooliganism and racism on the terraces. He even tried to change the name of the road from Cold Blow Lane to Montego Bay from memory. He really wanted to change everything from top to bottom which was maybe too ambitious as the club revelled in its 'no one likes us' image. The name of the ground, the name of the road, the song asking to 'let 'em all come down to The Den' and the hostile atmosphere all helped in its own way into making it a place opposing teams hated to go to. It was an advantage that has served the club well, even as it does in the New Den these days, it's still a cauldron. Gordon was always going to struggle to change too many things that had made the club what it was. In his wisdom, he invited a Panorama documentary to be made as the hooligan incidents had subsided. He is still incensed to this day about the one-sided portrayal and the fact that the production team plied fans with drink for the desired effect. It was a set-up and Panorama got what they wanted with some manufactured links and 'plants' to make better TV, obviously. The programme also showed the National Front distributing literature at games, which I'm sure I'd never seen before. It was all too much for Gordon who resigned at the end of 1977 and never returned.

Quite how the documentary that saw off Gordon also played a part in what happened later that season we will never know but, unfortunately, another indelible mark against the club occurred in March 1978, after we had both left. The side ended up later in the season going on a fine FA Cup run which saw them reach the sixth round with a home tie against high flying Ipswich Town. The scenes at that game were awful and you only have to look at the images to see that the game was hijacked by the far right that was on the up at that time, these weren't what I'd call true Millwall fans. Ipswich won 6-1 but the result was irrelevant, the scenes were among the worst ever witnessed and the damage to the club was irreparable as the media went to town and the bad reputation was reinforced indelibly and still exists in some form today.

When Gordon left, Jeff Burnige, the chairman told me to put in for the job but I knew it was a waste of time. I took over on a temporary basis for a handful of games and Jeff was already trying to tell me who to play so I thought bollocks to that. Saying that, I may have been better off listening to him as we lost all four games that I took charge over. I took four games in December, Fulham at home which we lost 3-0, Blackburn away which we lost 2-1, Spurs at home which we lost 3-1 and Cardiff away which we lost 4-1. A poor run of results and doing my 'on the job interview' no favours at all. For the third time, Fulham were to play a part in my final days at a club following their last day involvement in the Northampton and Charlton relegations in '66 and '72. The side had been struggling even before Gordon left so maybe he wanted away because he knew we were struggling anyway. We only had 14 points when he left at the start of December from a possible 36 so the team did well to finish safe in 16th place, albeit after we had long left. We'd managed to bring on young lads like Nicky Johns, Dave Mehmet and Chris Dibble as young prospects but, beyond that, there wasn't much to shout home about that season.

If I'm honest, I never really got on with the chairman at the best of times so it was always going to be a waste of time throwing my hat in the ring. I felt if they'd wanted me, they'd have offered it to me properly. They ended up giving it to my old foe from my playing days, ex-Crystal Palace midfielder George Petchey. I'd had a few run ins with him on the pitch marking him for Northampton over the years. Looking back, I'd have enjoyed giving management another crack with the experience learned since Charlton but it never materialised and another London club came knocking in QPR so it was going to be another new role, this time over in West London.

To this day, I'm not sure if the offer came because of Gordon who had strong links to Loftus Road having managed there or from someone on the coaching staff but it turned out to be a great move for me. I was offered the position of reserve team manager and was lucky enough to work with one of the best young squads I've ever worked with. It was also the club where I first worked alongside a certain Scots' boy called George Graham and a special working relationship was formed.

CHAPTER 9
The QPR Academy
1978 – 1982

Viv Anderson becomes the first black player to play for England and a certain Margaret Thatcher becomes Britain's first female Prime Minister. Four years later she led Britain to war with Argentina over the Falkland Isles. In America, former B-movie actor, Ronald Reagan, becomes president blazing the trail for anyone to reach the office of a world power many years later...

Ticker tape crowds see Argentina and Mario Kempes' goals win the World Cup in '78 on home soil, with Holland finishing runners-up again while in '82 Italy beat West Germany in Spain as Paolo Rossi's goals steal the show.

Billy Joel is featuring heavily on my cassette player as the punk, mod or ska music coming from the boys' rooms is just a din. John Lennon is tragically gunned down in New York by a crazed fan. Diana Ross and Stevie Wonder are keeping the Motown spirit alive. Good ole Johnny Logan, under the Irish flag (but he wasn't really Irish), scooped the Eurovision Song Contest with 'What's another Year?'

Blockbusters like 'Jaws' and 'Star Wars' hit the screens and Peter Sellers underlines his comic genius in The Pink Panther films. One of my favourites, Robert De Niro is at his best in the brutal 'Deer Hunter' and a year later is unrecognisable as boxing legend Jake La Motta in 'Raging Bull'. Harrison Ford dons his fedora for the first time as Indiana Jones.

I drove a very plain four door navy Renault 9 to death in those days racing through the centre of town to Shepherds Bush and Greenford. To survive that journey every day you had to be bold...and quick. For a while, as I couldn't sell the bloody thing, I had a red Austin Princess 1.8 which handled like a speedboat. I refused to slag it and admit defeat but the boys gave me plenty of stick at home. I also rekindled my love of air cooled VW's with an Orange Camper van which I loved.

Another new London club and another new role, this time working with the younger lads coming through, what I already knew was, an excellent youth system at Loftus Road. I was confident in my coaching ability but wondered how I'd get on with lads who may be a bit more fragile and maybe want continual encouragement. The first team was third bottom in the old First Division when I joined at the beginning of 1978 and not pulling up any trees. They had international players like Phil Parkes, Stan Bowles, Gerry Francis and Billy Hamilton in the side so they were definitely underachieving for some reason. They finished third bottom and got relegated, so a poor season for the club, but from my point of view and the lads coming through, it was a great opportunity to make a difference. Frank Sibley was manager when I joined but he was sacked in March '78 as the side headed for relegation. Alec Stock took over as caretaker manager for the last two months of the season only to be replaced by Steve Burtenshaw in time for the 1978-79 season. It was hardly a stable environment at the club and the chairman, Jim Gregory, was a fiery character alright. Jim carried a huge wad of cash at all times and was a real wheeler-dealer type, literally as he was a local car dealer. He loved the club even if he was a Fulham supporter deep down. He'd tried to buy Fulham in the past but failed so QPR was the next best thing. He didn't hold back with his thirst for appointments so it was often best to just keep your head down.

It was soon very apparent that we had an embarrassment of riches at QPR of young players who were either ready or nearly ready. We had a fantastic set of players coming through the system at that time with almost all of them making the grade with the first team. If you compare that with the club now and, indeed, many of the top London clubs, it is unrecognisable to the superb production line that existed then at Loftus Road. The reserve team I managed in the Football Combination League had players right the way through it that went on to play for the first team.

We had players like Peter Hucker, Warren Neil, Ian Dawes, Alan MacDonald who is sadly no longer with us, Gary Waddock, Gary Micklewhite, Wayne Fereday, Steve Burke, David Kerslake and Ian Stewart. Then, of course, we had the two jewels up front, Clive Allen and Paul 'Sarge' Goddard. There were plenty of others too but these 'core' players went on to play many games in the Football League and at the top level. A good number of these lads went on to play at international level too. To get that many players all making the grade is unbelievably rare and, much like the youth system at Millwall as I'd seen, the club was punching above its weight but the lads knew they had a great chance to make it there rather than say at Arsenal or Tottenham.

In order to produce players of this quality you need a bit of luck with the 'crop' shall we say but you also need a first class scouting and coaching set-up and we certainly had this at QPR. Unsung names behind the scenes who found these lads from here, there and everywhere and managed to get them to come across to Loftus Road when other clubs may have been pushing for them to sign. Nowadays you get players who are lifted from other clubs at the drop of a hat and big money can change hands for young boys who have done nothing in the game yet have the so-called 'potential' to make the grade. The nearest thing to a QPR nowadays is maybe somewhere like Southampton who have churned out the likes of Walcott, Bale, Oxlade-Chamberlain, Chambers, Ward-Prowse and Shaw. Southampton has been forced to sell on all of these with the exception of Ward-Prowse though and, although most of the QPR lads moved on eventually, they all came through together and stayed for some time. These days it just would not be allowed to happen.

There is definitely a big slice of fortune in youth development and it does make me laugh now when I hear about this superb Academy with the latest coaching methods and thinking that will definitely churn out quality players. Now, I agree that you need the facilities and a clear coaching ethos, if you like, but if you think you'll get quality no matter what, then you are deluded. Give these lads the best possible environment yes, but sometimes the raw materials are sadly lacking. There has been a surge of Belgian players recently all playing in the top European Leagues like Courtois, Benteke, Dembele, Alderweireld, Vertonghen, De Bruyne and Eden Hazard of course. Every club then starts to look at their set-up, what can we copy and how are they doing it? When the Belgian head coach was asked for the secret to their success, he simply said 'luck'. He's right but there's an industry and network set up now to support the science so good luck to them I say.

Take Pep Guardiola who inherited some of the best players ever to pull on a pair of boots via the much heralded, La Masia. Players like Pique, Puyol, Busquets, Xavi, Iniesta and the jewel in the crown, Messi. Will a group of players ever come through like that again? Unlikely. Was Guardiola fortunate to be there at the right time? You bet he was, which enabled him to create his own legend accordingly. Any coach or manager who loves football would give their right arm to work with players like these. I've not seen many recently from La Masia to rival those players. Unfortunately, there is so much tripe spouted by people who have never coached or played the game about where we are going wrong in this country. Do me a favour. The new FA centre at Burton looks a great facility to give yourself the best chance with the cream of the crop and the U19, U20 and U21 sides are all bearing fruit lately. Clearly something is working with the junior sides and now people are looking at our way of developing players. It's a hot topic right now as there is always this gripe that the best young lads here never force their way into the first teams to the detriment of the national side. Well, the EPL is massive business and the best players come for the money, so the homegrown players just have to be better. Belgium managed it – with luck!

I think things have improved but there's still plenty of bullshit around the game. Put football people in charge of our beloved game, not stuffed shirts or the former head of some huge company. This is football and those that know the game were ignored for years, like Bobby Moore as highlighted earlier. It takes time and my old favourites at the FAI are probably lagging even further behind the FA. There's some talent coming through definitely like Kane, Rashford, Dele Alli, Calvert-Lewin, Loftus-Cheek and even younger lads like Foden at Man City so something must be working alongside the raw materials. Gareth Southgate looks to be trying to bring in different methods too and linking the new with the past so keep the faith I'd say. The Irish squads are always going to benefit from players in the English system and the Premier League here as the Irish League is nowhere near as strong. The likes of Seamus Coleman, Shane Duffy, Robbie Brady and Harry Arter have all improved the international side by playing regularly in the Premier or Championship as younger players. Maybe we don't have the big names of years gone past but, as I've alluded to, these things have always been cyclical and always will be. We'll be back I'm sure.

Back to QPR, my role in the system was to back up those who found these gems and to work alongside John Collins who had nurtured the lads through the youth team before a certain George Graham worked his magic. I would then prepare them for the real stuff, toughen them up or, in the case of lads dropping down from the first team, massage their egos and get them back on track. I had to work closely with the first team manager above and the youth team manager below so it was a good learning curve for me in the art of diplomacy both up to the first and down to the youth team. I saw a host of first team managers come and go as Jim Gregory didn't mess about bringing in new bosses so I worked alongside Frank Sibley, Steve Burtenshaw, Tommy Doherty and finally Terry Venables. All very different characters so I had to change my ways accordingly. Terry was probably the best coach I've seen so it was no surprise to me when he went on to enjoy success at Spurs, Barcelona and England. A sharp football brain who planted certain thoughts about the game in both George's and my mind.

At QPR, we had a tight-knit group of coaches who all loved

the game and wanted to succeed in bringing these lads through. That may seem like an obvious statement but you would be surprised how many coaches just do it as a job and not necessarily for the love of the game or to ensure player progression. Egos can get in the way with coaches and managers but, at QPR, we had something special, a group of players that were hungry to succeed and a group of young and ambitious coaches that wanted to bring them through and win things. John Collins went on to work at other clubs before he stopped working in football and, speaking to him recently, he doesn't even watch games on TV these days, so maybe the intensity was all used up at QPR. George obviously went on to be one of the most successful modern-day managers in the game and his best man, Terry, also had a fantastic career, widely regarded as one of the best coaches around. It was the perfect storm and although hardly in the same league as a Barca crop, in our way we were enjoying real success with local lads at a club that could not compete financially with the big boys at that time.

I am a firm believer that George owes a great deal to the insight of Terry while we were at QPR. He agreed with that assessment recently when we met. I'm sure this makes Arsenal fans smile a little to think a Tottenham man helped George to success at Highbury. They were the best of pals and Terry brought George in to QPR to give him his first proper coaching job. Well, he took to it straight away and just soaked up the knowledge from Terry who was very forward-thinking in his approach to the game. Coaches are always looking to others to learn from and take things from and, in Terry, we had one of the best. His sessions were superb and the players responded well to them. George was known as a laid-back footballer, a luxury if you like but on the training pitch he was the complete opposite. Highly focused and very clear in getting his point across to the players, an excellent communicator. If they didn't get what he was saying, then he would soon let them know about it.

George became a different character as a coach and it's amazing how some players go the other way and wilt under the spotlight of stepping up to be a coach while others, like

George, grow with the responsibility. I've seen a fair few players who had plenty to say in the dressing room with the audience around them but put them in front of the same players trying to put a session on or explain something on the board and they fold like a pack of cards. You are either good at communication or you're not and to be a good coach or manager, you have to get your point across in a way that players of, varying football intelligence it's fair to say, will understand. Some players will get things straight away and others won't, that's just how it is so you have to find a way that works for all. Terry and George were both very good at doing this and it was no surprise to me that both had continued success.

Little did we know it, but we were blessed with a fertile environment that continually churned out top players. We had a good crop of players over two to three years and as the side wasn't signing big names or running away with the leagues we were in, it allowed chances for the younger lads. I am a firm believer that the fact we were forced to play younger players early on alongside a sound coaching support system created the healthy environment to produce the successful youth systems at QPR, Millwall and Arsenal. If all of those clubs had been flying, those players may have been moved on. It's a fine line though, as some players may struggle in a side that isn't winning. The environment was healthy though, especially in the old Second Division, and the lads were mentally tough enough. What QPR wouldn't give to have a young Clive Allen or a Paul Goddard coming through the system now without having to fork out millions for that type of player.

Clive was a pure goal machine but he was a player who worked continually to improve on the training ground. When the rest of the lads had gone in for a shower before necking one of Doris' legendary crusty rolls at Greenford, Clive would ask me for extra training and shooting practice. His goalscoring record is phenomenal. For any young lads who only really know football from Premier League days and don't know about Clive and his record, look him up. He averaged better than a goal every two games for his main clubs QPR and Tottenham and scored 49 goals in one season at Spurs back in 1986-87. The hardest thing to do in football is to stick the ball in the net. I would say he is the best goalscorer I had the pleasure of working with and I worked with some good forwards like Halesy at Charlton, Stevie Lovell at Millwall and not to mention the likes of a young Teddy Sheringham at Millwall, Alan Smith at Arsenal and Peter Crouch at Tottenham.

They were all top forwards but very different to Clive who was a born goalscorer, he'd get tap-ins and goals out of nothing and he had that single-minded desire to score more than anyone else and that selfish streak that forwards need. As a contrast in 'Sarge' Goddard, he had the perfect foil. Paul was a very clever footballer who was never going to score as many goals as Clive but he would chip in with his fair share and would provide assists and good all-round build-up play. With these two playing up top we were a feared side in the old Combination Reserve Team League and romped to the title, my first trophy as a manager.

Which brings me to one occasion that Ian Stewart recently reminded me of. 'Stewy' now works at the Northern Ireland FA and we had a bit of an 'issue', shall we say, later on when he joined Millwall (see next chapter). We had two games to play in the Combination League, one season, and looked nailed on to win the league which, as a coach wanting to do the right thing, would be a good feather in my cap aside from bringing all these lads through. We were away to Bristol Rovers midweek which wasn't the best journey but we were all confident as we were flying and had a good side out that night. We even had the experienced John 'Budgie' Burridge in goal who was mad as a March hare and perfect for these midweek games away as he was so lively and bubbly he got everyone going. Budgie used to come off the pitch after a warm up caked in mud and sweating his nuts off. Not the full ticket but then 'keepers never are, a strange old breed. For an example of his pre-match warm up, type in 'John Burridge warm up' in YouTube. Crackers he was.

We are all chirping away on the coach with the usual piss

taking and card games going on. The coach pulls up at the ground and it is pitch black, not a soul there, which seemed odd. We bundle off the coach and I try to find someone around the place but there's no one to be seen. I look up at the ground and we are at Bristol City, not Bristol Rovers. Well, the driver got both barrels and some more the dozy twat. Not good preparation for an important game for us as we turned up at Rovers a little later than planned. It went downhill from there and we got well beat. We were abysmal, no fight or endeavour which I was not going to stand for. Fair enough, if you get outplayed but not outfought with a lack of any effort.

I went berserk in the dressing room after the game and tore into the lads for letting themselves and the club down. Any nurturing or understanding that these young players were on a path to bigger and better things went right out of the window as I wanted to win the league and couldn't understand why these lot didn't. I may have gone over the top but they could never say I didn't care. I told a few lads that they had gone missing and that they could forget about making the grade if they couldn't do the business at Bristol Rovers on a Tuesday night. Stewy was a quiet Northern Irish lad who had some real talent and eventually went on to have a fine international career. He has since told me he sat there and wondered if he was on his way out of the club.

Now, when someone is going mental in a dressing room and laying down the law you just avoid eye contact and nod when it is needed. As someone giving out the bollocking you want one of them to just say something back to you, to roll their eyes or smirk at the wrong time and you will be on them quicker than Ali on Liston. Thankfully, for the lads and for me, that night not one person said anything back and we drove to Loftus Road in a hushed silence the whole way. I told Ron Berry, the kit man, to tell them all they could forget about getting the usual fish and chips on the way home, we were going straight back. As we approached West London I told Ron to tell them all to report for training in the morning. Usually they would get the day off after a midweek game but not after that shite. I didn't say a word the whole way back, still fuming and thinking of how they would pay for performing so badly.

Well, I got to the training ground at Greenford early and set up for a session of just working their bollocks off. They all got changed and were waiting in the dressing room at 10.00am not sure of what was in store and not sure of where I was as I had driven up the road. I told Ron to let them all know that I was two miles away up at Horsenden Hill which has some great hills and inclines for a bunch of lads who didn't fancy running in Bristol. They were all told to report to the meeting point regardless of injury and niggles as I was having none of their excuses. They ran from the ground to the Hill and Stewy reckons I still had steam coming from my ears, in fact he said I resembled Mussolini. If only Mussolini had driven the bus we would have at least got to Bristol Rovers ground on time the night before like his famous punctual rail system.

I told them right from the off that, because they didn't want to run the previous night, they would be running their bollocks off today. No one chirped back or moaned as they knew it would only mean more running. Well, they were sick of the sight of the steep hill by the end of the session as they ran up it repeatedly. I could see them all trying to guess on how long the session would be, how much more they would be doing and so on. None of them saw this session coming though as they all thought after the mammoth hill session they would be jogging back gently to Greenford but no, we went on a long run down the canal and out to Northolt before heading back to the training ground. Not many of them were chatting now and they were bolloxed. They thought that was it but no, we knocked out a load of sit ups to the point that the abs seize up and you can't pull yourself up.

The reason I mention this old school punishment is that it still sticks in Stewy's mind. This was a lesson that was meant to hurt, it wasn't going to be a gentle examination of what went wrong in front of a screen in a nice warm room, this was early 1980s and this was the way it was or it was the highway.

They worked very hard for over four hours that day, on the day after a game away to Bristol and a late night getting back. If you did that now as a coach you would probably get sacked but I guarantee all of those lads remember it still and they never swung the lead again for me. We won the league in the end and maybe it was a little excessive but as far as I was concerned it was a valuable lesson that would stand them in good stead. If I cared about winning the reserve team league and getting in good habits, then so should they.

When I joined the club in 1978, as well as the internationals I've mentioned, we had some very good players in the first team like stalwart Ian Gillard, Dave Clement, God rest his soul, Don Givens and Don Masson. We had the classy midfielder Gerry Francis who was a great player and we had the one and only Stan Bowles. Now Bowlsey was something else, he was a complete maverick as he's commonly referred to. We'd start training every day at 10.00am and Stan would slowly jog out at 9.58 with his socks down but never ever late. He had so much ability it was a joke, he could win 10-15 games a season on his own. Stan is another like Alan Hudson, Peter Osgood and Glenn Hoddle who should have played a stack of games for England and had teams built around them. Stan won just five England caps at a time when the national side were definitely not overloaded with talent. People are often wary of characters in the game but he was good as gold, much as he wanted to entertain, he also wanted to win.

The stories of Stan's gambling are legendary and all true. We went to Ascot one year for a bit of bonding and he had three grand in his pocket back when it was a lot of money. I asked him all day to give me £2,000 and I would give it back to him when we got back. 'No, Theo, it doesn't work like that,' he kept saying, adding, 'this is what I can afford to lose.' He gave me one cast iron tip and I put £50 on and was shitting myself until it came home. Stan just smiled. I doubt he even came out on top that day but he never changed, he was exactly the same; easy come, easy go with Stan. Another time at the ground the security guy let some toe rag in by accident who rifled through everyone's gear, nicking a fair few quid and a watch out of Stan's bag. He was so laid-back about it all though, he told the security lad not to worry and he just got on with it. That was Stan, lovely fella and a great talent, he just liked a bet that's all. I saw him recently at his benefit match and sadly he's battling Alzheimer's but he still had that maverick twinkle in his eyes. Everyone turned up for the man which says it all.

Frank Sibley, the manager, struggled in his first season at the club following Dave Sexton's move to Manchester United. By the time I'd joined, at the start of 1978, they were down the bottom along with Newcastle and Leicester who were rock bottom. They rallied a little in the second half with some better results with experienced players like Johnny Hollins pulling them along but the side finished fourth bottom, just pipping West Ham by one point who were relegated with Newcastle and Leicester. Cloughie's Forest romped home that year also winning the League Cup before picking up the European Cup the following year. For me, it meant I had an opportunity to push my lads through for the next season as we had a few that were ready as well as Clive and Sarge who had already broken in to the side.

Frank was gone at the end of the season, he couldn't really argue I guess, and Alec Stock came in temporarily without taking a game weirdly enough. I didn't even have time to mention the bung he'd offered me for Paul Went, back in 1972 and, by the start of the season, Steve Burtenshaw was in charge. I still speak to Steve, a likeable football man who didn't really have much joy at QPR, and only lasted the one season. The side finished third bottom with only 25 points, three points above second bottom Birmingham City, and were relegated to the old Second Division. It was a changeover from the previous season at the top as Bob Paisley's Liverpool beat Forest to the title but Cloughie picked up the first of his back to back European Cups.

Jim Gregory's revolving door spun again and Steve was soon gone to be replaced by The Doc, Tommy Docherty. Sarge was now a regular in the squad and Clive had forced his way into the reckoning too but it was tough to throw more young lads into a struggling side. Peter Hucker had gone on to play between the sticks also, alongside Derek Richardson sharing the No.1 shirt. Both great lads, Peter used to get called Ronald McDonald as he had a mass of frizzy hair and I called him 'Bollocks' affectionately. If you went on a run it was 'bollocks', if you put on some shooting for him it was 'bollocks' so I just called him by his favourite word.

I got on great with Tommy, a typical Scottish football character, sharp as a tack, with a great sense of humour and a very astute football brain. There were high hopes for the club when The Doc joined having had some success at big clubs like Chelsea and Man Utd where he'd been relegated and then promoted but blink and he was gone. I can only assume he clashed with the chairman as they were both fiery characters but he was out 29 days into the season and Terry Venables was appointed.

Straight away the atmosphere at the club changed and Terry got everyone pulling in one direction with clear coaching philosophies, changing the playing staff and, thankfully, promoting a few lads from my Football Combination side. Gary Waddock made his way into midfield, a 100 per cent committed player, ideal to set the tone for a side in games and Ian 'Frank' Muir made his debut up front as Clive Allen was sold to Arsenal for big money (before famously going to Crystal Palace without playing a game). Paul Goddard was also sold on to West Ham so the club had made a nice few quid on the best homegrown talent. The reliable and tidy Ian Dawes had forced his way into the squad to replace Ian Gillard at left back and, on the other side, Warren Neil slotted in at right back with good pace and ability. I'd recommended Wayne Fereday who was a pacey winger who could chase pigeons and cross the ball all game and midfielder Gary Micklewhite who lived two minutes from me and was a very good all-round player. Then we had left sided wingers Steve Burke and Ian Stewart also banging on the door, two players with stacks of ability. An amazing progression of young lads all playing in the Second Division and more than holding their own.

Chris Woods had signed in the summer who went on to play for England and playmaker Tony Currie also joined for an embarrassment of riches alongside Bowlsey and Gerry Francis. Terry Fenwick signed from Terry's old club, Crystal Palace, along with Budgie who I'm sure was brought in to raise moral with his infectious personality, a few sandwiches short of a packed lunch that boy. Even Gordon Hill, who'd left Millwall as I'd joined in 1975, signed for us from Derby County. Centre back Steve Wicks had signed the season before from Derby to play alongside the colossus Bobby Hazell signed from Wolves. We also had Glenn 'Dickie' Roeder at centre back with the best step over shuffle seen by any defender driving forward. My old Charlton signing Mick Flanagan joined from Crystal Palace and, all of a sudden, there was a good mix of youth and experience with the young lads really keeping the older lads on their toes. You can't have 11 young lads together but, by the same token, you can't have 11 old ones. The balance looked right.

I used to share the driving duties all the way across town from SE London to the training ground at Greenford with Gary Micklewhite who went to school with my two eldest boys. It was a nightmare journey right through town and out the other side through rush hour traffic. To make the time fly we had Stevie Burke in the back who was in digs nearby and then Bobby Hazell used to share the driving when he lodged with Burkey. Steve is one of the funniest lads I've ever worked with in football, he'd played for Forest with Cloughie and did a perfect impression of him. Everyone was an 'egg' and he played juvenile jokes all day long. Not always the most sophisticated humour, or politically correct now, but you couldn't help but laugh at him.

Every day, without fail, he would say to Gary in the front of the car, 'Biddly bee Mick-le-whiiiite,' after the noise that the little metal robot in the Buck Rogers' TV programme made. Gary had a similar type of side to side walk and, like the TV robot, he wasn't that tall, well Burkey latched on to it. One day, he wound up Bobby Hazel in the car park at Greenford and he was chased around the cars, Bob was livid and wanted to kill him. He picked the wrong man that day and stayed clear from then on always sitting in the back of Bob's big Volvo. Gary and I were laughing when Peter Hucker got injured during one game and Burkey had to go in goal. The first cross that came in, Burkey shouted out at the top of his voice 'Banksy's ball,' as he caught it. That's him; never taking anything seriously but he had stacks of ability as well.

Whenever he scored in training or in games he'd shout out 'Latttcccch-ford' as he loved the old Everton forward Bob Latchford. He was a typical wind-up merchant who used repetition continually, a man after my own heart. We had a big lad, shall we say, called Jock who managed the kit at Loftus Road and Burkey drove him mad. Whenever he saw poor old Jock he'd say, 'Starring Jock Skinner as Frank Cannon,' after the big-boned 1970s' American detective on TV. Jock, fair play, would just laugh every time. Burkey was merciless and crackers. One of his favourites coming around Parliament Square would be, 'Anyone got the time?' with Big Ben looming over us. He soon learned not to fart in my car though, when I kicked him out at Park Lane one day with only 50 pence in his pocket. Every time he got close to the car I just drove off again. God knows where he is now, probably a head teacher or an MP!

The young lads coming through more than held their own and impressed everyone including Terry as the side finished a credible eighth in the 1980-81 season while West Ham won the Second Division title with John Lyall's FA Cup winning side from the year before. The chairman and board then made a very bold move at the end of the season by digging up the pitch, which was always a bog in winter, and replacing it with the latest plastic Astroturf pitch. Now this stuff was not the nice bouncy 3 and 4G surfaces you get today, it was a thin layer of plastic turf with loads of sand brushed in on top of a rock hard sub-base. Horrible bone-shaking stuff. We were the first to lay the Omniturf system, soon to be followed by Oldham, Luton and Preston who all had some success with it too.

The players hated it and I dread to think how many knee injuries it caused over the years, plenty of lads suffered. The bounce on the ball was ridiculous, if you put too much on a pass you were never catching it, there was no 'check' on the ball like there is on grass, it was forever going out of play. The lads all wore 'pimples' or trainers basically with loads of tiny rubber studs to help you stop but they didn't work. The burns from sliding removed layers of skin as the sand was like glass so players ended up staying on their feet as much as possible or it was nights of stuck sheets to gammon-like grazes. Opposition hated it too and the lads definitely learned how to use it to their advantage as the results over the following three seasons proved.

That '81-82 season Terry guided the side to fifth place only two points off the third-place promotion spot, while Luton won the league. Tragically, former right back and excellent youth product Dave Clement took his own life in March '82 after breaking his leg whilst playing for Wimbledon. Dave's son, Paul, managed Swansea and is the former Real Madrid coach, Dave would have been a very proud dad.

The club went on a great FA Cup run that probably affected their league results beating West Brom in the semi to play Spurs in the final. Argentinian Ossie Ardilles and Ricardo Villa withdrew from the Spurs squad as the Falklands War was being fought at the time. We took Spurs to a replay with Gary Micklewhite having a great strike disallowed, losing 1-0 to an early Glenn Hoddle penalty. The squads for both games included 'keeper Peter Hucker who was Man of the Match in the first game, Warren Neill at right back, Gary Waddock in midfield, Clive Allen up front, Gary Micklewhite and the crackpot Burkey on the bench. The fact that six of my 'lads' were playing in the FA Cup Final made me a very proud coach indeed as I watched high up in the stands with Sheila, both guests of the club.

The following year in the 1982-83 season, Terry achieved what he had threatened the previous season by winning promotion back to the top flight at a canter from Wolves. More of the reserve team lads had forced their way into the squad with 'keeper Graham Benstead, Dawsey, Warren Neil and Wayne Fereday now all regulars. Ray Wilkins' younger brother, Dean, was pushing Gary Waddock and Gary

Micklewhite for a starting shirt in midfield while Burkey was also a regular up front with Ian Stewart and Ian 'Frank' Muir.

We also managed to progress a big Northern Ireland centre back, Alan McDonald, into the first team. Hard as nails, he liked the odd cigarette and a pint, a real old school centre back and excellent defender. You wouldn't want to run into Big Mac on a dark night in Belfast, he broke my nose in a challenge playing five-a-side once and swore it was an accident but I'm not so sure! Alan went on to play 476 times for QPR and gained 52 caps for Northern Ireland. Sadly, another no longer with us, Alan passed away in 2012, aged just 48. The coaches at the club were all so proud of these lads and, by the time I'd left for a return to Millwall in December '82, at least 14 players had made it to the first team, many of them in the top flight. The reserve side was left in good shape too with more players to come through later. How many sides now have that level of homegrown talent?

When Terry had arrived from Crystal Palace in 1980 he persuaded his good pal George Graham to join him as youth team manager. George had ended his playing career at Palace at 32 suffering with an ankle injury before a short spell playing in the sun for California Surf. Now, for some reason, I have always got on great with Scottish lads with my two best friends in football, Joe Kiernan and Johnny Kurila, both coming from north of the border. George was no different, he was nearly 10 years younger than me but we got on straight from the off. Straight-talking, private and a very sharp football brain, we'd talk every day about football, coaching, the players we thought would make it and so on. Straight away we had a mutual respect and trust for each other which all management teams must have. George fed his trusted youth team lads to me and he knew I would look after them and help them along. I'd watch his sessions and people probably don't realise just how good a coach he was because he was such a successful manager. He was keen to help the lads, meticulous and detailed, a good communicator and very engaging.

In December 1982 George walked in to the coaches' room at Greenford with a mug of tea in his hand as I got changed on my own and he said out of the blue, 'I've just accepted the Millwall job, Theo, what do you think of that?'

I just laughed and said, 'They'll eat you alive, George.'

To which he replied, 'Well, I don't know why you're laughing because you're coming with me!' That was it, my interview and offer of a job all rolled into one and a partnership that lasted 10 years, with a fair few trophies, was born. It was a pivotal moment in both our careers and I was heading back to The Den.

CHAPTER 10
Strolling Back to The Den
1983 – 86

Maggie gets a second term beating a fragmented Labour party led by the left wing ideals of Michael Foot, who is then replaced by Neil Kinnock. CND march on London in protest at nuclear weapons and Gerry Adams takes on the leadership of Sinn Fein – weeks later Harrods and Oxford Street are bombed by the IRA. The Brinks Mat bullion robbery is pulled off at Heathrow with the best part of £26m never recovered. Unemployment tops 3.2m, a post-war high whilst initial plans are drawn up for a Channel Tunnel between England and France. Wapping riots at the new premises of Rupert Murdoch's newspaper headquarters as a global recession looms in the background.

England fail to make the Euro '84 finals as Maggie hits football hooligans hard with Wolves' Subway Army members arrested in one swoop. Liverpool dominate the top flight winning title no. 16 in '86. Argentina win the '86 World Cup in Mexico beating West Germany in the final as England exit at the quarter finals beaten by both the treachery and brilliance of Diego Maradona. Gary Lineker heads to Barca and Ian Rush goes to Juventus but gets loaned back to Liverpool.

Plans start on the development of the derelict London Docklands on the Isle of Dogs which gets financial benefits from an Enterprise Zone subsidy. The Docks are redeveloped, so it's claimed, with dirty money from criminals.

Good music seems harder and harder to find as the sounds blaring out from the kids' bedrooms does nothing for me. Stevie Wonder, Billy Joel and Lionel Richie are still releasing singles but not the standard of songs they once were. Pacino plays it over the top in 'Scarface' while Harrison Ford is still cracking his Bullwhip as Indiana Jones in his third outing. Tom Cruise fights Russian MiG jets in 'Top Gun' and Eddie Murphy plays namesake Axel Foley in 'Beverley Hills Cop', giving any future dressing room that I enter, a ready-made nickname.

I had been given youth team scout Bob Pearson's old Renault 18, another plain navy one and on account of Bob's heavy smoking habit, it reeked of fags all the time I had it, no matter how often I cleaned it.

Back to working near home again in South East London to The Den and the romantically named Cold Blow Lane, this time a little older and wiser. The club was probably in a worse position than when I'd left back in December 1977 and the old ground was definitely looking a bit worn around the edges. The big names like Kitch, Seasy, Tony Hazell and Ray Evans had gone but there were still some familiar faces like stalwart Billy Neil behind the scenes or 'wee Toodle' as I called him, the ex-player who basically ran the club as a general manager. Billy is yet another Scots lad I've always got on with, they really do make great football people, passionate and straight-talking which I've always identified with. Then we had former '77 player Roger Cross and wily Bob Pearson running the hugely successful youth system which was the envy of other clubs, constantly producing players and winning things.

The side was in big trouble when we walked through the old blue metal gates in December 1982, languishing rock bottom of the old Third Division. Kitch had briefly taken over the reins from Peter Anderson who finished ninth in his first season but the side struggled in his second season with a terrible run of 15 games without a win. It all ended in very strange circumstances for Peter as chairman Alan Thorne, not one for holding back, had suspended him and his assistant on a Friday before a home game against Wrexham. Alan was livid that Peter had dropped Alan West and Dave Martin along with two recent 'big' signings in Trevor Aylott and Sam Allardyce.

As a result, Alan asked Kitch and Roger Cross to take the

side on the Saturday and they managed to get a 1-1 draw with all four players reinstated after fitness tests. That was the final act for Peter who was told to leave the ground when he turned up at midday for the game. By all accounts he'd been uncontactable since announcing the side on the Friday which made Alan even more livid. Kitch took over for the next four games but it hadn't worked out so the job was linked to a number of names before George was appointed.

George told me recently that he'd been doing a training session at Loftus Road for about an hour, one day, as this fella in a suit watched from the stands. He just thought he was a visitor to the club but, as it turned out, it was Alan Thorne who had heard very good things about George so he wanted to see for himself. He introduced himself as the Millwall chairman, said he liked what he saw and would be in touch. Not long after we were walking into The Den wondering what we had let ourselves in for. Aside from the club's position we soon found out the boardroom was at war and that the chairman was threatening to shut the club if the crowd trouble continued (his windscreen had been smashed at a recent friendly at the ground). The club was losing money every week, gates were down and Alan's threats were very real with a huge overdraft keeping the club going in the background.

We had a good run through the list of players and decided to give the existing squad a chance to prove themselves but, after a couple of games, we soon realised the size of the job in hand. I'll never forget George working out what we needed in a meeting with the chairman who nearly fell off his chair when he was told we needed seven players or we were going down to the Fourth Division. We'd seen enough of the squad to know that we needed an urgent list of targets and a list of players to offload.

It was a big task for us both, and we had to be fairly ruthless, but with the club nailed on to go down, no one could really complain. The recent short-lived England manager, and back then a big name signing for the club, Sam Allardyce, didn't last long. George has never been one for reputations and, much like the Far East 'sting' recently, Big Sam didn't see it coming. Big centre forward Trevor Aylott, who was another signing made by Peter Anderson, followed Sam on his way out of the club. Trevor looked the part and had been successful at Barnsley before signing for Millwall, but his face just didn't fit down at The Den. On one occasion, after a game, in the Vice President's bar, one fan started tearing into him after a toothless display. Millwall fans just won't tolerate anyone not seen to be putting it on the line for the club and this fan told big, strapping Trevor to his face what he thought of him. Goalkeeper Paul Sansome, defender Paul Roberts and midfielder Austin Hayes were all moved on at various times as George made room for the new lads needed as we searched high and low for undiscovered gems.

The first two brought in were experienced goalkeeper Peter Wells from Southampton and a young full back from Crystal Palace, Steve Lovell. Lovers had been at Palace with George as a youth player and turned out to be a key player as we turned it around thanks to a masterstroke by George repackaging him as a centre forward. We agreed loan deals for both as a way of minimising costs while changing the squad at the same time before we eventually signed both on a free in the end. Then we picked up a player from Colchester to create a spark with the fans, Kevin Bremner, for just £25,000. Brems would literally run all day and through anything which the fans loved him for. One game he was on the floor after a tackle and as the defender went to kick it, he stuck his head there to block the ball. Tackling with your head is as good as a goal at The Den.

Then two of the best signings we made came from Essex side Southend United after watching centre back Dave Cusack and winger Anton Otulakowski. George, in his wisdom, decided to watch them in action from the terraces at Roots Hall thinking no one would spot him. Well, of course, he got plenty of stick as the Shrimpers' fans knew he was scouting for players. He didn't do that again. Cusey was a classy centre back, strong in the air and a great reader of the game, a snip at £30,000, while little Anton was as tricky as they come on and off the pitch, also £30,000. Ask any fan from that time and they would put both these two players in their favourite list I'm sure. Anton was a former gymnast who could run and literally trip himself up 'winning' so many penalties it was unreal. It's funny how you would go mad if an opponent tricked a ref but with the club struggling and in need of every bit of luck possible, we loved the little Polish gymnast when he did it.

We brought in Mickey Nutton from Chelsea, in March, for £60,000, a quick, mobile centre back perfect to play alongside Cusey and we swapped forward Dean Horrix with hardworking midfielder Dean White at Gillingham. We then used our old contacts to get reserve team winger Ian Stewart on loan from QPR. As mentioned in the last chapter, Stewy was a top player who went on to score that famous Northern Ireland goal in the 1-0 win over Germany in '82 but, as he found out one day, I didn't care how good he was if he didn't follow my rules in the car. I'd always objected to lads farting in my car and Burkey was one of the main culprits back at QPR slowly winding the window down and wafting it out because he knew I'd go crackers. It became a way of winding me up but this time I didn't see the funny side, although I laughed when Ian mentioned it recently.

We were heading to training from the ground, me driving a couple of lads, with Stewy in the back, along the Old Kent Road. Ian did this fart that stunk the whole car out. I pulled the car over and he was trying not to laugh while I turn around and tell him to get out of the car, swearing away at him. He thought I was joking at first, which made me even more angry, but soon realised as I was going wild at him. I ended up getting out of the car, opening the back door and dragging him out onto the pavement. By now, he knew I was deadly serious and was pleading in his Ulster accent, 'Aahh come on now, Theo, I have no money or anything.'

I told him, 'Bollix to you, I've told you before, don't ever fart in my car,' and drove off leaving our recently signed star winger on his own in a rough part of town. It turns out he had to walk back to the ground, grab his gear and head off to the train station. George got wind of it, no pun intended, after asking where he was and ended up driving after him to persuade him to come back.

He was not happy but he'd signed a loan deal so he was stuck with the wild coach. He ended up striking a deal with George that he would train with QPR during the week and then just turn up on matchdays to play. I was happy enough with that as he wouldn't be stinking out the car and no one ever farted again in my car. If you ever see that famous goal against Germany, or the photo of him after saluting the fans, think of him traipsing along Old Kent Road in his training gear and George driving round New Cross looking for him. All because of a fart but, as Stewy said recently, it was a belter.

Aside from problems in my car we were still in the shit in the league and from being rock bottom in the New Year we then went on a four game losing streak in March which prompted the flurry of more signings. No one gave us a chance, we were dead certs to go down. Then something just clicked and we won four on the spin with all the new lads, including fartarse Stewy, all playing in a new look side. Only three players had survived the clear out with left back David Stride, forward Dean Neal who we knew from QPR and midfield stalwart Nicky Chatterton. Experienced defender Lawrie Madden and dyed in the wool midfielder Andy Massey were kept, along with promising young lads Alan McCleary, Dave Martin, Nicky Coleman and a certain player by the name of Teddy Sheringham. In the last 13 games after that terrible run in March we won nine, drew three and lost just the one game. It was a remarkable turnaround. It was title winning form after hitting rock bottom.

That frantic period of rebuilding was the start of it all for us both, when George made his name as a manager who gets results and makes great signings. I know George is very proud of what we achieved at the coal face there with limited funds and hunting around for bargains. We ended up finishing in 17th spot having to win to be safe on the last day at bottom side Chesterfield. We managed to win the game thanks to a second half penalty from Cusey. We still did it the hard way as we were forced to play over 50 mins with 10 men having lost Dean White to a red card just before half-time.

Anyone who supported Millwall then will tell you, we were as good as down in March but we pulled off our first footballing miracle. Had we gone down into the old Fourth who knows how our careers would have panned out.

In amongst this relegation dogfight we had a side story that had been rumbling after early season progress under Peter Anderson in the Football League Trophy. The FL Trophy was a competition for a random group of two sides from the First Division, three from the Second, 13 from the Third and 14 from the Fourth. Someone at the FA must have had a heavy lunch one day then devised that format by the looks of it. It was only known for two seasons by that name before being called the Full Members Cup, so we were in an elite group.

The club had played three regional games at the start of the season beating Brentford and Crystal Palace but losing to Wimbledon. This was still enough to put us into a North/South one off game against Bradford City at home for our first game. We won on penalties and then beat Reading 3-1 away in the semi eight weeks later before drawing Lincoln City away in the Final at the beginning of April. Dean Neal, who I worked with at QPR, scored two and young defensive prospect Alan McLeary scored the third. We had Sam Allardyce playing in one of his last games for the club and a very young Teddy Sheringham on the bench along with Roger Wynter, both stars of the televised Indoor Soccer Six Wembley tournament the following year which we also won. At Lincoln that day we had the 'old guard' of Paul Sansome, Keith Stevens, Paul Roberts, Andy Massey, Paul Robinson and David Martin in a squad that had no fewer than ten homegrown players.

George played a completely different side to the 'League' side with all the new signings which gave these real Millwall boys the impetus to impress and win something for their club. It could have all backfired but, as was often the case with George, it didn't. It was a very strange competition but it helped unite the club and turned out to be our first trophy together as a management team. Of course, it was followed by some more prestigious ones later but it was no less important in terms of effect and significance at that time. It really helped lift the club, the fans didn't care as they just love to win against the odds and we were a struggling Third Division side. The win was three games into our unbelievable end of season run so in terms of our management partnership it was, as it turned out, probably our version of the 'Mark Robins moment' for Sir Alex before they went on the road to glory. The usual League players came back in with something to prove and we never looked back. Keeping the club up that season is, without a doubt, one of our best achievements as a management duo, just ask George. We now had some results to back us up for next season with more changes planned already.

With some breathing space between May and August 1983 after the miracle escape we worked tirelessly on issues off the pitch so we were in a better place for the start of the year. As I said at the start of this chapter, the club was in a worse situation than when I'd left in '77. The old ground was really tired and had fallen behind really in terms of facilities being up to date. The chairman had plans to redevelop the ground as a retail area with Asda but that fell through as he looked to unlock some money for the club from the space around the ground. He had an issue with the Cold Blow Lane entrance, wanting to make it more appealing. For those who remember the old route into the ground will know that the brick tunnels, the narrow roads and the wasteland car parks almost gave you a 1-0 lead before a ball was kicked. It wasn't a warm welcome for the faint-hearted but that was the charm of the place, it was a fortress for the club through the years especially on a cold winter's night.

George and I did agree, however, that we needed to improve some areas around the ground and set about bringing in new ideas to a neglected facility. I managed to persuade a local builder, Ollie McGuinness, to build a new gym/physio room as there was no such facility believe it or not. Ollie did it all at virtually no cost with plenty of his own money and it transformed the area giving players somewhere to have their rehabilitation, and the dressing rooms got a good makeover. He obviously had plenty of wood effect panelling as this went on the walls all over the place in real '80s style but it was great to have new areas that the players could use.

Then George had a brainwave on one of our many training sessions over at Woolwich Barracks after chatting to a couple of the officers there. He agreed with them that he would take the soldiers who were in a bit of trouble, for whatever reason, and set them up with paint and brushes to give the whole ground a facelift. He reminded me recently that he'd go and buy a crate of lager at the end of the week and they were happy as Larry to get away from the doghouse at the barracks and get some beers for their efforts. George chatted with them one day and, as we walked past, said, 'Great job lads, well done.'

He then walked in the dressing room and said, 'Theo, go and tell that lad he's not done those railings in the corner.' That was George, never missed a trick but I had been asked to pass on the bad news. They made a great job of the whole ground and, along with some new dugouts supplied by Paul Scally, another local businessman, the ground looked 100 per cent improved come August and the new season. To this day, there have always been strong links with the military at The Den and George had pulled off another masterstroke calling in a favour or two for nothing.

On the field we strengthened again signing Peter Wells permanently on a free as he'd more than proved himself, then a key signing in Stevie Lowndes from Newport County for £55,000. Lowndsey was an exciting, quick winger who had been part of the Newport side that reached the quarter finals of the European Cup Winners' Cup in '81 and was a recently capped Welsh international. He turned out to be a crucial player for the way we played, with him and Anton out wide supplying the balls for Brems, Dean Neal or, as it turned out, Lovers up front. George spotted something in Lovers that no one else had and convinced him in the second half of the season he could convert from being a full back as he had a lovely right foot and was strong in the air, good tools for a centre forward. Not many players manage that switch. Kevin Phillips is another who started life as a right back for Baldock Town before scoring goals all through his career as a pro. We had tried to bring in various forwards unsuccessfully including beanpole Ross Jenkins from Watford and Northern Irish international Bobby Campbell from Bradford, but we had one under our noses all along.

We struck gold with Lovers who cost us nothing at all. We shipped out five players including Big Sam, forward Bobby Shinton and Lawrie Madden to reduce the size of the squad and work with a core of 19 which really helped everyone feel part of the plans for the season. We also picked up the crackpot Burkey in October on loan from QPR to replace Stewy who went the other way as QPR wanted too much money for the flatulent winger. We looked like we had solved our attacking problems and preseason was going well as we now had more time to get our ideas across to our new squad. Our friendlies were disrupted, however, as we had to play all of our friendlies away while pitch improvements were completed. Then just to let us know that the old hooligan element was still there we had a reminder in a friendly at Kent side Tonbridge's ground.

There were a few arrests as fighting broke out and the game itself was a waste of time really as we won 7-0. Four other games that we'd planned had to be cancelled on police advice following the Tonbridge game so our plans were severely hampered. We also lost goalkeeper Peter Wells to a broken hand, picked up in a game at Braintree, so it quickly turned into terrible preparation for our first full season. That said, we were still much improved and were unlucky not to force our way into the top spots over the season but for a few poor results. The new lads settled in well with Cusey, Mickey Nutton, Brems, Anton and Dean White all featuring heavily. Dean Neal was still the main goalscorer and Anton picked up the Player of The Year as we ended up in a respectable ninth place.

That season saw the introduction of a highly talented young forward by the name of Teddy Sheringham who made a handful of appearances, mainly from the bench, even scoring a couple of goals. Anyone could see he had bags of ability, always seemed to have time on the ball and just a touch of class. For some reason though, and it happened with some other high-profile players, George saw something he didn't like and ended up sending him out on loan. Maybe it was Teddy's languid style and George felt that he didn't work hard enough but, let's not forget, George himself was known as 'Stroller' when he played. George can always say he gave him his pro debut, I guess, but I think Teddy ended up more than proving him wrong in a glittering career winning everything on offer. I think for that reason we have to put Teddy in the 'one that got away' folder. He wasn't the first though and wouldn't be the last to fall by the wayside and prove a manager wrong.

We were making real progress on the field and with a couple more players we felt we would be very close to challenging for the league. We were getting our ideas across well on the training pitch with a group of lads who were all hungry for success as they hadn't experienced it. They all knew the ethos of the team was hard graft, hunt in packs and attack with width and pace. Nothing too scientific but they knew if you were caught not putting a shift in you were out. We had a bit of a battle with Cusey over the season as there was talk of him going back to Southend as player-manager and he asked to go on the transfer list. Dave was a wily pro and his little Polish partner in crime, Anton, was no different, both active with the PFA at the time. George knew he had to deal with them a little differently or they'd have cried foul and have the PFA in without a doubt. As it turned out, they were good as gold and two of the best players we had at the club. Cusey elected to stay, thankfully, which was like a new signing for the 1984-85 season.

Off the field the chairman was still shooting from the hip about the Millwall 'fan problem' and trying desperately to get development plans off the ground to bring some money in as the club was in serious debt. He tried to get a community run sports centre and a separate shopping centre built, which would have been great for the club, but he faced stumbling blocks everywhere including gas and electricity diversions as well as council problems. To add to the problems, George had been hauled in front of the FA at the start of the season on disciplinary charges which he played down publicly in his usual way. We were never going to stop our side from being aggressive as it was a key feature of the team, besides this was Millwall.

Then, in May 1984, we made what George has since described as his best signing, in midfielder Les Briley from Aldershot. Trusted scout Bob Pearson had gone to a game to watch their lively forward Dale Banton and he came back to say he didn't fancy Banton but the lad Briley in central midfield was excellent. We checked it out ourselves and, sure enough, he was spot on. Les was just what we needed, much like Terry Brisley many years before. He linked defence and attack well, was aggressive, a leader and had a good range of passing. We stole him for £20,000, with Andy Massey going the other way, and he became the catalyst that season. We did more shrewd business getting ex-youth player Tony Kinsella back from Ipswich on a free, snapping up experienced centre back Lindsay Smith for his second spell from Plymouth for £17,500 and a last-minute swoop in August for left back Bill Roffey from neighbours Orient on a free. Bill became rhyming slang, soon after, for a coffee and used to need the widest shorts for his big strong arse but he was another excellent signing, very steady with a lovely left foot. From memory an American Football side wanted him to be a specialist kicker but they probably couldn't get pants big enough for his big old jacksy!

We were quietly confident with our carefully improved squad but managed to stay under the radar which was just how we liked it. Sure enough, we hit the ground running winning 13 out of the opening 23 games, losing only four matches. We were difficult to beat, awkward to play against, hardworking but dangerous and, in November, we signed a player who epitomised all of those attributes. John Fashanu, or 'Fash the Bash' as he became known, had played against us for Lincoln and we both felt he roughed up centre backs who would usually do that to the forwards. We signed John for £55,000 and, although he was raw in some ways, he won

171

a fair few points for us just by being impossible to play against, an absolute nuisance who was a skilled martial arts expert. I lost count of the times I saw him work the channel to chase a ball and whack his marker as he ran yet refs rarely booked him, they were probably too scared. We played Fash in most games and mixed up his partners depending on the opposition but usually always Fash as he frightened the life out of sides and he was very effective for us.

He was a lovely, bubbly lad too in and around the dressing room but not always the best trainer so we clashed a few times. Les Briley reminded me recently of the time we'd put on a shooting drill and you'd think Fash as a forward would love that but, no, he thought if he blazed his shot over the bar as far as possible, he could have a rest retrieving his ball. You can't kid a kidder so I'd just make him do some extra shuttles at the end, the big dope. Another time, we were doing some body work in the gym one day and I could see him stretching his back and hanging back. I shout over, 'Come on, Fash, in you get.'

He pulled a pained expression and came back with, 'I've got a bit of a strain, Theo.'

I latched straight on to him and said, 'Fash, do me a favour will you and get yourself in here.'

He carried on protesting and said he was off for treatment so I was now halfway to madness, raising my voice and swearing at him, as I walked over and, then, bang, he threw the red rag, leaning forward as he said, 'Why, what are you going to do about it?' Well, before I knew it I had him up against the wall and you could see he was shocked that someone would take him on especially giving a few inches advantage. The lads had to pull me off him which is probably just as well as I'm no black belt but I never had another problem from Fash, he even admitted he was taken aback in his book.

He damaged our nice new physio room too when the physio Joe Miller, or Joe the Crow as he was known on account of his limping gait, told him to piss off out of his room as he wasn't injured. Fash jumped off the treatment table and went to chin Joe, who was only about 5 foot 7.

Luckily for Joe he ducked, Fash punched a hole in the door, thanks to his martial arts power, and Joe scarpered to safety. Now, Joe was never the quickest getting out to an injured player but put a 6 foot 4 wild-eyed black belt behind him and he turned into Linford Christie!

On the field, we kicked on again in the new year going on a 10 game winning streak from February, and it looked like we would walk the league, but a patchier spell followed until a closing run of five wins and a draw from our last six games saw us finish as runners-up. Lovers, the converted full back, ended up as top scorer with 27 goals with both Dean Neal and Brems sharing second spot. Fash didn't score as many but probably bashed up 27 more centre backs than the others as we became a side to be feared. The core of the side was the same most weeks and that stability was a key part of our success. The resurgent Paul Sansome was virtually ever-present in goal behind Bill Roffey, Paul Hinshelwood, Keith Stevens, Lindsay Smith and Cusey at the back. In midfield we had skipper Les Briley and Nicky Chatterton in the engine room while Lowndsey and Anton were the skilful game winners out wide. Around the squad we had young players like Alan McCleary and Nicky Coleman pushing for a start. The core was only 15 or 16 though and it proved to be decisive as the side picked itself most weeks.

It would be remiss of me to talk about the 1984-85 season without mentioning the elephant in the room which had been the terrible scenes at Luton in the FA Cup. We'd had a great run in the cup that season which proved we had the side to cope with the better teams. We started off with a comfortable win on the south coast against non-league Weymouth before beating another part time side, Enfield, who had a very good side that year down at The Den. Then we drew local rivals Crystal Palace with a number of links between the clubs not least of all George who ended his career there. We drew at Selhurst Park before going through 2-1 at home, thanks to Les and Lovers, then we were pulled out of the hat to play Chelsea at Stamford Bridge. The rivalry between both clubs is huge and Chelsea were a top six First Division side and, in Kerry Dixon and David Speedie, had one of the best forward partnerships around.

The game was electric and the Chelsea fans gave Fash stick all game including some awful racist abuse but you'll struggle to find a mentally tougher lad. I won't go into all of it but it's the worst I think I've ever witnessed at a football game but he had the last word scoring our equaliser on the night. Steve Lovell had put us in front but Chelsea had gone 2-1 up through Nigel Spackman and Paul Canoville before Fash replied. Lovers then slotted home from the penalty spot with 20 minutes to go as we'd come to expect to put us in front but with three minutes to go they were awarded a penalty that would have made it 3-3. David Speedie stepped up but missed and the scenes at the end were unbelievable, I can still see the joy on the fans' faces and I'm sure George was secretly delighted to put one over one of his old clubs.

We then drew First Division side Leicester at home, with Gary Lineker and Alan Smith, a deadly pairing, up front. We kept them relatively quiet all game and beat them comfortably 2-0 with Fash and Alan McLeary scoring the goals to take us into the sixth round. I remember saying to George after the game that if we ever get a few quid to spend we should sign Alan Smith as he looked a top player that day. I can only assume Gary Lineker had a quiet game! We got drawn out of the hat to play Luton Town away, who were a good side back then under David Pleat, but no one predicted the terrible scenes on the night of the game. We were 90 minutes from the semi-finals and we really felt we could beat anyone in a one-off game. They had Mick Harford, Brian Stein, Ricky Hill and Peter Nicholas in their side, all good First Division players. We felt, though, that the two sides we had beaten in the last two rounds, Chelsea and Leicester, were better so why couldn't we win again?

The build up to the game was the same as any other but obviously plans were afoot to create chaos that night and undoubtedly the culprits were not all regular Millwall fans. I'm not saying that Millwall fans weren't involved because they were, but there were other fans from rival clubs who were there just to stoke up the fighting which was proved following details of the arrests made. Kenilworth Road, for those who haven't been there, is one of those old Football League grounds that sits smack bang in the middle of houses and shops with some turnstiles actually in the middle of a row of terraced houses. Luton, for some reason, operated a 'pay at the gate' policy instead of ticket allocation which is a recipe for disaster. The club had told Luton before the game to make it all ticket but they ignored the club's advice.

Throw in the fact that thousands of 'extra' Millwall fans were making the trip exceeding the usual home gate for an evening game, so an afternoon of drink was possible, and you had the perfect storm. We knew trouble was brewing as you get a feeling from the atmosphere in the build up and warm up on the pitch. We could see more and more Millwall fans filling the stands and just swarming around to the Luton ends, unopposed. Nowadays it just wouldn't happen as you'd have ticket allocations, police segregation to and from the ground and separation on the terraces with a police presence.

Well, as we know, the whole area around the ground was vandalised, the Millwall fans forced Luton's fans out of their own stands and they spilled onto the pitch even throwing missiles at Les Sealey in the Luton goal. The ref took the players off and George went out to appeal for calm which worked for a short while at least to allow the game to be restarted. As for the game, I couldn't tell you much other than Brian Stein scored and the players had to sprint off at the final whistle. All hell broke loose after the game as fans fought with police and threw anything they could get their hands on including seats ripped out of the stands. It was a black day for the club, and for football in general, and marked the start of a trio of terrible events with the fire at Bradford and then Heysel disaster within two months in what was a terrible season for English football.

We were embarrassed to have been part of it all and it really affected the club which had been trying to make progress. If nothing else that terrible period eventually heralded the improvement of football stadia, as membership schemes and pre-allocations came in and the management of fans in and out of stadiums changed forever. It still needed an avoidable and awful tragedy at Hillsborough four years later for things to really change. Why did it take these awful events for the authorities to take action? The hooligan problem wasn't a new one and, as ever, it mirrored the problems in society going back to the social unrest of the '70s.

Arrests were made on the night and on the days that followed as fans were identified from TV footage. Posters of offenders even appeared around the ground, complete with known addresses, which was not the smartest move by the club. One fella who was plastered around the ground made it into the ground one day, walked past the commercial offices and up the stairs to our offices where he found George sat behind his desk. Journalists had been turning up at his address knocking on his door and asking questions. He was not a happy man. George was definitely caught unawares and sat there until he'd calmed down, promising that they would take the posters down. The lad eventually left but not before throwing a few expletives in and pointing away and it prompted George to request that the door entry system was upgraded. This was life at The Den during those times. It was established afterwards that the game had been subject to organised hooliganism similar to the events that so upset Gordon Jago years before in the infamous Panorama programme.

It definitely knocked us off our stride a little in the league until we realised we still had a job to do and we needed to continue our good form in the league to get out of the Third Division. We were up already before our last game at The Den which we won 2-0 against Plymouth and, as the game neared the end, you could see most of the players edging to the right so they were closer to the tunnel a bit like a sloping snooker table. They had no chance as the whistle blew as the fans wanted to be part of the celebrations and took their shirts, their shorts, the lot. Fash shit himself as one fan cut his shirt off with a knife, probably instructed to by Joe the Crow. It was great for the fans and the club, the chairman who had put his hand in his pocket and for us as a team. George and

I enjoyed a nice few drinks afterwards, very satisfied with what we had achieved in two and a half seasons. The club was back in the second tier and we had a side more than capable of winning games in that league. Not many sides would fancy playing us in the Second Division that's for sure.

We added a few new faces without going mad so we were giving the side that got us there a chance in the Second Division. We signed a centre back from Lincoln called Alan Walker, who was tough as teak, and another from Lincoln who, like Fash, was physically very strong. We'd spotted Walks play against us and he'd caught our eye as an out and out defender who was powerful in the air and looked to dominate whoever he was marking. We eventually lost Cusey to Doncaster where he went as player-manager which was a blow and Lindsay Smith was 31 now and struggling with a few knocks. We had Mickey Nutton back from injury who was a classy, mobile centre back while young Alan McLeary was a great prospect but we felt, at 20 years of age, we would need to blood him into the side. We felt Walks was an important signing for us, filling Cusey's shoes, and we only paid £32,500 at a tribunal. He soon received his nickname after letting it slip he felt weary one day in the car on the way to training. That was it, he is still called 'Weary' by me to this day.

We then splashed out a bit for us in bringing Robert Wilson from Fulham for £57,500 who we hoped would bring some higher league experience, a few goals and good ability in the middle of midfield. We brought him in to play alongside 'Spam' Briley as Nicky Chattterton, who'd been a great servant in midfield, was now 31. Robert and Nicky ended up sharing duties alongside Les who was the mainstay in the centre of the park. Les made the transition from the Fourth Division, where we had signed him, to the Second Division look easy which is a rare quality. Paul Sansome was proving to be steady and reliable in goal, keeping Peter Wells out of the team and the Welsh duo of Lowndsey and Lovers were excellent playing in almost every game. Lovers was top scorer again that year proving the season before was no fluke and his defending days were long behind him. He even ended up playing up front with legends Ian Rush and Mark Hughes for Wales thanks to his goals for us.

Dean Neal had been moved on to Southend so we lost a number of valuable goals there and Brems moved on to Reading. We looked to Fash to chip in with a few goals and, thankfully, Robert Wilson did chip in with plenty of goals as we'd hoped. The decision to let Teddy go on loan was maybe a bit rash in hindsight as he could have made a really dangerous pairing with Lovers but George wanted us to play a certain way and Fash fitted the bill. Keith Stevens was as reliable and aggressive as ever as regular right back which are attributes that have made him a cult hero down at The Den. On the other side Paul Hinshelwood had made the left back shirt his own after a solid season in our promotion side. George had always recognised the need for a few out and out winners in his sides rather the odd one or two. Very few players over George's time at Millwall, Arsenal, Leeds or Tottenham have been what you'd call luxury players. It just didn't wash with George and a fair few players, good players mind, just fell by the wayside.

We lost Anton to injury for half of the season at the start and we definitely missed his bit of magic and ability to turn a game, never mind win a fair few penalties. We more than held our own that season though, finishing a very respectable ninth above some so-called bigger clubs with more money like Leeds, 'Boro and Sunderland. Our home form, as it normally was at the old Den or indeed still is at the New Den, was very good and pushed us up the league. My old club Charlton won promotion that year with the Wimbledon Crazy Gang and a very good Norwich side won the title. They spanked us 6-1 at Carrow Road, just before Christmas, and I was getting more and more frustrated as the goals went in. I started to shout and bollock a few and the Norwich faithful started giving me a bit of stick so I gave them a volley of abuse back. No doubt a few of them remembered the time I got involved in 'cushion-gate' when I was at Charlton so a couple of seat cushions start heading my way. The red mist descended again and I threw them back, not having learned from before. The linesman spotted me and the Norwich fans made sure the ref soon knew what had happened. I got sent off, much to the delight of the Canaries fans. Not only had I been humiliated by our performance but by myself too so I had to sit there and take the abuse, definitely not a career highlight.

We finished quite strongly again, which had become a bit of a pattern for our sides, and both the chairman and the fans seemed happy with where the club was heading. As usual, at the end of the season, I started to think about where we could improve and push for promotion next year but little did I know we would be moving to one of the biggest clubs in the land and I was to reach my professional pinnacle.

Chapter 11
Marble Halls and Heated Floors
1986 – 1990

Britain and France announce plans to construct a tunnel under the English Channel, the Wapping riots rumble on at News International, Rupert Murdoch's HQ. Mexico hosts the World Cup which is won by Argentina, captained by Diego Maradona who had scored one scandalous goal and one wonder goal in the 2-1 quarter final defeat of England – Italy hosted the 1990 World Cup won by Germany who beat England on penalties in a crushing semi-final defeat – Gazza shone and sobbed.

Black Monday '87 wipes £50bn off the value of shares on the London Stock Exchange sending the UK into a long period of recession. '87 storm wreaks havoc in the UK. Poll Tax introduced and demonstration riots occur as a result. Football identity card scheme is introduced for fans by the government to combat hooliganism. Sky TV airs for the first time in February 1989. IRA step up their bombing campaigns – Maggie looks to 'clean up' New Age Travelers and ravers with multiple arrests.

GCSEs replace 'O' Levels for 16 year olds at secondary school – the M25 is opened – Maggie gets a third term – AIDS epidemic becomes major concern at a rate of one person a day contracting the disease in the UK – the tragedy of Hillsborough Stadium occurs resulting in the tragic and avoidable deaths of 96 Liverpool fans in their FA Cup semi-final – perimeter fencing starts to come down.

My favourite Paul Newman returned to his old character 'Fast Eddie' Felson to team up with a young Tom Cruise as pool playing hustlers in 'The Color of Money'. Kevin Costner leads an all-star cast in the excellent 'Untouchables' and Axel Foley returns to Beverley Hills to give more people more nickname ammunition. Martin Scorsese's 'Goodfellas' goes down as a worthy successor to 'The Godfather'.

We were still listening to the old favourites on our Hi-Fi so still Diana Ross, Billy Joel, Stevie and Phil Collins but nothing new excited us. Paul was fully into something called House music in 1988 and the so-called 'Rave Culture' – the Berlin Wall comes down – Cold War ends – Maggie loses leadership of the Tory Party to John Major as there is a social uprising against the Tories. With this 'House' music continually blaring out of Paul's bedroom and his regular disappearances up town for the whole weekend, I tell Adrian's friend Ian Bishop of West Ham, 'He's definitely smoking that ecstasy, Bish.'

Arsenal gave me a Burgundy Ford Sierra which suited me fine punting round the M25 to London Colney or Highbury. I'm not sure David Rocastle appreciated my music on the stereo though, as we travelled in from SE London.

Unbeknownst to me, George had been in for an interview at Arsenal on the back of our success at Millwall but, by all accounts, they were interested in some big names in front of George like Terry Venables and, apparently, Alex Ferguson. Even so, George told me at the end of the 1985-86 season that he had a great chance of getting it but he was very cautious and told me to keep it firmly under my hat. Arsenal had been treading water under Don Howe for a while prior to his resignation after just over two years in charge. Don, who was a fantastic coach, had taken the job on from Terry Neill after his seven years in charge with some mixed results despite plenty of cup final appearances but just the one trophy picked up, the FA Cup.

Steve Burtenshaw had taken the reins temporarily from Don in March '86 and managed to get the club to seventh place in the table as Liverpool won the league once more. The club and supporters demanded trophies as it had been far too long, seven years to be exact, despite three consecutive appearances from 1978-80 in the FA Cup and a Fairs Cup appearance in 1980. Don will forever be remembered for introducing some fine young talent into the side like Paul Davis, Tony Adams, David Rocastle and Niall

Quinn. George knew all about the next group of young players coming through as he still had strong links at the club and he told me more than once that there was great scope to wake up the sleeping giant that was The Arsenal.

Now, to be honest, when he told me he was in for the hot seat at Arsenal I thought that was it for our partnership and I began thinking about staying on in some role at Millwall. Although we'd worked so well together I just assumed that George would team up with his old pal and former Arsenal captain, Frank McClintock who was manager at Brentford at the time. When I mentioned this to George recently he said the thought never crossed his mind and there was no way he would take anyone else as we made a great team. I'm so glad he did as I'm immensely grateful to George for taking me to both Millwall and Arsenal. We had the best of times together with huge success and highs in, what will always be, the pinnacle of my career.

George had come from a working-class background in Coatbridge to play for some of the biggest clubs, winning trophies and playing for his country. I had left a similar upbringing in Dublin to play in all four divisions, win promotions and have the privilege of playing for my country. Now these two Celtic working-class boys were to be placed in charge of the Mighty Arsenal with its marble halls and heated floors. Arsenal is football royalty, it really is. It was a huge thing for me, personally, and it still makes the hair stand up at the back of my neck when I think about Highbury. I have been lucky to work at some terrific clubs but Arsenal was something else. Anyone who has played for Arsenal, or worked there, will say the same, it really stays with you.

Peter Hill-Wood, the Arsenal chairman back then, offered the job to George and I can still remember the phone call he made to this day. George calmly told me that he'd accepted the offer and I was going as his assistant, assuming, of course, that I wanted to. There was no thinking time required, Arsenal was one of the biggest clubs in football, never mind English football, and they always will be. I said yes immediately, you dream about joining clubs like Arsenal,

Manchester United or Liverpool – teams that I grew up with as they held preseason visits to Ireland. George signed off with one piece of advice which was to stay in and not answer the phone until it was all announced. He didn't want anything leaked without the club announcing so I had to wait impatiently until I told anyone, apart from Sheila obviously.

We met up to run through the current squad seeing how we were set for the season. I had to keep telling myself these were now our players as they were household names, the likes of which we had never worked with. Would we be able to handle their egos? Would they respect us, two fellas just starting out really? Would they listen to our instructions? We needn't have worried as each one of them responded in the right way, they were hungry for success. Even now it impresses me, John Lukic in goal with defenders like Viv Anderson, Tommy Caton, David O'Leary, Kenny Sansom and a 20-year-old Tony Adams. Midfielders like Graham Rix, Steve Williams, Paul Davis, Stewart Robson and David Rocastle. Up front you had the North Bank darling, Charlie Nicholas, and Tony Woodcock. A side littered with internationals while we'd been hunting bargains in the lower leagues for four years. What really set George's eyes ablaze with excitement though, were the young lads coming through as well as Tony Adams, David Rocastle and Stewart Robson. He knew all about them, what they were good at, which ones would make it and when they would be ready. I knew then we were in good shape to build on.

We had two exceptional centre backs who were both 20 years old and who had broken into the side the season before, Tony and Martin Keown. Both aggressive, both excellent readers of the game despite their age, both very strong in the air and both quick enough, although Martin was slightly faster, whereas Tony was maybe slightly better on the ball. It was soon evident there was not much between them, but George was very clear and certain. He said Tony was born to be a captain and leader right from the start and boy, was he proved right. There was a South London boy named Michael Thomas who really excited me – he had the lot, pace, power and skill but was playing full back then. We both really liked his potential, we felt he could be as good as he wanted to be. His good mate, as they grew up together through local school football, was David Rocastle who was an exciting attacking midfielder. More of David later, who was the player I was closest to out of the many hundreds I worked with. I make no excuses for that as he was just one lovely boy.

Then there was the supporting cast, if you like, with midfielder Martin Hayes who had broken into the side and scored a fair few goals. Hayesy was a clever footballer and very underrated. There was a tall gangly Dublin lad who was very effective and as good on the deck as he was in the air, 20-year-old Niall Quinn. We had an exciting young lad called Paul Merson coming through, only 18 but had everyone talking as he had great feet, pace and an eye for goal. I had heard all about Merse from a relative of his who was a Millwall regular and he was always telling me to sign him. Tony Woodcock was still at the club but was struggling after a bad injury so we'd definitely need some young lads up front. Our notes at the end of the discussion were very positive. A very good 'keeper, six or seven international level, experienced players and eight or nine players, all about 20, coming through and ready to play. I went home with my head spinning with the possibilities of what we could do with this squad and George felt the same.

I will never forget the first session we had with the squad at London Colney, George and I speak about it often. We gathered the lads together after an introductory session and sat them down on the sunlit, manicured grass, explained who was doing what on the backroom staff and to just listen in for 10 minutes. George calmly explained, in his excellent way of communicating, what we expected of them all. As was always the way with George, he was very clear, there were no hesitations or wishy-washy instructions. No one was to call him George, as some remembered him from his playing days, it was to be Boss or Gaffer. We wanted everyone to stay and prove their worth, and everyone, including the younger lads, would get a crack. We felt the side had underperformed, given the quality, and we would not accept anything less than top levels of performance. You can sometimes see older pros roll their eyes and go 'here we go, the same old bollocks' but not this time. We were right, they had been treading water, some of them were nearing the end of their careers and the rest were young and hungry. Both old and young wanted to prove themselves. George finished with some simple instructions, he wanted to see 'wet shirts through hard work' at every training session and every game. Nothing less would do.

Players go away usually after these kinds of talks and mull it over. The older lads probably thought, can I raise my levels a notch or two and stay in the side or am I going to struggle? The younger lads probably thought, I've got a chance here, this fella is a straight shooter and he'll play me if I do well. Both of those reactions, in the main, occurred. They all responded well even if Charlie did call George by his name one day in the halls at Highbury. He didn't do it again and for all of his 'Champagne' image, Charlie was always very professional when it came to the football. We had no trouble with him whatsoever, a lively, bubbly lad and great to have around the place. There is a bit of a myth that George couldn't wait to get shot of Charlie but it's not true at all, Charlie was a key part of our first season.

We were giving everyone a fair crack, we'd have been stupid to get rid of players as there was so much quality already there. The first signing was a modest one with Perry Groves, a player we'd been tracking for some time since Millwall days, for only £50,000 from Colchester United. Colchester had another player we really fancied called Tony Adcock who'd scored bags of goals but they wanted too much money and he ended up going to Man City. Grovesy was as quick as you like, a constant threat out wide and stretched defences as they worried about his pace. He used to drive me mad in training, the little shite, as he'd whack me and then run around like road runner knowing that I couldn't catch him. Hardly one of the marquee signings of today but what a good value signing he turned out to be and great to have around the place, a real character.

Tony Woodcock was moved on after being told by George he would struggle to hold down a place and Martin Keown forced the issue with his contract. I walked back to the offices one day after training as George had told me to go and talk with him. Martin was waiting outside George's office so I stopped to ask him in but before I could say anything he said, 'I haven't come to fucking speak to you.' I could see he was obviously a bit stressed and had some things on his mind so I just left him to it as I knew where this was headed. George had already made his mind up on Tony over Martin so it would only end one way. Eventually, he sat down with him and, after George had laid his cards on the table, Martin explained that he wanted away. George and I were talking recently about Martin and the excellent career he had but do chuckle when he talks about Arsenal and current players' loyalties as he had asked to leave his beloved Arsenal rather than fight for the shirt!

For our first game, it was fine as we only had Manchester United at a packed Highbury so not exactly a big game! It was a wee bit different from our last game at The Den against Barnsley in only a matter of weeks. Charlie got us off to a flyer with the only goal of the game in front of 41,000 at Highbury in the blazing sunshine. It doesn't get much better than that, football Utopia. At Highbury they even had glass ornate dugouts that you could stand up in. To anyone who has sat in a dugout, and this was my office for 30 odd years, this was a luxury. These things were a work of art, white painted metal work and 360 degree clear view thanks to glass all around including the roof. Some wealthy fan probably has them in his back garden now, I suspect. At Highbury there was a real camber on the pitch too so at pitch side you lost the lower legs and the ball as players ran along the opposite touchline. Not ideal for watching but great for the pitch drainage.

The stadium and pitch were, in football terms, just perfect. The stands were famous listed art deco structures, with ends that were household names on all four sides. At either end behind the goals you had The Clock End where the away fans stood and the North Bank for the home fans, packed to the rafters for every game. The West and East stands were on both long sides and on two levels housing the corporate areas, bars, the offices, the dressing rooms, the dugouts and the paddock behind the dugouts. In the main areas of the East Stand were the famous marble halls. The main entrance was always manned by a commissionaire called Nobby, kitted out in hat and uniform like a posh hotel. Just inside the entrance you had legendary manager Herbert Chapman's bust as a constant reminder of past glories in the '30s. As you entered through the big front door, on the left you had all the offices and on the right was the big oak door leading to the dressing rooms and offices under the stands. Beyond the dressing rooms were the management offices, the physio room and kit room, all of it served with underfloor heating to go with the undersoil heating under the pitch. Now, I will generally adapt to any surroundings but this place was more like a hotel with the marble, the timber panelling and ornate fittings. It just felt too posh for football.

Whenever I coached at non-league grounds in later years when Paul played at Ramsgate or Greenwich Borough, I'd ask if we could leave the wet training gear on the heated floor like Highbury. It never got much of a laugh on those freezing wet winter nights but it seemed a shame not to mention it. I tried to treat Highbury like normal on the outside while inside I was blown away every time I walked through the halls. You walked down a small number of steps to the narrow tunnel under the stand then back up to the pitch, packed with fans on a matchday. I'd take the lads out for a warm up before a game and just soak up the atmosphere on the pitch.

One of the drills I did every week was to take a few balls out to the flanks and cross balls for John Lukic to pluck out of the air and then have a few close-range shots to make sure he was warmed up and ready to play, always in front of the North Bank. Now, at some point, I'm not sure when, a few fans started singing out, 'Theo, give us a ball, Theo, Theo, give us a ball.' I couldn't believe the famous Arsenal North Bank were singing my name, so of course I played to the crowd and smashed a ball into the packed end. This happened every home game from then on and became our little pre-match ritual during my time at the club. They never took the piss and always threw the ball back. I doubt Bouldy would be allowed to do it now though without some clearance from The Head of Footballs, or similar, signing it off.

That first side we picked against Manchester United was very different to how it ended the season with players like Stewart Robson and Graham Rix in midfield, Quinny up front with Charlie. By the end of the season Stewart had gone and Rixy was out injured whilst Grovesy and Merse had edged in front of Quinny. We started the first half of the season really well, having won 15 and drawn six out of the first 24 games in the league. I remember every week when George and I would have our regular catch ups, we couldn't get over how good things looked. We expected it to be much harder without being flash about it. At Millwall we'd needed to duck and dive, constantly work at fine tuning the squad until we got to be a serious Second Division side. Here, we'd been given the raw materials at the start, we'd changed a few subtle things, worked the lads hard and we were getting immediate results.

In November we were top and we actually started to think we could win the league the more the season went on. We were right in the mix and the side was settled and picking itself now. Steve Williams and Paul Davis were the regulars in central midfield and as good as you could wish for. Out wide we had young lads David Rocastle and Martin Hayes who were perfect for how we played our pressing game and attacking out wide when the ball was turned over. The back four of Viv, David O'Leary, Tony and Kenny Sansom is as good as any Arsenal defence, before or since, and John Lukic was already one of the best 'keepers in the league. Up front was probably the one unit that needed some improvement as we weren't quite prolific enough but we had some targets in mind. No sooner had we even considered going on to win the league than we were brought back to reality with some poor results and we fell away.

We had two good runs in the FA Cup and Littlewoods Cup losing to Watford in the quarter final of the former whilst drawing North London rivals Tottenham in the semi of the latter. We lost the first leg at home, thanks to my old QPR forward Clive Allen netting the only goal of the game, so we had to go to White Hart Lane to win and force a replay. We managed to win 2-1 in the second leg thanks to goals from Viv and Quinny in response to another goal from Clive. We were then required to play another game at White Hart Lane in a replay. Now, whenever I speak to Arsenal fans from that time they mention this game as much as any other. We weren't expected to win and the atmosphere was unbelievable that night, both of my younger sons, Sean and Paul, were in the away end. Clive scored yet again and we managed to pull one back from squad player and substitute Ian Allinson. Towards the end of the game David Rocastle sent the fans wild with a late winner squeezing home a rebound under Ray Clemence from close range. Both goals were at the away end and I can still see the whole end bouncing at the whistle with celebrations that went on for ages afterwards. This was to be a key moment, as it turned out, and it is fitting that it was David who put us into the final.

David is one of those rarities who unites opponents and teammates alike. It's no secret how much he was loved by everyone at the club, the fans, the employees, the players, you name it. Straight away I found him to be this lovely friendly South East London boy with impeccable manners and always smiling. When I found out he lived locally, as he came from nearby Brockley, I used to get him to head to our house and travel in every day with me to training and games. He'd sit in the front room, never late and waiting patiently chatting to Sheila or Paul who would be on his way to school. The lads at Arsenal soon spotted that we got on great and started ribbing the pair of us saying that I never dug him out, that he was the 'son of Theo' and so on. They were probably right, I never had cause to dig him out, he had bags of talent, a huge heart and never ever went missing in games, he was my kind of player. As Paul Davis said recently, he was just a special person David, everybody loved him.

We were in a Wembley Final in our first season and the club was clearly hungry for success and the fans were delighted to have some potential glory. We had Liverpool though, the best side in the land for many a year, on a beautiful, sunny April day. There is nothing better than a Wembley Final and I've been lucky to be involved in a few at the old stadium. They're great occasions, the suits being measured up, the preparation, the hotel stay, the coach journey in with all your family going to support you. The adrenaline is flowing and the day just flies along. This was our first Wembley appearance as a management team but it just felt right. We were kitted out in immaculate Aquascutum Club Blazers, trousers and shirts all as you would expect of Arsenal. George, who is always immaculate, knew exactly how we should be turned out and we looked like winners already.

We were playing in our famous red home colours with Liverpool in their change kit of white. The game is a bit of a blur and, after Ian Rush had scored, you felt that the remarkable record of Liverpool never losing when he scored would continue. But up popped Charlie with two of the scrappiest goals you'll see to win a final, the winner taking a deflection of my old mate Ronnie Whelan after Grovesy, on as sub, had set him up following a blistering run down the left. I don't think the ball hit the back of the net as Grobbelaar was wrong footed and it barely trickled over the line. Did we care? Did we bollocks. It was meant to be Rushy's emotional farewell before he headed to Italy having signed for Juventus who loaned him back for the season, so we spoiled those plans.

It's a closely guarded secret for years but I recall watching Ian Rush for Chester as a skinny whippet of a player in the late '70s when I was with QPR. The general gist of my report was that he was very quick, a bit lightweight and just okay. Thankfully, someone at Liverpool saw the real Rushy who went on to be one of the best goalscorers of all-time. What do I know? Imagine Clive Allen and Ian Rush up front? It would never have worked as they'd have run out of balls for their hat-tricks.

Not for the first time, as it turned out, we ended up ruining the Liverpool party. The trophy was the first at Arsenal for eight years since Alan Sunderland scored his famous winner in the FA Cup in '79. The club was able to puff out its chest again and dare to dream a little. You could really feel the lift around the place. We were delighted, a cup win at Wembley, a quarter final in the FA Cup and a fourth place finish in the league. Hayesy was top scorer with 26 goals in all competitions, a great return for someone who played most of the time wide left, even if he did take all the penalties. Tony Adams capped a fine first full season and won the PFA Young Player of the Year which was thoroughly deserved. Not bad for our first season and we knew where we could improve the side so we got busy once more lining up players.

We were a little concerned about both full backs, Viv and Kenny, not in terms of their performances but they were both around 30, Kenny just under and Viv just over. They were still on top of their game but George knew players inside out and he knew they would be looking for a good deal to see out their best days at the club. Both had enjoyed excellent seasons and were big characters at the club, we certainly didn't want either to leave. In my view, Kenny was up there with the best in the world at the time at left back and Viv was one of the best right backs in the league so we'd be mad to just let them go.

Kenny had his demons even then, and is tackling them very publicly now, but his performances in those first two seasons for us really set us on the way. I can remember Rixy and Kenny betting on anything, and I mean anything, on the coach, it could be a raindrop reaching the bottom of the window first, you name it. At the time Kenny was captain of England and Arsenal but I think he only drove a Montego which may have had something to do with his gambling. I have nothing but good things to say about Kenny though, a bubbly chirpy South East Londoner who was a top professional, leader and winner on the pitch. I wish him well on his battle with addiction, I really do.

We'd been watching a young full back at Wimbledon, Nigel Winterburn, and he was perfect fit for us. Nigel was very mobile, tenacious, good energy and good going forward. Okay, he was very one footed and his right foot was a 'swinger' but he had a lovely left foot so he ran around the ball when he needed to rather than use his cheddar slice. We paid £350,000 for him which raised a few eyebrows at the time and he didn't play for a while, signed as cover for both full backs really despite his one footed preference. When you study it now he was a hell of a signing, playing over 400 games for the club and getting capped for England. As we feared, we lost Viv to Alex Ferguson's new look Man Utd which was a real blow, we tried desperately to keep him but he'd already made his mind up. We started the season with young Michael Thomas at right back, who was more than able, but you could tell Mickey didn't really want to play there. Nigel had to play in the ressies and bide his time, not making his full debut until the new year in a similar way to how Liverpool used to blood new signings and stick them in the reserves.

Next was the main problem area, as we saw it, up front. We had Merse coming through but he was probably still not the finished article and two lads in the youth system, Kevin Campbell and Andrew Cole, but neither of them really ready for a lengthy run. Quinny was young and raw back then but showed definite flashes of the quality that he later displayed at Sunderland and Man City. We felt we needed another option to play with Charlie, Merse or Hayesy and we now had a few quid so we returned to the player I'd told George to sign at Millwall, Alan Smith. We actually signed Smudger the season before, costing the club £750,000 which, for George, was a huge fee but we both knew we'd signed a top player. Leicester were reluctant to part with Smudger having lost Gary Lineker two seasons before so we struck a deal to loan him back for the rest of the 1986-87 season. Again, we saw all of this squad building along the lines of the Liverpool way creating cover for positions and blooding players into the 'Arsenal' way and more importantly, our way. It was all strategic with planned targets rather than the quick fixes you are expected to secure now. It was definitely a healthier environment to grow sides back then.

We also picked up a bargain buy from Watford, in the summer, in Kevin Richardson for just £200,000. Richo had won the lot at Everton playing in a host of positions and he was a hell of a player for us, anyone who thinks otherwise is talking out of their jacksy. Kevin was a manager's dream who could do a job in two or three positions and do more than a job too. He was still young and we saw him as a long term replacement for Rixy, who was picking up a few injuries, and Kevin could also cover more than one position. I had a lot of time for Kevin who became a key player in the short time he was at the club, the very definition of an unsung hero. Ask any of the lads who played with Kevin what he was like, as they knew better than any. No fancy stepovers or tricks just a very accomplished and smart footballer. Halfway through the season we signed Lee Dixon for £375,000 from Stoke, another we'd watched plenty and knew would fit into the side ethos. George always talks about the time he met Lee in a service station on the motorway and how hungry he came across to work hard and succeed. His Stoke defensive teammate, Steve Bould, followed soon after for a similar fee of £390,000. Bouldy was different class, one of the best around and what a snip. These players we were picking up, with the exception of Kevin maybe, were all starved of success and willing to work their bollocks off to get there. We didn't want the players who'd been there, seen it, done it; we wanted players that craved success. In Grovesy, Nigel, Smudger, Lee, Bouldy and also Kevin, we had bags of desire and willing.

Towards the end of the season we made another crucial signing in Brian Marwood from Sheffield Wednesday for £800,000, as Hayesy was missing games through injury. Brian was another who had impressed, caught our eye with his old-fashioned wing play and crossing which would really suit Smudger or Quinny up front. Brian completed the sixth signing since taking over as we quietly set the side up for the following season with one eye on some ageing players in Kenny, Rixy and Charlie who might join Viv, Martin Keown and Stewart Robson and move on. As a management pair, I would be close to the lads and try to get a 'feel' for how happy they were, if they agreed with what was being asked of them and so on. In a way you are the front-line counsellor and it isn't a sneaky way of obtaining information, it's just what you have to do. You are acting as a filter, as they'd tell me things they'd never tell the Ayatollah, as they called George in private. George only needed snippets to come to a decision and we both knew footballers inside out. It worked well, we were often described as Fire and Ice by players. We felt well set-up for the season throughout the squad with plenty of cover patiently biding their time and plenty of versatility.

We started the 1987-88 season a little patchy but with Liverpool at home then Man U and QPR away it was a tough start. Then it clicked in a 6-0 thumping of Portsmouth at Highbury with Smudger getting a hat-trick in only his third game. We drew the next game away to Luton then went on an amazing 14 game winning streak as things just started to fall into place. There were four League Cup wins in that run but derby wins over Wimbledon, West Ham, Charlton and the big one, Tottenham, at the Lane. Things were going far too well again as we raced to the top of the table then we had a shocking November and December only recovering by the end of January '88 which killed off any chances we had for the League. As for the season before we had reached the Quarter Final of the FA Cup losing to Nottingham Forest this time and we also reached the Final of the Littlewoods Cup again, beating league title holders Everton over two legs 4-1. This win really made people sit up and was a sign of things to come, as Arsenal were a force once more.

Quinny was being used less and less due to Smudger's form and David Hillier reminded me recently of a midweek game we'd arranged with a Charlton side at Welling United's ground at that time. I took a mixed side of first teamers and young lads with Niall on the bench as we might need him at the weekend with the first team. After an early injury he had to go on but was moping around clearly unhappy at having to play on a cold night for the reserves so I ended up taking him back off. This made him even more pissed off and we had a 10 minute slanging match in the dressing room after the game, all these young lads looking at their boots until I snapped and said, 'Let's take this outside.' Not for the first time, I was giving a few inches away in height and reach but Quinny decided not to take it further. I ended up buying all the lads a drink in the bar including the big ole Dub and we buried the hatchet. I told him he'd shown better aggression in the dressing room so I'd report back to George positively. He got me back one day rugby tackling me on the training ground, the crafty bugger.

That fine win over Everton in the semi-final was soon forgotten in the Final against Luton Town as we lost 3-2 in 'one of those games'. Never mind it 'just' being the League Cup, this defeat ranked up there with the relegations at Northampton and Charlton and the defeat to Spain in the '66 World Cup. It stung like hell and I didn't want to feel that way again, I'm a terrible loser for days on end. There were nearly 96,000 people there watching on another glorious sunny Wembley day at the old stadium. We were in good shape, possibly better in some key areas than the season before, but we had lost David O'Leary to injury before the game and we pulled in young Gus Caesar to play centre back. This was to prove a critical factor in how the game went, unfortunately.

We should never have lost, no disrespect to Luton, we were the better side and we were coasting at 2-1 through Hayesy and Smudger after Brian Stein had put them in front. Then David got fouled in the box for a penalty which would have made it 3-1 and been game over. Now, Hayesy used to be the penalty taker but hadn't played much that year so Mickey Thomas was the designated penalty taker but he'd missed the last penalty. Who grabs the ball? Silly bollocks Winterburn. God knows why, he'd never taken a penalty before and everyone knows left footers don't make good penalty takers. Inevitably, his effort was saved by stand-in 'keeper Andy Dibble, it's all so football clichéd looking back now. Gus then made a mistake at the back as the last man getting caught in two minds to clear it, allowing Danny Wilson to equalise and then, sure enough, Brian Stein scored the winner in the last minute. If Gus is reading this he still owes me a few quid in bonus payments, but then so does the little shit Winterburn!

In the month leading up to the final George fell out with Stevie Williams. I remember discussing it a few times with George and putting the case forward for Willo to play, especially in the final with the big wide open spaces of Wembley and Steve's excellent passing range. George was not for turning once he'd made his mind up though, and he rarely admits an error, but he will openly admit these days that Steve should have played that day as his class would have told in a big game. We finished sixth in the league in a season that showed real promise but ended in disappointment. The title stayed in Merseyside, this time the red half and the disappointment of the final and our falling away in the league really helped the hunger of the side the following year.

The squad had really settled down, all the bigger names like Charlie, Viv, Kenny, Rixy and now Willo had all been moved on. We had no big stars now but we had a talented, hardworking, hungry side full of legs. No one was ever carried, no one just got by in games. Everyone always thinks their team has the best atmosphere, something I always ribbed my eldest for; he played for stacks of non-league clubs and every single one had a 'great set of lads'. But we really did have a special bond, not one 'egg' as madcap Burkey would say. It was part of my job to keep the spirit going and keep things light so nicknames were thrown out to those that could either handle it or needed a bit of stick. Now, anyone who knows me knows that once you've got a nickname, that's it for life.

John's was simply 'Lukey' so a bit unimaginative but they're a funny old lot those goalkeepers so probably for the best really. We'd stay at hotels and he was always disputing something on the bill saying he didn't have what had been charged against his room. Lee Dixon was usually called Dicko or Son of George by everyone else as he got on so well with him. He got christened 'Wiggy' by me as he had that sort of hair that flew in the wind. I don't think he was too keen on it and it looks like he has more hair these days on the box.

Nigel escaped a piss-take name as Nigel is bad enough, I guess, so 'Nutty' or 'Nidge' was as bad as he got. Tony was the skipper but he still got one and 'Rodders' from Only Fools and Horses was a pretty good match. O'Leary was imaginatively called Paddy, not by me I might add, he got a respectful bye from me. Similarly, David Rocastle was always David to me, not Rocky. Mickey was too tough to dig out so we all left him alone and both Richo and Davo were never going to be the types to bite so they were left alone. Hayesy was christened Albert Tatlock after the old Corrie character as he always looked miserable as sin, old before his time was Hayesy.

I don't think Merse would have noticed if we'd given him a nickname so he dodged that bullet. Smudger had a special one after coming off one game because of a muscle twinge, saying in his Brummie accent, 'I've got a spasm, Theo.' That was it, he got called Spaz for ever more which drew some funny looks and was probably misunderstood by most. Grovesy was just the little shithouse or Ginger bollocks, not much thought went into those. One of my favourites was for a young 'keeper at the club called Alan Miller who went on to play for Middlesbrough and West Brom. I called him Maxie every day, I bet he'd never even heard of the old Music Hall cheeky chappie Max Miller but we laughed about it recently. New signings Brian Marwood and Steve Bould escaped any nicknames for a week or two before I christened Brian 'Bumsy' on account of his big wide arse. Bouldy gave a look if you dug him out and was definitely not one to wind-up so he didn't need cutting down. He was wild as a badger especially after a beer or two. It's important to have this environment though giving some common ground with all the different characters in a dressing room. It can be a brutal place to be but always a great laugh. Some lads would be prime targets for getting cut down as they were just too lively, like Grovesy or Nigel, and then others, like Davo or Richo, would just sit back and take it all in, never biting. Every day was a blast though, I loved going to work.

I mentioned two lads earlier who were coming through the ressies and scoring for fun, Kevin Campbell and Andrew

Cole. Kevin was a year older and a real physical player with pace, power and an eye for goals. Andy was very slight, lightning quick and deadly in front of goal. They were chalk and cheese players and different off the pitch too, Kevin very outgoing whilst Andy was a wee bit quieter but had that self-belief forwards have. We knew all about both of them and had really high hopes for them at the club. I had a £50 bet with Kevin every season about how many he'd score and every year I'd kiss goodbye to a nifty as he took it off me laughing away.

I've heard all sorts of rubbish about Andy who was never any trouble at all, I think he just wanted to play in that single-minded way that forwards need to have. George, as we know, was not one for changing his mind and after one particular chat George decided to let Andy go. He went out on loan to Fulham and then Bristol City where, of course, he scored quick goals attracting interest from Newcastle. He then went on to become one of the best goalscorers in Premier League history winning the lot so I'd say this was big mistake number two made by us, well, George, to go with Teddy at Millwall. Both went on to win the league at Man Utd many times over and both featured in that remarkable treble year in '99. Unbelievable really, we let both of them slip through our hands but I'm sure they aren't too fussed.

We had the squad we had worked hard to create, the best we had ever worked with and we felt good about the season. We had been at the club for two whole seasons and had made our plans clear for the squad so each player, new or old, knew what was expected of them. It sounds obvious but it is not always the case judging from how some sides are sent out. I hear the phrases DNA and identity now which is well and good but in simple terms it is giving everyone a clear role. This is what we expect of you in the team, if you can provide anything additional without upsetting the overall team objectives, great but make sure you do the basic role well. None of the players that year were in doubt due to continued drills, sessions and countless discussions during training when George or I would stop and explain over and over. No areas were left open to interpretation. For some players wanting to express themselves, with varying results, this type of management would not work but for this hungry and willing group, they believed in the objectives and they believed in George.

People talk about the famous Arsenal back four and the clinical effectiveness of the unit, even making its way into the brilliant Full Monty film. There are no wonders of coaching or innovative methods to detail, just very good and very clear instructions. We worked so hard on game situations, breaking them down into sessions repeated to the point of autopilot reactions at the risk of driving the lads to distraction. If you ask the players now I'm sure they'd say it was boring as hell to go through but I bet they never get bored of looking at their medals.

Take throw-ins, for example, how much can you coach about a seemingly basic part of the game? Well, think about how many times a ball goes off in a game, where it goes off changes the objective both with and without the ball, what are you looking to achieve? Do you want to get the ball under control and down to play or do you want to progress further up the field? Do you want to create a goal scoring opportunity, or prevent one, so which players are to be involved around the ball and so on? It became a routine to work on every week to the point of groans from the players but they knew as soon as the ball went off what was to be expected. Nothing was to be off the cuff and if they didn't do it on a Saturday they got an almighty bollocking alright and they didn't do it again. These days, it's quite obvious to me that this type of coaching is not being followed as other aspects are considered more important. That's fine if you want to leave yourself open to chance but we didn't subscribe to that school of thought and it worked.

We entered into the season, therefore, with a clear coaching philosophy and a carefully selected squad hungry for success. It was a very good side, don't let anyone kid you otherwise. The early signs were good as we spanked Fash and his Wimbledon Crazy Gang 5-1 at their place with Smudger getting a hat-trick. We had a little patchy spell before really hitting our stride in a run of 11 unbeaten games where the side picked itself which is a great feeling for a manager. In that run we played our rivals Liverpool twice in the first of five key games we were to have over the course of the season making our future and history forever entwined.

It always rankled George how you'd play out of your skin against them, win or lose by the odd goal, yet they never gave you any credit. That was just the Liverpool way, engrained at the club by Shankly and years of winning the lot. No one could be as good as they were and boy did it wind George up. He'd smile and accept the drinks in the boot room then come out swearing and steaming about, '...those bastards are up to their old games, Theo.' I'd chuckle to myself as George had a similar mentality, he wasn't one to offer credit to a rival but it just made us more determined to knock them off their perch long before Sir Alex famously said the same years later.

The core of the side was constant and if we got an injury say to O'Leary then Bouldy came in, if Davo was injured then Kevin Richardson came in. It wasn't a weakness to lose a player or two and, of course, you need to keep the changes down and get lucky over a season but anyone coming in would be very similar and they all knew the drills. There were no weak spots in the core squad of 16 and if you look at how many players were used that season and think of squad numbers now, it is incomparable. If we played in the League Cup, same side. If we played in the FA Cup, same side. You'd get sacked for overusing the assets now if you did that but I've never understood how players get tired if they play more than 40 games. The phrase 'winning becomes a habit' is well used for a reason, why lose momentum just to have a rest that you don't need?

Anyone who plays or is involved in a side that wins things will talk about getting in 'the zone' and it's true. It absorbs you on a daily basis, you look to the next game, think of nothing else, win that game and just go straight to the next. No dwelling on the victory or time for backslaps, just on to the next. Come December we were all in that almost meditative state just rolling over sides and expecting to.

Lukey was in fine form, I'd say the best in the league at the time. The back four was immense as a unit, be it O'Leary or Bouldy with Tony they were like a single unit at times rather than four separate parts. Much like my old Northampton side this was the bedrock for the team to achieve success. In midfield Davo was in and out with injury that year so Richo played more with Mickey in the middle and we had David on the right with Brian Marwood on the left as our wide outlets. Smudger and Merse were a dangerous pairing up front with all-round intelligence from Alan and a bit of magic from Merse. We had Hayesy, Grovesy, Kevin Campbell and Quinny to come in or off the bench but that was it. We didn't need any more.

We beat all the so-called top sides that year like United, Everton, Forest, Spurs and we were practically honours even with Liverpool. We never felt inferior, we were The Arsenal and the club had its pride back. We were flying and then Liverpool just hit their top gears, going on a remarkable run as we had a few poor results losing by the odd goal. It was heading for a dramatic race between the two of us but we were still in the driving seat. Then the terrible events of Hillsborough occurred in April as Liverpool pursued another League and Cup double. Many millions of words have been written about what happened that day, and the terrible injustices that followed, but it still strikes sadness to the core of me that people went to watch a game of football and, due to proven negligence, never came back. So tragic and so avoidable. It rocked all of our lads obviously, how could you not be affected? We were snapped out of that meditative state we were in, as this went beyond kicking a leather bag of air about, this was life. The season was put on hold, the clocks really stopped and Liverpool FC showed their class with Kenny being the ultimate symbol of dignified honour. The ball was taken away as a mark of respect.

It started again after a fortnight break in a strange atmosphere of whether it was right or not but it was generally agreed that the honourable thing to do would be to play. Liverpool picked up remarkably on the swell of emotion while we struggled after initially picking up two wins and we suffered a terrible defeat to Derby followed by a draw against Wimbledon, both at home. The atmosphere after the Wimbledon game was deathly silent, we looked a beaten side in the dressing room as we'd handed the baton to Liverpool. You start to entertain thoughts that maybe it's right that they win the league, for the club, for the fans, for the 96. Then from somewhere it kicks in and you find yourself going around rallying the side, snapping them back as best you can, convinced it wasn't over and managing to pull some enthusiasm from the depths of your character as well as theirs. Even if you don't fully believe it, that's just what you have to do. Never ever give up or why bother in the first place? George was bitterly disappointed too but said a few words, said it wasn't over, just a wee bit tougher now and we would prepare for one last go with no pressure of expectation.

The events at Hillsborough and the two week break meant the fixtures were rearranged and, just by chance, we were scheduled to finish the season away at Liverpool, pitting us against the top side in a strange twist of fate. It was a Friday night and it was a live televised game in the days before general games being on and the blanket Sky coverage. In short, this was a real one-off event and, as it turned out, one that will never ever be repeated. We had over a week to prepare for the game having played Wimbledon on the Wednesday the week before while Liverpool beat Everton in the FA Cup on the following Saturday. The week off definitely helped us to prepare for this one-off 'final' type of game but not to the point of an advantage as Liverpool were on fire at the time.

By the Tuesday in that final week we knew we had to win by two clear goals as Liverpool had wiped the goal difference winning 5-1 against West Ham. George was still very relaxed in the build-up, just ask anyone who was involved, and this helped keep the pressure off the lads. If I'm completely honest, I didn't give us much chance but I would never show that outwardly and there was always a small chance that we could pull it off.

George and I spoke about the game during the week a fair

few times, obviously. The first bombshell he dropped on me was that we would play with three centre backs and look to push on the full backs. We had literally only played that way a handful of times and we definitely hadn't spent hours working on it at the training ground as we did everything else. I was a little dubious but agreed we would need to push higher on John Barnes who really made them tick, so, in many ways, it was three at the back not five as many have claimed since.

George, who was great at coming up with counter tactics and game management, knew this would throw the Reds who may have expected all-out attack from the kick off. The second curveball was that we would not be staying over as he wanted to keep it lighter, to prevent the feeling of being on Liverpool's patch and being weighed down by their 'territory'. He kept talking about the Naked Ape by Desmond Morris and the rules of territory, which meant little to me, but I understood what he meant about not feeling like an imposter. This flew in the face of all preparation protocol as generally you wanted to be relaxed, in good time and have a good night's sleep. George wanted it to feel less of a big event with time to overthink so, again, he pulled a masterstroke even if it seemed risky at the time. It was all about the placement of pressure, lightening it on our side and placing it on their side. Pressure can do very strange things to even the most experienced footballer.

We travelled up early by coach and checked in at a local hotel for our pre-match meal and let the lads walk the journey off. The papers were full of reports about us having no chance including the now infamous article on the back of The Mirror with Graeme Souness saying it was a 'waste of time' for us to even consider winning. All of this added to the siege mentality and gave another shift in the balance of pressure. If the experts didn't expect us to win then we had nothing to lose. As the opening chapter details, pressure can make human beings act in unusual ways and it definitely played a large part in the outcome that night.

We boarded the coach again, feeling recharged and headed to the ground in good spirits. At the ground, George went through the game plan in his usual clear, calm way and you could see a few strange looks when he confirmed the side again. Tony on the left, David O'Leary in the middle of the three and Bouldy on the right. Martin Hayes was the unlucky one dropped from the last game and put on the bench with Grovesy. Now, people don't believe me when I say the game went exactly as George predicted but it really did. He said as long as we kept a clean sheet and kept them quiet we would get a chance in the second half and if we scored they'd panic. He said that the game could be won in the last 15 minutes. The lads probably thought we were crackers but he had me believing it by now and you could see they felt some assurance of what was expected.

Ken Friar arranged for bouquets to be taken out by each player at the kick off to hand to Liverpool fans which was a typically classy Arsenal gesture which the home crowd really appreciated. It was only right that we acknowledged the Hillsborough '96 victims and it just diffused the situation by addressing it so we could settle down to the football side. I'd like to think that this formed a unique bond between the two clubs that exists to this day as there was a mutual respect on and off the pitch that night. It never felt nasty or disrespectful on both sides, including in the dugout where my old mate Ronnie Moran was sat with manager Kenny Dalglish.

The game plan worked a treat with it being goalless at half-time which George reassured the lads in the dressing room, was perfect. He said we could now be more expansive and apply more pressure as the game wore on and, sure enough, Smudger scored early on in the second. He glanced on a left foot inswinging free kick with the faintest of headers from a Nigel cross. Liverpool captain Ronnie Whelan had given away a foul for the free kick for the goal prompting David Rocastle to respond with a pumped fist to get the lads going. Thinking about it, what with the Littlewoods deflection in '87 and the build-up to our first goal in '89, Ronnie has been a great Dub friend to me.

Grovesy came on for Bouldy and Hayesy came on for

Merse as we injected some fresh legs and pace for the second half. We had a couple of half chances including a really good chance in the box for Mickey but he poked his effort with his right when he should probably have gone with his left. Then, with seconds on the clock, Mickey famously did what Mickey does best and created history with his right foot flick past Grobbelaar. Cue pandemonium on the bench, me whacking my head on the top of the dugout and then George telling us all to calm down and sit back down. Calm down? That was impossible. The message went out to the lads too and Tony made a great challenge on McMahon before Mickey rolled it back to Lukey as they sent their last cross in. One long punt downfield and Steve Nicol just runs the ball out as the ref blows for full time. That's it, all over. We'd only gone and won it.

George and I embraced each other, there were hugs all round, stacks of emotion and uncontained joy. Brian Marwood, Paul Davis, Kevin Campbell, Niall Quinn, Alan Miller all in their club blazers supporting the lads on the pitch, all part of it. Then you gather yourself, gather your emotions to shake hands with Kenny, Ronnie and Roy Evans. George was so calm still while we're all going mental, I think he was just in shock and couldn't quite believe it, always wanting to be in control of the situation. The events on the pitch after are just a blur, the away end was bouncing, there were all sorts of people on the pitch, it was chaos. We paraded the trophy and the Liverpool fans stayed to clap us off the pitch which blew me away, a really classy gesture amidst all of that emotion and disappointment.

We finally got to the dressing room, champagne laid on by Kenny being sprayed and drunk all over the place, non-stop singing and we eventually got back on the coach surrounded by fans all the way home. We ended up near the ground in a bar called Winners, from memory, with a load of fans, drinking through the night side by side. I don't remember much after the game but I remember getting back to the ground in the early hours and there were fans in the street singing and dancing just as depicted in the Nick Hornby film Fever Pitch. The goodwill extended to the local police force too as I'd attempted to get into my car in my stupidity and the local bobby spotted me, saying, 'Theo, I'll take you home, best you leave your car there.' I bumped into the same PC not long ago and we shared a laugh about it now. Thank God he was looking out for me that night.

At some point, I don't know when, I'd agreed to appear on TV-AM in the morning so after only a couple of hours' sleep and still half drunk, I was ferried to the studios at Camden and propped up on a chair. I have no idea what I said or how I didn't throw up but I think I managed to get away with it with plenty of make-up to cover my white-faced pallor. The parade through Islington was hastily arranged as no one actually thought we'd win and it was mobbed. It had been a long period of 18 years since the last league win and grown men were in tears kissing and hugging us all. That was the day that a new Arsenal was born no matter what the club then went on to achieve with Arsene Wenger and his remarkable sides. We had halted the mighty Liverpool, we'd done it with homegrown lads, some key signings, hard work and tactical knowledge. The club had its pride back.

How do you follow that the next season? That's the mark of true champions like Jack Nicklaus or the Liverpool sides of the 70s and 80s, to keep on winning and keep up that desire to win. We felt the squad was in good shape, we had Kevin Campbell pushing to start as a replacement for Quinny who had departed for Manchester City. We signed Colin Pates halfway through the season as cover at the back and midfielder Siggi Jonsson from Sheffield Wednesday but he had a terrible time with injuries and, both Colin and Siggi for example, hardly played. It was a strange season as we weren't far off with the side, just maybe a couple of signings like Liverpool used to or Man U did in their dominating period. We finished in fourth position long before it was a Champions League spot as Liverpool bounced back to win the title beating Aston Villa and Spurs above us.

It was during that season that we had an unsettling situation regarding the goalkeeping position and I'm certain this was the beginning of the end for George and I, although he denied it recently. George really fancied signing David Seaman at QPR and was looking to pay £1m for him as well as John Lukic in exchange. I didn't agree with him on the deal as Lukey had been exceptional since we'd joined the club and definitely wasn't a weak link. I just didn't see the value in paying out £1m, back when it was a lot of money, for a position that really wasn't a problem. I can remember one heated discussion which ended with him half-jokingly saying, 'What do you know about 'keepers anyway?' Ultimately, with the career David Seaman went on to have, I can see that he was right to want to sign him but let's not forget Lukey went on to win the league at Leeds in 1991-92. How many goalkeepers have done that with two sides? I can't think of any.

John mentioned it one day and said he didn't want to leave so I told him to stay and fight for his contract. The deal fell through and it probably rankled George that Lukey had approached me and dug his heels in. Another player to fall foul of George's iron fist was the Anfield hero, Mickey Thomas. They'd fallen out over something or other, maybe contract terms or a difference of opinion on how and where he should be playing as Michael was a confident boy who wanted to play a freer game than George would permit. As a result, Mickey was told to train on his own so we would work one-on-one at the ground while the rest of the side trained without him. This is a surefire way to hurt a player, take him away from the other lads and either get him gone or to toe the line.

As with John, Michael would talk to me in private and say he'd had enough, that he wanted to go, he couldn't work with George and so on. I managed to talk him round, said that George definitely wanted him to stay but he didn't like people stepping out of line. Mickey and George sorted out their differences and he stayed another season before heading to Liverpool, of all places, and I know when we spoke recently he said he loved his time at Anfield so maybe I shouldn't have talked him round after all. It was probably around this time that Mickey started to do impersonations of George wearing his long coat in the dressing room saying 'another 20 minutes and you're coming off son' which I'm sure George may not have appreciated.

We went on a tour of Scandinavia at the end of that 1990-91 season and, while we were on a ferry, George dropped his bombshell as we sat on our own. He felt I was maybe too close to the players, that it was time to freshen it up so I was to swap places with Stewart Houston who managed the reserves. I didn't see it coming, I have to admit. I was hurt and disappointed as I loved my job, I loved the club and I loved the players. It was, and still is, the pinnacle of my career. I don't remember my exact response but it was along the lines of 'bollocks to you' as I didn't want to swallow my pride and drop down a notch. Again, with hindsight, I could have gone away and thought about it, weighed it all up and realised I probably had a job for life at the club much like Pat Rice has performed admirably.

But no, it stung like hell and I was thinking hot for a long while after. I know George found it very tough, he even said so in his book and thankfully it hasn't affected our friendship in the long run. Whether he was right, I'd still say no, as I felt we were still a great partnership and in Stewart there was undoubtedly a different dynamic with maybe less resistance, which is not always a healthy environment. I know speaking to most of the players over the years, they could never understand why the partnership was split up and a fair few called to see what was going on. These things do happen, unfortunately, and nothing lasts forever but I felt we still had a good couple of years in us.

As often happens in life and football, by a strange twist of fate my old club Northampton Town sacked their manager and my former teammate Graham Carr after relegation to the old Fourth Division. I knew the chairman, Dick Underwood, very well having struck up a connection back when I played and he was a young fan. We both discussed the vacant manager's job and my situation which Dick couldn't quite believe as he thought I was at Arsenal to stay. We spoke in general terms and I went to meet him to talk in more detail. Believe it or not, Dick offered me a far better salary at

Fourth Division Northampton than I was on as assistant manager at Arsenal. It struck a chord with me at a time when I felt in need of that kind of offer, not the money, which was a bonus, but a return to my beloved Northampton and a real desire for me to return. It wasn't a hard decision at the time but whether it was the right decision is debatable given the alternative of staying at Arsenal.

I'll never forget my time at Arsenal, I never got tired or bored of the place. How could I? It was a dream come true and when I left Dublin nearly 40 years earlier I would never have imagined I'd end up coaching at a place like Highbury. I'll never forget the conversation I had with David Rocastle when he found out. He was absolutely gutted, which I found really touching, and we were both quite emotional. David just couldn't understand why and was genuinely surprised as we were such a strong partnership. David gave me a signed England shirt saying, 'To Theo, you will always be my no. 1 coach, wishing you every success as manager of Northampton Town, from your stepson Dave 'Rocky' Rocastle'. His dad passed away when David was only five and he used to call me Dad as a mark of affection and to wind-up the lads who called him the 'son of Theo'. The shirt is one of my prized possessions hanging next to my Spanish Luis Suarez shirt from the fateful 1965 game. It broke my heart when David passed away, aged only 33, from cancer, so young and such a great lad. It still upsets me now.

Other lads called and couldn't understand why. Kevin Richardson even went into print saying some lovely things and that I had been a big part of our success. You always hope that people appreciate what you do and I've never been one who needed to be told continually but it's always great to hear especially from people you hold in high regard. Kevin left the following season after some contract disputes with George but took the time to mention that it 'was a big loss' when I went to Northampton as he felt I had a 'wonderful way about me and was always laughing and smiling'. When all is said and done, you'd rather be remembered for those attributes rather than for being a nasty bastard, surely, and Mammy's old saying, 'it's nice to be important but it's more important to be nice', springs to mind.

When we spoke to Tony Adams recently he also said he never understood why George changed things as it worked so well as we were different. He felt Stewart was too similar and the lads used to say they missed the attributes I brought in. As Tony said to me recently, 'It is one of the hardest jobs in the world to motivate football professionals on a wet February morning when they don't want to train.' Tony is 100 per cent right, a coach must always be in a positive mood otherwise it rubs off on the squad and will have an adverse effect on the session. You aren't allowed to be low key, you always have to be on the front foot. Tony reminded me that I used to always demonstrate my penalty technique cleaning my boot on the back of my sock before striking the ball, aside from all the other things I showed him! Tony is that football rarity, someone not afraid to show his emotions as he has been through so much in his life and he told me, 'There are not enough Theo Foleys in football anymore.' Now, it doesn't get much better than that from someone who knows the ups and downs of both life and football.

To this day, when I catch up with lads like Mickey, Lukey or Davo, they still never knew the full story and they just thought I'd moved on to try my hand again at management. I would never have left Arsenal had I not been asked to step down, no offence to my beloved Northampton. The warmth is still there whenever we meet up, like at the recent 89 Film Premiere, which says so much about the atmosphere we had at the time. I know everyone thinks they have a great team spirit but five minutes in our company and you can see why they were such a unit on the pitch. We all revert to type straight away and the mickey-taking starts, but always in a good-natured way, never nasty. For all the honour and the trophies from my time at Arsenal, I'm just as proud of the connections and relationships formed with a superb bunch of human beings who just happened to be excellent footballers too.

CHAPTER 12
The Prodigal Son Returns
1990 – 1997

Nelson Mandela is released from prison after 27 years as the anti-apartheid movement gathers pace and the world says no more – the Berlin wall officially and physically comes down. Back home, Poll Tax riots occur across the UK in protest at the 'one size fits all' Community Charge introduced by Maggie Thatcher, which signalled the beginning of the end for the Iron Lady. Workers from the UK and France meet 40 metres under the Channel seabed as the Eurotunnel nears completion, just in time for the opening of the Euro Disney theme park. Strangeways Prison is under siege for 25 days as the nation basks in a heatwave.

The AIDs epidemic is still very high on the world's agenda as Freddie Mercury becomes a high-profile casualty of the deadly disease. The USSR starts to break up in '91 granting independence to many regions and modern-day Russia is born. A referendum is held in South Africa and, at last, Apartheid is dismantled. The Balkan War starts in the former Yugoslavia. The 'Birmingham Six' are released after 16 years of incarceration as something called the 'internet' undergoes a relaunch with the introduction of the World Wide Web, all far too late for me to embrace it.

The 'Godfather III' tries to recapture past glories but comes up short. Julia Roberts and Richard Gere enjoy huge success in 'Pretty Woman', effectively a new take on Cinderella. Spielberg hits hearts and minds with the highly emotional 'Schindler's List'. The film 'Titanic' sweeps all awards after release in '97 while UK film 'The Full Monty' is a major box office surprise. I'm still clinging to my old favourites in the tape decks, so Billy Joel, Elton John and Rod Stewart get plenty of airtime. The 'Big O' Roy Orbison was still releasing hits but the charts are getting more and more of a rotten din.

America re-enters the space race as the Shuttle undertakes its maiden voyage in '92 while the riots and social unrest rumble on the UK. OJ Simpson plays out a police chase live on TV in '94. Tension circulates around North Korea and planned nuclear inspections as Russia moves tanks into Chechnya. A major shift in public attitudes to the spending levels of the Royal Family in the UK results in the introduction of Income Tax for the first time on the Royal Family in '92. Coal mines are closing down regularly and Sunday trading means Britain is open for business in '94. The National Lottery is launched along with the Eurostar in 1994 as the IRA announce a cease in all operations. Rogue Trader Nick Leeson brings down Barings Bank in '95 and Brixton riots again.

Ayrton Senna tragically dies in the San Marino GP in '94, the same year his country, Brazil, win the World Cup. England host the Euros two years later and the nation is swept along on a wave of summer euphoria as Terry Venables' excellent side reach the semi-finals losing, all too predictably, to Germany on penalties. Princess Diana dies in a car crash in Paris as Tony Blair's New Labour take over in '97. Scotland and Wales edge towards independence.

I'm given a new silver Ford Granada 2.0 Ghia by Northampton FC which is great for trekking up the M1 on my weekly commute to the East Midlands.

In a coincidental sequence of events, I soon found myself heading back to my true footballing home of Northampton. The scene of my best playing days, the Town I loved so much back in the '60s and somewhere I've always held dear to my heart. It was an honour to be offered the job and the chance to follow in the large footsteps of my managing guru, Dave Bowen. Did I think it through fully? Nowhere near enough. Was my decision clouded by a wee bit of anger and disappointment? Almost definitely. Aside from all of that, as ever, I tackled it head on and just looked forward to another new role and chapter in my career, which is exactly what this is, I guess. How it all ended at Arsenal was very disappointing but that was in the past now so I set about making a fist of it.

Arsenal had been the fairytale chapter, now it was back to nuts and bolts and look to get the Cobblers back on the up.

Apart from the odd game as caretaker at Millwall in '78, this was my first management role since getting sacked at Charlton in '74. I felt much better prepared, I'd worked alongside the likes of Gordon Jago, Terry Venables and then very closely with George, obviously, at Millwall and Arsenal. I had learned a lot since the mixed success at Charlton where my greatest achievement really had been the players I'd signed rather than the results on the pitch. I'd had an additional 16 years of coaching and not only that, coaching at the very top level. This required some readjustment and lowering of expectation as Northampton were three leagues lower than Arsenal. I'd coached in all three top leagues now though and I felt ready for the challenge.

Maybe there was some self-imposed pressure forced on me as I returned to my footballing home, older and wiser, with success behind me. Added to which, I didn't have the excuse of youth and that 'first job' tag now that I had at Charlton. Throw in the fact that the Cobblers fans who remembered me would be nostalgic for the success of old while the younger fans would only know the recent success achieved at Millwall and Arsenal. Either way, they probably expected success, so it was a clear challenge but it didn't worry me. I still had the appetite for a football challenge.

The back story to my eventual appointment is a rare old tale as, way back when we gained promotion to the First Division back in 1965, I'd thrown my shirt into the crowd to a young lad near the front. Some 25 years later that young lad became the chairman who was to entice me back to the club. Dick Underwood had been a lifelong fan and successful businessman so was a prime candidate to be the chairman. Having appointed my old Cobbler's teammate Graham Carr five years earlier, Graham had been sacked after relegation to the Fourth Division. Dick went looking to recapture the spirit of '65 again by throwing an offer my way.

Little did he know but it was a perfect time really, as George had dropped his bombshell at the exact same period that Northampton were looking for a new manager. With 25 years passing since I'd thrown my sweat soaked no. 2 Claret and White jersey to a young fan, that same Cobbler's fan, now a local businessman and the chairman, threw me a management lifeline. It's remarkable how life plays out like this sometimes. Dick was a likeable fella and seemed to have the club at heart. He wanted to restore some pride back in the old club. It all seemed very positive as these things often are when a club is trying to sell itself. It didn't take much selling as I knew the club very well and I was flattered by the courtship, to be honest.

With my personal deal sorted, we then sorted out the finer details. I could use a flat when I needed to as a break from the long commute from SE London to East Midlands and I was given a new Granada for the journey. I made an early appointment in Bryan Carnaby as youth coach who was a great lad I knew from our time together at Millwall. Carn was an ex-pro who was very keen on fitness as well as injury rehabilitation so he would be a key figure in getting the lads fit for the season. Then it was time to choose an assistant to work alongside me closely, someone who knew the game, knew the club, someone I could trust.

There were very few that ticked all of those boxes and I only ever had one man in mind, the King from our time together as First Division teammates, Joe Kiernan. I knew better than anyone that you want someone that isn't always going to agree with you as a no. 2, but someone who believes in a similar football ethos and Joe was that man. He was delighted to return to the club and was excited to be a part of a new chapter in our combined history. I also managed to get Billy Best along as a coach, another player from our First Division days, one of the younger lads from that side. Billy was another I could rely on, he was super keen and also delighted to be involved. I was more than happy with my backroom team.

We got busy straight away, tracking players, drawing up lists, pooling Joe's knowledge of the local game, as he'd ended up playing for Ron Atkinson's Kettering Town side, and my own knowledge of the lower leagues. As an avid watcher of all games of football, I'd picked up plenty of player knowledge watching my eldest son Adrian play in the Southern League. There were plenty of players in those non-leagues who were well able for the Fourth Division and they generally had a hunger to prove themselves in the pro game. I had a list of four or five that I'd seen a few times and knew they were a safe enough bet if I could persuade them to sign.

We picked out Terry Angus from VS Rugby who was a big, strong, quick centre back who my son Adrian had played against plenty of times and he kept recommending him. Terry turned out to be a great signing for us, playing over three seasons for the club before going on to play for Fulham for another four years. We picked up another lad from non-league in Kevin Wilkin, a forward we signed from Cambridge City, another of Adrian's opponents. I'd seen both many times and they'd stood out so they were calculated risks really and low-cost transfers too, so the club was more than happy. I had high hopes for both of them who were, in my opinion, really good signings and would hopefully prove I still had the knack to find another Flanagan, Hales or Powell.

We had a few older experienced lads who we were going to need, undoubtedly, like Bobby Barnes, a winger who had top flight experience with West Ham and Peter Gleasure in goal who, ironically, had been sold by Millwall when George and myself joined the club. These things happen in football, it can be awkward for a bit but Peter knew the situation was different here and that he would be needed. He probably thought, not that arsehole again, but he never admitted it. We had some solid pros like Stevie Brown, Stuart Beavon and Phil Chard so there was definitely a good framework to work with. We inherited experienced centre back Steve Terry who had been signed from Hull and had top flight experience with Watford.

Before the season started I was approached by a publisher to complete a book as part of their suite of fitness books for various sports. Soccer (Fit for The Game) it was called. It was just a bit of pin money and quite a simple book really as it detailed various drills to get in shape for football based on exercises I'd picked up over the years. They picked out the two new lads Terry Angus and Kevin Wilkin as their live models for the exercise photos. The book is still available in a few bad bookshops and has the feel of a secondary school text book now, let's just say it hasn't aged very well. Despite the army-style exercises, the drills are still pretty good if you can look past the dated presentation. The lads ripped into Kevin and Terry for their 'modelling' exploits but they got paid a few quid for their troubles so weren't too fussed.

As I did every single year, drawing on the methods of the great Dave Bowen, I put the squad through its paces during preseason and made sure we were as fit as could be. We didn't need to consult the Fit for Soccer book though. The inclusion of a few new lads usually helps lift the mood of a preseason as they are so keen to impress they drag some life out of the old cynics, and so it proved again. We looked in pretty good shape and started the season really well. We won four and drew one in our first five games but were soon brought back down by the romance of the Fourth Division, as it was then, visiting the likes of Aldershot, Scarborough and Peterborough. We soon worked things out though, and what we needed to do to win games in the league, usually relying on the age-old requirements of hard graft and organisation, no wonder tactics. There was little merit in playing out from the back or through the lines in that League and, as has always been the case since football began, if you had someone who nicked a goal or two, you were in with a chance. We looked strong at the back, solid in the middle of the park with Bobby Barnes still a match-winner on his day and we had Kevin Wilkin up front who looked a real threat. We were top of the league come February and things were really clicking into place. It was all going much better second time around as a manager.

Now, as I'd seen George do before, with the team doing well it would have been ideal to have made a signing or two and kicked on but I was told in no uncertain terms that the well was dry. Alarm bells should have rung then but we took it on board and knuckled down. Inevitably, we suffered with injuries and fell away in the last three months. Kevin Wilkin ruptured his cruciate ligament which was a key injury loss as we lost him for the best part of a year. We ended up on a terrible run winning only one in the last ten and rumours about the club's stability began to surface. We really should have won the league at a canter and, at times, we were by far the best side in the league but we really were just limping along for the last two months. Meanwhile, in the First Division, Arsenal were beating Liverpool to the league title again in a contrast of fortunes at either end of the game.

The financial uncertainty really derailed the plans we had made and we had to scrap the players we had earmarked to get us out of the league. There is nothing worse for a manager than having your hands tied and being forced to keep hold of players that you just don't fancy. We had four or five that we could improve on but we didn't have any money whatsoever to spend and we were actually asked to reduce the wage bill. Our only option was to play a few of the younger lads and move the higher wages on, it really was a dire situation.

When you hear Jose or Conté moan about not having a world class third striker it is a bit different but similar in some ways, just to a somewhat different level. When you end up having to play midfielders or wide men up front and such like, you've had it. You might get away with it for the odd game, but a few games? No chance. If you are a carpenter you can't make a lovely piece of joinery with one saw, you need all the tools to do the job. With football though, you get slaughtered for making excuses, so you just bite down and hope it improves. It didn't, it got worse.

I don't know the ins and outs of it all but it was definitely tied into the deal struck on the ground as it was shared with the County Cricket Club, the bowls club you name it. Instead of making sure the club had a major stake in the main asset of the ground, they came out completely and lost any say in it or any revenue stream. Ever since, the club has lurched from one close shave to another and nearly went under again three years ago but, thankfully, they now seem more stable at their new stadium, Sixfields, with new financial backers on board. We didn't have any financial saviours that season though, and near the end we were bringing in YTS lads. I'd even asked youngest son Paul to sign as he was playing for non-league Fisher Athletic at the time. He was due to sign for Trevor Gould at Aylesbury for a few quid at the time but, as it turned out, he ruptured his cruciate ligament against Dartford, so neither move happened.

It was a desperate situation playing young lads who were miles away from being ready and, I'll be honest, it was a relief when they sacked me. They also sacked the coaching staff and ten players as administrators took over the running of the club. I was told to hand my car back and I was followed all the way home like I was going to steal the bloody thing. Needless to say, I'd been working for weeks without getting paid and, to this day, I'm still owed money but I guess I've had a few biscuits with my half-time coffee whenever I've gone back! I'm still owed a fair few Rich Teas I reckon. However, there are no bad feelings these days with the club and, more than anything, I'm just pleased it is still going as it was touch and go back then with large debts.

At the time though, it all ended a little sourly. Dick Underwood, the chairman, moved on and a new fella stepped in to take over. Joe, Billy, Carn and I all went back to our old lives looking for new jobs. That's life and that's lower league football unfortunately. It was hardly the romantic return for me as the old First Division captain leading the club back to former glories but I'd given it my all. In our first season I'd even picked up two Barclays Manager of the Month awards with jeroboams of champagne and commemorative plates to mark the awards.

The plates were proudly displayed on the wall in my dining room for years but, little did I know, one of them had been glued back together without my knowledge. One day, the two youngest were messing around and Paul had launched a banana for some reason at Sean's head. Sean ducked out of the way and the fruit missile apparently hit the plate sending it towards the floor and into pieces. Paul avoided a good rollicking by carefully gluing it all back together and Sheila was sworn to secrecy for years.

To be fair, everyone gave it their best shot and if Joe, Billy and I could have put our boots on and played we would have, such was our love for the club. I don't really regret giving it a go but, as I said before, if I'd stood back and considered the options carefully, staying put at Arsenal would have been the safer bet. The club finished 16th that season finishing with a stack of youth team players but safe enough due to the points they had in the bag already.

It was time to find a new job again, the second time I'd managed and ended up getting sacked, this time in half the four years I'd been given at Charlton. I was a better manager this time round but at a club that wasn't financially stable and just couldn't be helped. If it was the other way around and Charlton had been the second club managed it could have all been so different. Ah well, who knows what hand you're going to get dealt.

Usually, when you are on the floor, the only way to go is up but after a brief spell at Fulham, working with the youth team which I loved, I ended up as assistant manager to Peter Taylor at Southend United and it all felt very similar to Northampton. In between, I had worked a season at Fulham as youth team manager. I wasn't too keen on taking on the youth team as I'd not worked with young lads for many years but, as it turned out, it was just the tonic to raise the spirits. Fulham was a real old football club right down to the old stands and the cottage dressing rooms. It really restored my faith in the game again. The young lads were great, all super keen and willing to listen. We had a great spirit at the club and a couple of lads did make it through the ranks.

Halfway through the season at Fulham, I lost my dear Mammy, having reached 91 years of age despite smoking Sweet Aftons every day of her adult life. One formidable lady was Agnes Foley and, just like Daddy, an iron-willed character with a 'Foley' look that would wither the toughest recipient. Always immaculate, a fine-looking lady who ran the house and the family in true Irish matriarch style. If she wasn't making a dress, she was keeping the peat on the fire or cooking up a feast of food that seemed to last for hours.

She had a heart the size of Dublin and I can still see her walking along waving and crying as my ferry left Dublin Port, every time too mind. As with my Da, I love and miss her dearly and, in return, I know she was very proud of her youngest boy who made the grade at soccer. These characters make us the people we are, instilling all of the important traits into our make-up. As an example of our traits, one continual debate between us would be over who would pay the food or drinks bill, Mammy waving a fiver or tenner, as it was then, saying, 'Go 'way,' and trying to stuff the note in my pocket. This was a ritual played out continually for minutes at a time, neither willing to give in, stuffing notes here and there or giving it secretly to the unsuspecting children. Like many others who have lost their parents, what I wouldn't give for another five minutes with them both.

Having seen the season out at Fulham, I answered the call and stepped back into the pro league, agreeing to join Peter Taylor in June 1994 in, what turned out to be, the end of the pier at Southend. Peter had played with my eldest son, Adrian, at Dartford and was an excellent player even at the end of his career in non-league. He'd cut his management teeth at Dartford and as assistant at Watford before persuading me to join him down the A127 to the Essex coast with a bucket and spade in June '94.

Peter had struggled in his first season in the 1993-94 season finishing 16th in the old Second Division so I was under no illusions about the task in hand. What was encouraging though, was they had a couple of quality players like full back Chris Powell and Simon Royce in goal while Ricky Otto was a threat up front. The following season we somehow managed to persuade Ronnie Whelan to sign from Liverpool, probably on the back of Stan Collymore's transfer the other way the year before. Even a player of Ronnie's class couldn't turn things around and Peter resigned in February after a run of poor results.

The board asked Steve Thompson to take over until the end of the season and I was asked to stay on as assistant manager. The results really picked up and we managed to finish just below halfway in 13th spot. Steve decided not to take on the job, maybe knowing something we didn't, and Ronnie was asked to take the reins as player-manager with me assisting him on his first managerial job. Ronnie was a top player, that's for sure, but he would probably admit it was maybe too early for him especially having come from the top at Anfield down to Southend in such a short space of time. When we spoke recently about how he came to sign for Southend, Ronnie being Ronnie just said in his Dub brogue, 'No one else wanted me, Theo.' Can you believe that? A player like him, who had won everything in the game and, no disrespect to Southend, no bigger clubs wanted him.

Ronnie used all his connections and made a fair few signings, spent a few quid and, in doing so, created a rod for his own back really. Mike Marsh, his old teammate from Liverpool signed for £500,000 from Galatasaray as a showpiece signing. Mike had bags of ability but was struggling with an injury so the club never saw the best of him, unfortunately, and Ronnie had to pack up through injury also. We finished in 14th place which might have been okay if we hadn't spent so much money and, sure enough, the following year we really struggled.

It all came to a head away to Manchester City at Maine Road when little Georgi Kinkladze, of all people, clattered into our midfielder, Phil Gridelet, and both Ronnie and myself went wild at the ref. We both got sent to the stands, looking like a couple of Dub hooligans, tearing into the ref, maybe subconsciously looking for a way out. Well, the club went to town right enough and I was held mainly responsible being the more experienced of the two, can you believe that? Ronnie with all his trophies and medals in the top flight but little old me had led him astray!

We laugh about it now and Ronnie admitted recently that he wished he'd walked as a show of unity but I don't blame him at all, it was his first job in management so why would he jeopardise that. They put Ronnie on gardening leave, whatever that is, and I was gone, but strangely enough not too upset just embarrassed really as we'd let ourselves down. I don't think Ronnie even had a garden at the time! We both ended up in front of an FA Disciplinary Committee, not for my first time but it was to be my last. I'm not sure why I ever attended these as they were kangaroo courts that had decided what punishment was due long before they clapped eyes on you. All for show.

Ronnie was reinstated and saw out the last three months of the season but the club finished bottom and were relegated to the old Third Division in '97. Ronnie was sacked so went out to Greece and Cyprus to manage with more success than we had managed together at Southend but, in a way, the stint in Essex marked the end of both our management careers. Ronnie was, and still is, a gas character, a real Dub, I got on great with him. I knew his dad Ronnie Snr who played for St. Pats in Inchicore and Ronnie Jnr played for Home Farm like myself so I had a real connection with him. We were in the wrong place at the wrong time, unfortunately. Southend had sold Stan Collymore to Liverpool just before I'd joined the club, now if things had been different Ronnie could have supplied the passes for Stan to finish but we really were scratching around at times.

I believe the Irish FA were keen to bring Ronnie into their management set-up and I don't doubt the Southend experience tainted all of that. He's now a regular pundit on RTE back home so it worked out well in the end. From Arsenal to a Southend sacking, via Northampton, for me and straight from Liverpool to a Roots Hall sacking for Ronnie, we'd both slid down the football pole that's for sure. With my tail between my legs I headed out of Essex and started a 'softer role' scouting for Spurs appointed by David Pleat and, thankfully, a brighter chapter of my career was to follow.

CHAPTER 13
From a Gunner to a Cockerel
1997 – 2004

Good Friday Agreement signed to mark beginning of Peace Process between the UK and Ireland. That outpost of Britishness, Rolls Royce, becomes a German firm after being purchased by BMW. The Dome, the London Eye and the wobbly bridge are all built for the Millennium Celebrations. Queen Elizabeth celebrates her Golden Jubilee.

Osama Bin Laden becomes a person of interest and real concern to the Western World. The EU introduces a single currency, the Euro in '98. Bill Clinton denies any wrongdoing with an intern but ends up impeached before unleashing air strikes on Iraq following UN Weapons inspections. Putin takes over from Yeltsin as Russian President. America suffers double blow of Hurricane Katrina devastating New Orleans and the Twin Tower terrorist attacks as the world landscape changes forever. Saddam Hussein is captured and his regime toppled. Terrorist attacks increase across the globe.

France wins the World Cup in their own back yard and Wayne Rooney announces himself on the world stage. France follows up with the European Championship in Belgium and The Netherlands. Brazil win 2002 World Cup in Korea while Greece come from nowhere to win Euro 2004. Tom Hanks stars in the excellent World War II film, 'Saving Private Ryan' and the new Star Wars films don't go down well. Daniel Day-Lewis steals the show in 'Gangs of New York'. The Spice Girls explode onto the pop scene as I revert further and further to the old artists I love like Sinatra, Tony Bennett and Stevie Wonder. Britpop is all the rage.

I'm still not entirely sure how I came to end up at White Hart Lane but David Pleat was definitely instrumental in it as he knew I was available and had asked me to scout a few games. Before long, I'd been asked to fulfil a permanent role on the coaching staff as reserve team manager. Well, I jumped at the chance after the difficult stints endured at the sharp end of the game with two smaller clubs. I look back on my time at Spurs very fondly, especially as it was my last coaching role. I loved being back at a top club working with top quality players again.

It made little difference to me that I was a so-called 'Arsenal man' as Tottenham was a great club and it was just another job to me, I doubt many Spurs fans even noticed I'd been at Arsenal. When I joined, the side weren't pulling up any trees and my old QPR colleague, Gerry Francis, was nearing the end of his time as manager. Gerry had managed to bring a good side together and, I'd say, he was a little unlucky before resigning in November. There was some real quality in the side with players like Les Ferdinand, David Ginola, Darren Anderton and Sol Campbell. The side finished up in the bottom half when Christian Gross took over so they were definitely underachieving. They even brought in World Cup winner Jurgen Klinsmann but still only finished in 14th place.

In the reserves we had some top players pushing through including Sol Campbell who came through in my first year, even playing as a centre forward would you believe. Sol had the lot, pace, power, leadership so it was no surprise to see him become one of our best defenders of recent times. We had another one who probably had even more talent in Ledley King but he was blighted by injury. Ledley could play anywhere on the pitch, seriously. He was like a Rolls Royce, the lad, and the highest compliment I can give him was he reminded me of fellow Inchicore man, Paul McGrath, who was also hampered by injury throughout his career.

I don't doubt that Ledley would have been an England regular and captain had he not suffered with his knees. We also had Ian Walker in goal, Stephen Carr and Luke Young appearing for the reserves in the odd game. My job description was, as it had been all those years ago at QPR, to work with the first team above and the youth team below. It suited me fine and I really enjoyed working at a big club with all the facilities and top players again.

I was often asked to work with the first team lads especially as the managers chopped and changed during my time at the club. I struck up great friendships with both Les Ferdinand and David Ginola, who were both key players and great lads. Les is director of football at QPR now and I still enjoy catching up with him for a chat. He reminded me recently of a couple of incidents from the Spurs days that we were both laughing about.

Les was, and still is, an immaculate man so it's fitting that he's known as Sir Les. One day, at the training ground, I was one of the last people left in the shower room and I found a lovely leather bag of toiletries so I ploughed into the lot, smelling like a summer meadow by the time I'd finished. I slung it all into my bag and thought nothing of it. The next day I sauntered into the showers after training with my new toiletries under my arm and the double busy Ferdinand was straight on to me. 'That's a nice bit of gear, Theo, must have cost a few quid.'

So I'm now thinking where's he going with this, and come back with, 'Yep, Sheila bought it for me.' thinking that would get him off the scent, literally.

To which he replied, 'Oh right, has she been abroad then?'

Now I'm scrambling, in a bit of trouble. 'No, why's that Busy Bollocks?'

Then he hits me with, 'Because it's duty free and I bought it at the airport, you thief!' Well, that was it, to this day he still calls me Thief O'Foley, the busy egg.

He was also instrumental in running a book one day on our regular warm up routine where I took the lads for a jog and a stretch for a couple of laps at the Chigwell training ground. He said he'd have a £50 bet with me if I could keep quiet for the whole warm up. Well, the other lads were all involved in no time, Stephen Carr, Steffen Iversen, David Ginola, all the chirpy buggers. Before long, we'd got a few hundred quid in the pot. I only made it halfway round before saying, 'This is bollocks, I have to speak to do the warm up,' and they're all laughing and hooting saying I owe them £50. Luckily, they let me off the bet.

David was a great lad too and what a player. What people don't realise was the height and strength of him as he had such skill but no one could ever outmuscle him or kick him out of the game, even Dicko at Arsenal couldn't get into him. We got on great forging a friendship over our mutual love of golf. David hit a lovely ball, as you'd expect, and when he met someone who asked him a question he didn't like, he'd just shrug his shoulders and give it the old 'Je ne comprends pas' and look at me quizzically. As a former full back, I definitely would not have fancied marking him, he had so much talent with the ball at his feet and could go either way.

During one shooting session at Chigwell, he kept smashing his ball miles over the bar into the brambles behind the goal and taking ages to join the session again. I wandered over as he's making a meal of getting his ball and said, 'David, are you sure? Why do you keep kicking it over here?'

He just smiled and replied in his thick French accent, 'Fee-oh, it's these berries, I just can't stop eating them. Oh my goodness.' He was tucking into all of the wild blackberries in the bushes behind. Now anyone who knows me well knows I love a blackberry or a raspberry as well so I just laughed and joined him. I remember telling him to keep quiet about them and never to eat the ones low down. After a recent heart scare, it's good to see he is back working again in media, thank God.

Another lad that I always got on well with was Jamie Redknapp who, like Ledley, suffered with injuries too so played a few reserve games looking to reach full fitness. Jamie has established himself now as a regular pundit and team captain on A League of Their Own where he gets plenty of stick from Jack Whitehall and Freddie Flintoff. We run an annual golf day for Nicky Johns' Mr Brightside charity in memory of his youngest son, Stephen, who tragically passed away from bowel cancer. Every year for the past ten years, Jamie always sends tickets for the show or similar with no fuss or chasing up. Footballers get plenty of stick from people who don't know them and Jamie has always been tagged as one of the Liverpool Spice Boys but there are no sides to him, just like his dad, Harry, who is a real football man.

I'd get plenty of stick from my son, Paul, for 'selling out' after my time at rivals Arsenal but I wasn't going to bite on that one. I enjoyed working with the ressies, working closely with Chris Hughton who is one of the nicest fellas in football. When I got the job, Chris rang me at home to welcome me to the club and say how pleased he was I was joining and so on. Maybe it was the Ireland full back link but we clicked straight away and I really appreciated the warmth he'd shown by calling to welcome me to Spurs. All too often people in football are guarded and feathering their nest but not Chris, he's a straight shooter.

I've always followed Chris' career closely and his resilience is admirable having been unfairly dealt with, in my view, at Newcastle, Birmingham and Norwich. He's worked wonders again at Brighton who have the potential to be an established Premier League club so maybe he has found the right club for him at last. I've heard great things about the Academy set-up and training facilities, while their ground in Falmer is fantastic so I wish him all the best, one of life's good guys.

As mentioned, I worked under a few first team managers so helped out with the firsts when needed especially with David Pleat when he stepped in a couple of times. David has unbelievable knowledge on players and teams up and down the country or overseas. If there was a player worth a look in France, Germany or in the old Second Division, David knew all about them. A very sharp footballing brain. Gerry Francis left soon after I joined and Christian Gross took over with mixed results but gets credit for enticing Jurgen Klinsmann back for half a season who was world class. Christian was a nice enough fella but he always had that 'temporary' look about him, some people just never look secure. David Pleat steadied the ship before the club made what was a very surprising appointment to the Spurs faithful in '98. They committed a cardinal sin in the eyes of many fans and appointed an Arsenal man, George Graham of all people.

Now George had been at Leeds for two seasons without

recreating the success we had at Highbury and it was only four years since he'd left Arsenal under a cloud. It's fair to say, therefore, he was not the fans' favourite appointment but, from my perspective, I was delighted as I knew George would improve things and more than that, the old team was back together. People assumed we had concocted this arrangement by getting me in first but it was pure coincidence. I wondered if it may seem a little odd working closely again after how it had ended at Highbury but I needn't have worried.

We both just got on with it as if nothing had happened and George was soon picking my brains for the inside line as I'd been there a year before him. He did what he does best, straight away, and set the side up to be organised, be difficult to play against and, in turn, win games. In no time he'd squeezed a little extra out of the players and we were on a good run in the Worthington Cup reaching the final only five months after he'd taken over. This was a big thing at White Hart Lane never mind it 'only' being the League Cup as the club had been starved of trophies for eight years, much like Arsenal had when we reached the same final under a different name in our first season. Both clubs had great cup pedigree and it's no coincidence to me that George, the master tactician, woke up those traditions in another sleeping club.

George had me in the dugout for the game, which was a nice touch, and we were back at the old Wembley again after appearances in the Littlewoods Cup, the Makita tournament and the Charity Shield, all for Arsenal. This time we were there with the Lilywhites and it was great to be involved in another big game together, suited and booted in the sunshine, with our families watching on from the famous old stands. We were favourites to win that day against Martin O'Neill's Leicester side that were steady if not spectacular with the likes of Matt Elliot, Steve Guppy and Emile Heskey up front. We had a fair few match-winners that you'd expect to rise to the occasion, players like David Ginola, Darren Anderton and Les Ferdinand.

The game was a bit of a non-event though, with not much

to shout about apart from a couple of penalty appeals for fouls on Allan Nielsen. Then Robbie Savage duped the ref into sending poor old Justin Edinburgh off. Robbie being Robbie had whacked a couple already and caught Justin with a forearm body check on the halfway line and Justin gave him a swipe on the back of his blonde bob. Sure enough, good old Robbie waited a while before thinking, hang on, I can get him done here and clutched his face, nowhere near where his hair had been swished. Savage got a yellow but it didn't stop him having a run in later with Steffen Freund. He did well to stay away from Freundy who was definitely one to steer clear of.

Thankfully, after a great late run and shot from Steffen Iversen, we scored the only goal of the game when Nielsen nodded home the rebound from close range. It wasn't pretty but we won and who cares how you win in a final, especially with ten men. I'm sure the thousands of Spurs fans weren't bothered and I doubt they minded that the 'man in the coat' as they called George had masterminded it. Sol lifted the cup as captain that day, another who suffered later on having gone in the other direction to Arsenal.

The club went into the UEFA Cup the following season but only made it to the second round. George seemed to be improving things on the pitch but felt we needed two or three players to add to the big signing of Sergei Rebrov and really mount a challenge on the top clubs. He made this clear in the media which is commonplace these days but, at the time, the board didn't take kindly to being flushed out in public for holding the club back, boards rarely do. According to the club they issued written warnings for releasing what they deemed to be private information and sacked George in March 2001 just after we'd reached the semi-final of the FA Cup.

It was probably just as well as Arsene's new look Arsenal beat us 2-1. George has never really discussed it properly with me but I know he was really disappointed with the club and the fact he never took on another job speaks volumes. Losing George from management when he still had so much to offer the game is a travesty really. George could have straddled the onset of the Premier League no bother and, with more money to spend on transfers, I'm sure he could have really made a difference.

Glenn Hoddle took the job on and I stayed on working with Chris Hughton and the reserves. Ironically, the club allowed Glenn to delve into the market and sign Teddy Sheringham and Christian Ziege. Glenn had an almost identical season in 2001-02 to George's first with a Worthington Cup final appearance losing 2-1 to Blackburn Rovers and finishing ninth in the league. The following season, fellow Dubliner Robbie Keane signed for what was big money then at £7m from Leeds but, again, the side finished in a similar spot, 10th in the league.

Sir Les and Tim Sherwood were sold on as Glenn looked to rebuild the squad for 2002-03. With Stephen Carr and Robbie Keane, we had two lively Dubs around the place, driving everyone mad with wind ups. Robbie was a gas character and the chief busy around the place, he knew everything that went on. Glenn was sacked early on in the season after a poor start and David Pleat took over as caretaker again asking me to help out on the coaching side. The club shipped out a stack of players and regrouped for the next season making a few big money signings in Helder Postiga, Jermaine Defoe and Freddie Kanoute.

David did his level best but the club seemed very unsettled and, sure enough, another manager was brought in as the side finished around mid-table again. Jacques Santini lasted just a few weeks of the 2004-05 season and Martin Jol took over as I stepped down from full time work and carried on as a scout for Spurs and also for good friend Mick McCarthy at Wolves. I was 67 years of age and the old knees were struggling on the training ground so it was time to call it a day. The stopwatch, the whistle, the balls, the bibs and the cones all handed in as I thought about getting my golf handicap back down. More than anything I would miss the craic, the dressing room mickey-taking and the great characters I'd met in over 60 years of playing, coaching and managing. There really isn't a better life than getting paid to do what you love and I could not have asked for more, truth be told.

I scouted regularly and enjoyed keeping my hand in talking regularly to David Pleat or Mick at Wolves. I watched my namesake Theo Walcott as an exciting 16 year old for Southampton and had to correct my best ever assessment of Mark Penfold at Charlton. Walcott was playing at a different speed to everyone else and was fearless. I watched him about a dozen times and each time came away thinking, this lad is going to be a top player, repeatedly telling anyone that would listen at Tottenham to just sign him, however much they wanted. As we know, Arsenal signed him and, it's fair to say, he never really fulfilled his potential not helped by a couple of injuries mind. It gave the new North Bank fans a new Theo to sing about though.

I helped out the odd non-league club on the coaching side if they asked me to do a few sessions which took me to Stevenage Town, Greenwich Borough and son Paul's side VCD Athletic. It was the same atmosphere no matter what level it was and I loved being in amongst the mickey-taking again, but not the cold evenings. The attitude of these lads who do a day's work and then turn up on a cold night to train is what football is all about, a sheer love of the game. It was fitting, perhaps, that my last real involvement with a pro club had ended with a Wembley win in the sun for Tottenham with my old friend George by my side.

CHAPTER 14
Still Working
2004 – current day

The Premier League gets bigger each year as the TV money grows. England and The Republic of Ireland continue to disappoint in international tournaments. Terrorism and tensions grow the world over in ever- changing political landscapes and worrying times. My music tastes stay the same, however, as I resist any of the new sounds on offer with the possible exception of Amy Winehouse duetting with Tony Bennett or Gregory Porter singing Nat King Cole.

I loved 'The Shawshank Redemption' and 'Saving Private Ryan' but the best film seen for many a year can only be a very recent one, '89 The Film', detailing the true story of a fairytale ending to a football season at Anfield.

Manchester Utd dominate the Premier League with the odd challenge by Arsenal and, more recently, Chelsea and Man City. Spain, Germany and Brazil share the international spoils as Barca, Real and Bayern rule club football. Lionel Messi and Cristiano Ronaldo raise the bar, possibly higher than ever before.

I'm finally driving my dream car having now owned four Jags over the years...

I couldn't end on 13 chapters, so what am I doing now? I'm still in love with the game and will still watch any game of football with the same keen eye, be it a game over the park, watching my son, Paul, when he played or managed in non-league or my grandson and namesake, Theo, in junior football for Cray Wanderers. I watch any game that's on Sky Sports, much to Sheila's quiet and long-suffering dismay. In fact, I'll watch any golf tournament, boxing match or game of football that's on the box. I love it. As Paulie boy tells me regularly, I'm an absolute sport bore but there are worse things to be in life.

I am still working as a matchday host at Charlton Athletic which I really enjoy, getting to talk to people always willing to discuss the game in general. It's only five minutes journey down the road and it is a lovely way to watch a game of football amongst old friends. The club has suffered of late but things are looking up finally so I've not needed to submit my CV just yet. When Charlton are away, I head to Millwall with my son, Sean, who is a staunch Lions fan. We take his two boys, Connor and Theo, who are now big enough to be my minders if there's any trouble.

I have been fortunate enough to have been invited over to The Emirates for the odd game to see Ricey or Bouldy and was blown away when Arsene Wenger came over to our table and knew exactly who I was. Arsene is no fool, he is steeped in the history of the club and someone who took the club on from George. I share George's belief that Arsene has to go down as the best ever at Arsenal pipping Herbert Chapman and George himself which is not a popular view of late. Maybe his record has been tainted slightly but some of the sides and the players he has managed are up there with the very best ever seen on these shores.

In terms of our extended family, I get to dote on ten grandchildren (five boys, five girls) and two great grandchildren (two boys) so we've got enough for a five-a-side boys' and girls' team. I get to see my lovely daughter, Teresa, and her husband, Mark, in picturesque North Wales and see their children, Luke and Sophie. Grandson Bobbi-Jac can choose Wales or Ireland national football teams when he grows up and Luke's partner, Claire, is expecting again so more chances for someone to follow the trail.

We get out to California when we can to see eldest son, Adrian, his wife, Lisa and their son, Austin, who also tend to visit here at least once a year. Adrian is secretly running America, not that other fella in office, and we recently caught up with his son, Michael, over here who has just had a baby boy, Freddie, with his wife, Fran. I get to see Sean regularly as he lives down the road from us with Angie and their children; Connor, namesake Theo and Eliza. I'm pretty sure

Paul is fed up of the sight of me having slaved over this book for far too long but at least I get to see Chloe and their three girls; Clara, Maia and Esme regularly who look after me grand. Poor Sheila has to put up with me even more now as I don't get to play golf as much these days as my mobility is not so good and I have to admit I do miss playing with the lads up at Royal Blackheath or Shooters Hill.

I still keep in touch with almost all of the good friends named in this book, far too many of them have sadly passed away with very few of the Exeter, Northampton or Charlton sides I played in still alive. I've been fortunate to make great friends for life though, and that tops any achievements in the game it really does. Only recently, the majority of the Arsenal squad met up for the 89 Film Premiere and it was if nothing had changed, we're all just a few years older. After the film, the press wanted everyone together to take a team photo and I'd nipped off to the toilet. Well, the lads told them to all to wait for me, so they came and found me. That probably sums up that group perfectly. No one had greater billing, be it Tony or David or Mickey. I'm not so sure that exists so much these days in the top sides.

Every year George and all of the backroom staff from his old Arsenal team meet up for Christmas at a lovely restaurant in North London and reminisce over the times we had together. After all this time we still give out the same mickey-taking as ever, telling the same old stories and we disagree about football like we always did. It's a great way to spend the afternoon. Ricey, Steve Burtenshaw, Terry Murphy, Stewart Houston, Vic Akers, George and I represent Arsenal while poor old David Pleat gets a verbal bashing for his Spurs connections. We have a lovely time over a glass or two of vino.

There's still no shortage of football in my life, as you can see, and I still love the game just as much as I ever did back when I was kicking the ball around Dublin in the 1940s. I wouldn't change a second, all 60 years of it, I've had a rare old time.

Be lucky, Theo.

ABOUT THE AUTHORS

Theo Foley

Theo is a retired professional footballer who has played in all four divisions of the Football League and for the Republic of Ireland nine times. After an extended career coaching and managing professional sides in and around London for over 30 years, Theo now works as a corporate host at Charlton Athletic FC.

Theo is a keen golfer but he is still in love with the game that has given him so much joy and success for more than 60 years. His previous published works include coaching and fitness manuals.

Theo lives with Sheila, his wife of 58 years, in the same house he bought upon moving to Charlton in 1968. He is a grandfather of ten and has two great grandchildren.

Paul Foley

Paul grew up in a football family, where meal times involved discussing tactics with the salt and pepper pots with his two brothers and sister. School summer holidays were spent collecting balls every day at Queens Park Rangers' Greenford training ground for his father, Irish footballer, Theo Foley.

Paul has played non-league football for a number of Kent and South East London clubs. He is a Chartered Surveyor and Residential Developer operating in South East England. Paul is the father of three girls, only one of which has an interest in football.